SL.9.

A WHIFF OF NEWS

Peter Fairley

A WHIFF OF NEWS

The Memoirs of Peter Fairley

Foreword by
Sir Trevor McDonald

CLIFTON

Published by CLIFTON BOOKS, 1999

ISBN 1 84145 00 6

Typeset by Ace Filmsetting Ltd, Frome, Somerset
Printed and bound by Creative Print and Design Group, Wales.

Contents

Foreword

Sir Trevor McDonald, Chief ITN Newscaster

B y the time I joined ITN in the early 1970's, Peter Fairley was already on his way to becoming one of the towering figures in British Television journalism. In common with most brilliant reporters at ITN at that time, Sandy Gall, Peter Sissons, Anthony Carthew and Robert Southgate, to name only a very few, Peter had come to television having had a successful career with news agencies and then with the London *Evening Standard* in Fleet Street. This is the first great point of interest in *A Whiff of News* because, as the book makes abundantly clear by its amusing anecdotes, nothing like Fleet Street exists in the newspaper industry of today. And that remains true even when taken into account the extraordinary eccentricities, in more recent times, of newspaper owners like the late Robert Maxwell.

Those were the days when newspaper proprietors exercised a profound influence on the titles they owned and on the lives of the correspondents who worked for them. 'Lord Beaverbrook wants to know how you got the information' must have been a very familiar cry. Peter was told that by his Editor more specifically when, in April 1961, he scooped everyone with the news of the imminent firing of the Soviet rocket which launched Yuri Gagarin into space. His salary was virtually doubled just after that and a great career in journalism and a race between America and the Soviet Union were on the way.

As the book indicates, nothing like the old Fleet Street remains, when young reporting recruits were despatched in the 'office car' to find out more about robberies which may, or may not, have occurred. In the Fleet Street of that era, the proprietor's influence was decisive and the Editor's word was law. Peter Fairley discovered this when an assignment to report on a medical conference came up against the not insignificant fact that his wife was about to give birth to their first child. There was not the

slightest hesitation in the News Editor's mind about which oc-
currence the paper deemed the more important event. It was a
lesson Peter learned very quickly. Life, I would like to believe, is a
little different today.

In Fleet Street, Peter did all the customary things that young
reporters of his time were expected to do, reporting murders,
pursuing royalty and celebrities who wanted to keep out of the
spotlight, covering the court cases and standing vigil outside pris-
ons or Government offices. But, as far as I am concerned, the
thing which made his career so memorable was his fascination
with Science and, more precisely, with Space.

This is the side of Peter Fairley I saw, when I came to ITN in
the early 1970's, and the aspect of his career that makes his book
so interesting. I am absolutely sure that Peter had no idea of how
we saw him. At the ITN of those days we were young reporters
and newcomers, like me, were desperate for role models to help
pick our way through the thicket of difficulties involved in shaping a television career. And I never told Peter this, but we were
his biggest admirers. He was one of those we aspired to be like. In
the first place he had a 'Fleet Street' pedigree and in the second
place he was superb at what he did. I was fortunate to see Peter
Fairley at his best. I remember very clearly now those performances which made him a household name in Television.

This was the time when all the world was caught up in the
excitement of the Space Age and Peter was fortunate in the fact
that ITN realised the potential of reporting space thoroughly –
much more, in fact, because one of our Editors at the time had an
interest in space that bordered on the fanatic. But there was something equally important. For the first time, I think, television was
forced to confront the fact that it had something of a mission to
explain and to make complicated concepts and theories more
accessible to the general viewer. It is a responsibility we have taken
with great seriousness right up to the present time. But it was
only just coming to be appreciated then.

As his book describes, with the exploration of space, full of all
its scientific and human drama, Peter Fairley came into his own.
Never before had television tried to explain to an everyday audience, such complex mechanisms without the facility of all the
computer-generated graphics we have today. My abiding memories of Peter, at that time, involve seeing him performing faultlessly in the studio, demonstrating with models he himself

commissioned and, in some cases, helped to stitch together, how the new rocket science sent people in to space. Night after night, he would bring the drama to life and, mainly through this kind of explanation from Peter I think, the entire country soon understood and became consumed by the Space Age.

Peter Fairley's book does so again, with the grace, the relentless eye for detail and the humour of the best storyteller. It is a document of a time in a profession which, for better or worse, is always today the subject of tense controversy. *A Whiff of News* should be read by all aspiring journalists who will find it informative and a delight and *will* be read by all those, like me, who remember with fondness and nostalgia the great story of the Space Age and the enormous significance of the way television responded to it.

From Peter Snow:

'Watch out! This book is intoxicating. Open it up and out bubbles all the enthusiasm and vitality that made Peter Fairley the master of the art of reporting science on television. It's all there – the sense of fun, the encylopaedic knowledge – whether he's taking us on a journey to Texas or to the moon – and, above all, the relish he has for a good story. That is the most infectious quality of this book – and it is what made him such an inspiration to those who worked with him at ITN – his zest for a cracking good yarn. Stand by for a roller-coaster ride through a life of adventure with one of Britain's most colourful and resourceful writers – but fasten your seat belts!

From Alan Whicker:

Peter Fairley carries us at a gallop through an international career across the spectrum of British media: newspapers, magazines, radio, television. . . . Always correct, honest, unpushy – but enterprising and ever-alert for a story, his entertaining behind-the-scenes memories of news-in-the-making are an easy read. Fairley recaptures the exciting era during which communications advanced from Underwoods and pressing Button B . . . to space-age technology. While much of it happened, Fairley was watching.

From Peter Sissons:

Peter Fairley is the man who brought science reporting to a mass audience of newspaper readers and television viewers, during the years when the public imagination was gripped as never before by the programme to put a man on the moon. He didn't fail. He is the complete communicator of complex concepts, and his eye for what would caputre the imagination has rarely been equalled. 'A Whiff of News' is his colourful story. It contains a brilliant insight into those golden years for television when ITN was making its mark, and the spirit that made it the news outfit to beat. Told with humour, in the plain language that is his hallmark, there is much here that has not been told before. I was privileged to have aorked at ITN in those heady years, and to have learned from the great journalists and cameraman there. In 'A Whiff of News' Peter Fairley tells what went on – from his richly-earned vantage point among them.

What is a news sense?

T HE clues had been there for months; the warning to shipping to keep clear of a particular area in the Pacific where a
booster rocket might splash down, several features on aviation
medicine in *Soviet Weekly*; the mysterious behaviour of Soviet
delegates at a recent international space meeting. The only clue
that was missing was *when*?

But on the morning of April 10, 1961, my news sense and
desire not to be 'scooped' became so strong that I tapped out a
story which began as follows:

> Russia's first spaceman will circle the world just once before try-
> ing to come back. If he fails, he is likely to wait 24 hours – or
> another 16 sickening orbits – for a second chance. *The attempt is
> imminent.*

The story went on to describe the 'super-rocket' (more than
150 tons and developing nearly a million pounds of thrust) that
would 'streak up from a firing pad near the Aral Sea' with the
cosmonaut on top; the lay-out of his cockpit and foam-rubber
couch, his spacesuit, medical monitoring attachments and 'panic
button'. It also speculated on the identity of the first cosmonaut.

The *Evening Standard* of which I was then Science Correspondent, splashed the story all over the front and back pages of its last
two editions and I remember driving past the placards at Ludgate
Circus with doubt nagging to the point of feeling sick: 'Oh God,
suppose I'm wrong. . . .'

That evening the phone rang. It was my editor, the normally
ice-cool Charles Wintour. But he was anything but ice-cool. 'Lord
Beaverbrook wants to know how you got the information.' he
said warmly. 'Apparently, Moscow is abuzz with rumours that
the Russians are about to launch their first spaceman.'

When, two days later, they launched Yuri Gagarin it caught us all by surprise – not least me, who had always believed the accuracy of the word 'imminent' to depend on which cosmological timescale you were working to, and who had no more authority for his story than a 'news sense'.

I remember sitting at 8.15 a.m. at my desk and hearing a 'ping' from the *Reuters* machine in the nearby Teleprinter Room. 'Hey, Peter!' shouted the operator, as he tore off the first sheet of copy. 'SNAP', it read. 'Dateline, Moscow'.

The rest is a blur. I had given up smoking some 12 weeks previously and been finding great difficulty in typing any story without the 'prop' of lighting a cigarette first. That morning, there was no time to use a typewriter, much less struggle with withdrawal symptoms: the first edition of the *Evening Standard* closed at 8.50 a.m. There was nothing for it but to lift a phone on the desk and dictate words – 550 of them – straight-out of the head to a professional typist in the Copy Room. We made it with about a minute to spare.

Next day, April 13, a letter arrived from the Editor. 'Dear Fairley,' it read, 'Your work on the space story yesterday was a fine climax to the forecast you made so confidently on Monday. This sort of work not only does you great credit but does the prestige of the *Evening Standard* a lot of good also.'

To my relief, the details of the event were reasonably close to the forecast we had published – which was, perhaps, not surprising. Anyone who had studied the easy-to-come-by information about the US space programme realised that many aspects of a manned spaceflight would be bound to be the same, regardless of nationality.

But I didn't let on and was immediately rewarded by being upgraded to Expert. And Experts, I soon found, were allowed two things denied to mere reporters – Good Pay and the Right to Build an Empire.

It was a turning point. Not long afterwards, my salary was nearly doubled and before finally leaving the *Standard* I had graduated from a one-third share in the bottom drawer of a desk, to a whole desk, three filing cabinets, one book cupboard, a microfiche viewer, a personal secretary and an assistant (both of whom also had desks of their own).

'Expert' knowledge, particularly of the space scene, led to a whole new career in radio and television and a measure of fame, if not fortune.

Many people have asked: 'What *is* a news sense?' I am still trying to define it. Some people are born with one, others develop it. All I know is that it is something which steps up the pulse-rate, causes adrenaline to flow and makes the fingers turn to cotton wool as they fumble for a coin for the telephone or a notebook and pen. Somehow, it enables you to smell a story with all the acuity of a bloodhound picking up a scent. It also brings you into contact with fascinating people in all walks of life and gets you into funny – and sometimes embarrassing situations. At least, it did me.

It is certainly something which I would not wish to be without.

CHAPTER ONE
Cub Reporter

Dawn on June 10, 1954, had a real 'zing' to it – partly because it was sparkling clear and partly because it was my first day as a professional journalist.

Previously, I had dabbled in words in the Sutton Valence School magazine, launched the Sidney Sussex College journal *The Bull and the Porcupine*, spent an amateurish year as Sports Editor of *Varsity* (the Cambridge University newspaper) and sent the odd item on spec. to the William Hickey column at the *Daily Express*. I had even been paid five shillings by the *Kent Messenger* (at the rate of a penny per line published) for phoning in copy from one of their cricket reporters to his office (he dared not miss a ball) during a summer vacation.

But this was a Real Job – full-time work at the North, South and West London News Agency for the princely sum of six guineas a week – and I was, quite frankly, excited.

I was even more excited when I heard the fire engine.

A few months previously, I had spent a month of my Easter vacation on unpaid trial at the Agency under the wing of its then editor, George Markstein. George – who subsequently became Head of Scripts at Rediffusion, launching, among many series, *Callan* and *Armchair Theatre* – had a phobia about fire and fire engines. He used to shake like a jelly and flick his hands uncontrollably if a tip about a fire came in or was picked up from the emergency services' network, which the agency used to monitor (illegally). His voice would rise to a shriek. 'Get down there *pronto*,' he would shout to the reporter nearest the door.

Here I was, at 6.45 a.m. on Day One, with a fire almost literally in my lap. I could not believe my luck.

In those days, I rode a 'pop-pop' bike – a parachutist's foldaway Corgi motorcycle, painted silver and red, acquired from a fellow officer in the 8th Royal Tank Regiment in Catterick during my National Service. Its minuscule petrol consumption appealed to the impoverished agency, which had offered to contribute a penny a mile travelled (but not to and from work).

We were halfway across Westminster Bridge when the fire engine swept past, heading north. I opened every ounce of throttle and just about managed to keep on its tail as it turned and twisted through the side-roads. 'Thank God for the bike.' I thought as we finally braked in Pimlico. 'I'd never have found this fire otherwise.'

I looked around. Instead of a blazing building with escape ladders and people being rescued through dense smoke, the sun was reflecting brilliantly off the glass doors of – the fire station! And by then, I was late for work – on my very first morning.

George had taught me much of Fleet Street's fire jargon – engines were 'appliances', fires were 'blazes' which firemen 'tackled' or 'fought', smoke usually called for 'breathing apparatus' and you shouldn't mention the total of appliances attending a fire but, instead, multiply it by five to get the number of firemen. So the ideal fire report read something like 'Fifty firemen wearing breathing apparatus tackled a blaze in a warehouse in Deptford' – or wherever. The aim was to make the facts sound as dramatic as possible.

What George had unfortunately forgotten to teach me was that, when firemen were on their way to a fire, they had their helmets on. When they were returning, they had their helmets off . . . these were off.

I learned many things during the next eighteen months at that sweatshop of a news agency, where the Board of Directors had to approve any expenses greater than ten shillings a week. One thing was never to pooh-pooh one of George's hunches about a story – for he had a sharper news sense than anyone I have ever known.

Apart from illegally tuning in to the fire, police and ambulance networks and combing local London papers for possible follow-ups, much of our work came from national newspapers, who would usually have received a tip-off from some member of the public which needed checking – 'just in case, old boy'.

It seemed always to fall to me to make enquiries about children who had died in accidents. The agency working hours were 7 a.m. to *any* hour, then 9 a.m. to 1 p.m. with the rest of that day off. This rota alternated regardless of weekends or public

holidays. Sometimes as late as 9 p.m. I would 'pop-pop' off to
the bereaved and ring the bell.

I hated it. But I quickly learned that, far from intruding into
private grief, I was actually performing a service. The heartbro-
ken relatives really *wanted* a stranger's shoulder to cry on: and of
course, out would come the stories – 'new bike for his birthday
. . . ran to warn his sister . . . always shopped for her Gran' . . .
and so on and in would flow the cheques for the agency.

After a year and several pleading memos, my wages were raised
to a whole nine guineas a week. I probably should have quit then
but refrained for two reasons. First, my prospective father-in-law
had said I could marry his daughter when I was earning £10 a
week. Second, although Morley Richards (News Editor of the
Daily Express) had told me to 'come back in a year when you've
gained some hard, fast experience', I feared it would look more
like waiting for the kettle to boil than taking his advice if I re-
applied for a job in Fleet Street after precisely twelve months.

So I sold my Corgi, got married, moved aboard a houseboat
on Chelsea Reach and carried on with the crucifying routine.

Reward for perseverance was not long in coming. One of the
great frustrations of the job was that, although our stories were
aimed at national newspapers, we often found ourselves in competition with the papers' own reporters, who had been sent 'in
case it was a bit too big for you to handle, old boy'. On such
occasions, we had to be *first* with our copy if the Agency was to
be paid more than a pittance. But the Fleet Street mob could race
to the scene in taxis or chauffeur-driven cars, while we were re-
stricted to public transport, bicycle or foot.

The tables were turned on Easter Sunday in 1955 when, after
following up a road accident in Hampstead, I walked round the
corner of South Hill Park to find Ruth Ellis, a blonde model,
being taken into custody for the murder of her lover, racing driver
David Blakeley.

His body was still in the pub car park where she had shot him.
Many words of *my* copy were used in the national dailies, although in every case under someone else's by-line, because the
elite Crime Reporters arrived soon afterwards and took over –
'OK, old boy, thanks for your help.'

Ruth Ellis was subsequently found guilty, sentenced to death
and became the last woman to be hanged in Britain. Although the
agency did not have a specific 'order' to cover the scenes outside

Holloway Jail as dawn broke on execution morning, I was sent – 'just in case, old boy' – to join the ghouls and mourners outside the prison gates.

It was impossible not to be moved by the image of the rope around that beautiful neck, the silence of the crowd and the tolling of the prison chapel bell.

Fortunately, I have never had to attend another execution.

The boy who saved the Abbey

'Scoop' is a word used too freely, mostly by the public. To qualify as a 'scoop', a story has to be exclusive *and* important. Few journalists achieve many scoops in their careers, some none at all. It is largely a matter of luck – and 'news sense', of course.

The one which came my way around 5 p.m. on October 27, 1954, may not qualify on the second count but it certainly gave me great satisfaction.

I was riding a No. 11 bus past Westminster Abbey when not one but *four* fire engines screamed to a halt and the crews dashed inside. This time, the men's helmets were on. I leaped off the bus and followed them. The Abbey smelled of smoke and we were met by the Dean, who indicated that there had been a fire in the south triforium – the arcade above the choir stalls.

While the firemen were blanketing the smouldering embers, the Dean told me that a 12 year old City of London schoolboy had noticed smoke coming from the area and raised the alarm. He had then helped to douse it with a firebucket full of water.

'Where's the boy now?' I asked. 'He's still somewhere up there.' said the Dean. I felt the adrenaline surge again and the pulse race as I hurried off. Sure enough, the boy was still there with another lad and some adults, watching the firemen. 'Can we have a word?' I asked, steering him away from the others.

After 40 years, I cannot remember his name but I can still see his face. It was like an artist's illustration of the hero from one of Richmal Crompton's *Just William* books.

In those days, I used to carry an old German camera in my raincoat pocket – 'just in case, old boy' – so, after getting his story I led him outside the Abbey, took three or four pictures, gave him five shillings and suggested he went home and talked to nobody but his parents.

I phoned George at the office, who almost lost control. 'Stay where you are,' he shrieked, 'and ring back in five minutes'.

Twenty minutes later, after dictating the story to George, I was on my way (on another No. 11) to the *News Chronicle* offices in Fleet Street with the precious roll of film. It was the start of an exciting evening, during which I took the developed negatives on to four other newspapers. I became almost heady from the smell of print and the noise of newsrooms as I waited for copies to be taken.

Next day, every paper carried the story – virtually word for word as the agency had dictated – and four carried the picture. 'SCHOOLBOY SAVES ABBEY' . . . 'HERO OF THE ABBEY' . . . were two typical headlines. George told me it was 'a genuine scoop'.

A fortnight previously, the Directors had announced an incentive bonus scheme for us reporters. I was not privy to how much they had made out of selling the story *and* picture to Fleet Street but it must have been several hundred pounds and, in due course, I was told that I was to be the recipient of the first incentive bonus.

All staff were asked to report to the grimy offices in Ivor Place, Baker Street, at 11 a.m. the following Friday, regardless of shift. To everybody's amazement, sherry was produced. The Managing Director made a short speech and handed me a brown envelope, adding: 'Congratulations, Fairley – keep it up.' Everyone was keen to get at the Cyprus sherry, so I said nothing in return but crept down to the basement, which smelled strongly of dry rot, to open the envelope.

I was staring at a 10 shilling note.

Upstairs again, I took the MD aside. 'Look, I really do appreciate it but I must point out that my bus fares cost me two shillings and the price of the film was three and fourpence and I had to have a bite of supper while I was waiting for the '*Mail*' to finish with the pictures . . .'

'Oh, don't worry,' he interrupted, 'we'll pay your expenses as well.'

The final *dis*incentive came when George told me I was to be promoted to be a News Editor, but it would mean working indoors.

I hadn't become a reporter to sit at a desk. The windows were filthy and the desks covered in soot because the offices in Ivor Place were level with the point where all the steam locomotives lined up in Marylebone Station, spewing smoke.

Fires, murders, coroners' inquests, juvenile courts and council meetings may not be everybody's cup of tea but they were preferable to asphyxiation at a desk. So I refused. 'But it's promotion,' wailed the MD. 'I don't care. I don't want it,' I said.

In search of a new job

It was obvious, after that, that I had to go. I arranged another interview with Morley Richards at the *Express*, got out my best (and only) suit, assembled a few Press cuttings (including the Abbey story) and took another No. 11 along Fleet Street.

'Oh dear,' said Morley, much to my chagrin, 'you should have come back after a year. We've just taken on two new reporters and there are no more vacancies. We might be able to offer you a job in the library, if you want one. . . .'

I took my suit and Press cuttings up the narrow road beside the shiny black *Express* offices to a much older building with a clock projecting over its front door. *Evening Standard* it read. 'Have you an appointment?' queried the commissionnaire. 'No. But the News Editor of the *Express* told me I should come.'

It was a lie, of course. But within minutes I was in the presence – and presence is the right word – of Ronald Hyde, tall, distinguished and grey-haired, a legend in his time as the youngest man (at 21) ever to be appointed a Fleet Street News Editor. He had a reputation as a martinet. 'Do you do shorthand, dear boy?' he started.

I explained that I hadn't had time to learn shorthand – neither at Cambridge nor at the Agency – but had developed a kind of speed-writing with abbreviations. I said I was willing to go to night school.

The rest of the interview – and the one with the *Standard*'s Editor, Percy Elland, which followed 15 minutes later – is a complete blank, except that I know he, too, asked about shorthand and I forgot to produce my cuttings. I felt sick on the No. 11 bus back to Chelsea and told Vivienne, my wife, that I had 'definitely blown it'.

Next morning the postman delivered a letter to our houseboat. It was from Percy Elland. 'Glad to offer you a position on the staff at 16 guineas a week. When can you start?'

CHAPTER TWO

Footsteps on Fleet Street

I never did learn shorthand. It certainly would have been useful and might have saved a lot of stress, especially when reporting court proceedings, where accuracy was vital. But nobody insisted and, as well as speed-writing, I was lucky enough to have something of an 'audio memory' – I could remember exact words for several minutes afterwards. Besides which, life on the *Standard* – with nine editions going to press in eight hours – was too fast-moving and tiring for night school to have much appeal.

A taste of the hectic life that was to follow – and a lesson in the need for accuracy – came within 20 minutes of my joining the paper on Sept 5, 1955.

Feeling a bit like a schoolboy on his first day of term, I circum-navigated the vast Editorial floor and slid into a vacant chair by the long line of reporters' desks. 'Excuse me, that's my chair,' a woman's voice said. Viv Batchelor, one of the *Standard*'s most senior reporters, had arrived albeit a little late. I moved to another vacant chair. 'Sorry old chap, that's my desk.' Bill Roland, the Property Correspondent, was limping in even later. After the third try – this time it was Mark Wilson's sacred seat – I gave up and leaned against a pillar, hiding my embarrassment behind that morning's *Daily Herald*.

'Fairley – here!' A man with a squint and a shiny bullet for a head was waving a sheet of copy paper at me. He was the Deputy News Editor, Philip Grune, a man whose gruff manner concealed a thousand anecdotes and a warped sense of humour. 'Take the office car and get down there quick.'

The piece of paper bore a message – a 'tip' from a member of the public who had heard police cars arriving at the scene of a robbery. Such tips usually earned the sender between £2 and £10. This one stated that a dairy manager had been coshed on his way to the bank.

The Editor's chauffeur (no less) dropped me in the Dalston

side-street where the robbery was supposed to have occurred. It was empty, but I found several householders who had seen the police and a newsagent who could 'tell me everything'.

Yes, it *was* the local dairy manager who had been coshed. He had been pushing his bike up the hill towards the bank, as he did every Monday morning, with the weekend takings in the basket. Yes, he had been seriously hurt and was now in hospital. Yes, the police had come – in *two* cars. Yes, he did know how much was missing – about £2000 – one of the dairy workers had come into the shop and told him.

Did he by any chance know the manager's name? Oh yes indeed. It was Jim Grainger.

I ran to a callbox, scribbled four paragraphs in my brand-new notebook, phoned the office and dictated them. 'You'd better get over to the hospital and find out how the manager is.' Grune said.

At Whipps Cross Hospital, they were somewhat mystified. A check with Casualty failed to find any record of a Mr. Grainger having been admitted, much less treated. I began to feel queasy. I rang the dairy to check the manager's name. Yes, it was Grainger all right, but he was on holiday!

It turned out to be the *deputy* manager, one Ron Phillips, who had set out that morning and been coshed. My 'eye-witness' later admitted he had not seen Grainger's face – merely a figure pushing a bicycle with a bag on the handlebars at the time the manager usually went to the bank.

By now, it was 11.20 a.m. and the third edition of the *Standard* would be out on the streets, featuring the wrong name. There was nothing for it but to pick up the phone and issue the one word which no reporter likes to include in his vocabulary . . . 'CORRECTION'.

I quite expected to be fired. But when I returned to the office in abject misery, Phil Grune said, 'It can happen to anybody. Just don't let it happen again.' It was an important lesson: a reporter must always check – and if possible double-check – his facts. Accuracy thereafter became almost an obsession with me.

Although the coshing of a dairy manager and theft of £2000 would probably rate not even a paragraph in the *Evening Standard* today, it was the front page story lead that night. Which somehow made up for the fire engine debacle on Day One at the other place.

Never a dull moment

Life as a general reporter on a London evening newspaper can never be described as 'routine'. When I went temporarily blind some years later, the Editor told me he was ashamed of never having appreciated what a strain it must be to start each day without the slightest idea of what might happen to you or where you might end up. But that has never worried me. I enjoy serendipity.

A classic example of this came one Saturday morning in 1956 when there seemed to be no news around at all. I had read every morning paper, tidied my share of the desk drawer, up-dated my contacts book and drunk most of the coffee pot. I remember turning to Denise Richards, another general reporter, and saying, 'God, it's boring today – have you ever known it so quiet?'

Half an hour later, I was in the office car with cameraman Vic Drees en route for Croydon Airport. A chartered de Havilland Rapide was waiting, engines running. It flew us out over the North Sea to where a trawler was sinking.

It was primarily a picture story and I was not sorry to stay in my seat while Vic, legs astride and tethered only by his raincoat belt, stood at the open fuselage door taking his pictures. Round and round we went, only 50 feet above the pounding waves while the crew watched from a nearby lifeboat in numb disbelief as their livelihood disappeared – deck, handrails, winch and tackle, wheelhouse, funnel and finally the mast.

It was all over in 40 minutes. And by 2.30 p.m. I was back in my seat next to Denise, waiting for the teaboy to appear with the sixth edition containing (we hoped) my words and Vic's dramatic pictures.

'Did you say boring?' she mocked.

On another occasion, I was sent to Brighton to cover the opening of the annual conference of the British Medical Association. Knowing nothing about medicine or doctors, I was worried about the whole assignment and especially about spelling complex medical terms. The 'Press Room' was a large, flapping marquee, beside the conference hall, in which typewriters were set out on trestle tables.

Noting my frown and one-finger typing, one of the other reporters offered to vet my copy for accuracy before I phoned it to the *Standard*. He had a thin moustache, wore a blue blazer and told me his name was Alan Whicker (Alan was then working for *Exchange Telegraph,* one of the three Fleet Street news agencies whose reports were taken as gospel by all national newspapers).

I accepted gladly and felt confident, after three stories, that I had not made any boo-boos that day. 'Can I come back now?' I asked the News Desk at 5 p.m. when even the 'Stop Press' column had closed. Vivienne was at home on the houseboat, expecting our first child at any moment. 'Come back?' thundered Phil Grune, for it was him again in charge. 'When I send you to cover a conference, I expect you to cover the *whole* conference – not just one day of it.'

'But my wife's expecting a baby any time now,' I pleaded, 'and I haven't got any clothes or money with me.'

'Listen lad,' Grune went on – and he apologised years later, 'you've got to decide whether you want to be a reporter or somebody who takes time off when it suits him. We're running a newspaper, not a maternity home.'

I was close to tears. I rang my wife who said, 'Don't worry – I don't think it'll be tonight.' I thereupon went back to the Press Room. Alan Whicker saw my despair and asked what was wrong. 'Right.' he said immediately, 'I'll ring my hotel and see if they can squeeze you in there. In the meantime, here's £5 – go and buy yourself a razor and toothbrush.'

I covered the rest of the conference – the first of many BMA meetings, Vivienne gave birth to Josephine the day after I returned; and Alan and I have remained in contact ever since. Thereafter, I never stopped carrying a razor and toothbrush in my briefcase.

Search for an heiress

The Editor of the *Standard* at that time was Percy Elland, a bluff Yorkshireman with a twinkle in his eye, who believed that news stories should all have the same 'look' to them. He insisted that every story should be ruthlessly 'subbed' and bear no other attribution than '*Evening Standard* Reporter' – unless you had a 'scoop'.

It was 18 months before my name appeared as a by-line over a story.

Towards the end of January 1957, Fleet Street was headlining a society scandal – an heiress called Bobo Sigrist had eloped with a notorious playboy, years older than herself, named Greg Juarez. The couple had vanished. By the third day without 'hard news', the morning papers were getting really frustrated, the only clue being a report that they were aboard a yacht somewhere in the Caribbean.

If there was one thing Ronald Hyde, the *Standard*'s News Editor, liked more than following a cricket Test, it was a salacious piece of Society gossip – rumour had it that he had 'connections'.

'Fairley,' he called, 'I've got a little job for you.'

I was to ring the major hotels in all the Caribbean ports to try to locate Miss Sigrist. 'Bloody fool,' I thought to myself. 'How on earth does he expect me to find them by telephone from London when all the morning papers have reporters out in the Caribbean?' But a Hyde instruction had to be obeyed.

I started at 1.40 with an international directory of hotels and a word of explanation to the *Standard*'s switchboard. It seemed unlikely that, with her being an heiress, she and her beau would be shacked up in some one-star doss house. More likely, they would be in one of the grander hotels – *if*, that is, they were on dry land at all.

I ruled out Jamaica and Trinidad and started with Barbados. Four calls – no trace. Bermuda: two calls – no trace. Then I noticed in library cuttings that little Bobo had once been a guest at a Society 'do' on Paradise Island in the Bahamas. An atlas showed that Paradise Island was virtually part of Nassau.

I rang the Nassau Beach Hotel and asked for Miss Bobo Sigrist or Mr. Greg Juarez.

'Just a minute.' The operator replied.

Seconds later there was a clear, sweet, 'Hello.'

'Mrs. Juarez?' I queried.

'Yes, who's that?'

What made me say 'Mrs. Juarez' instead of 'Miss Sigrist' I shall never know. But she told me at the end that that was what made her accept the call and continue with the interview. Greg and she had got married and she wanted them to be taken seriously.

My speed-writing went wild and I could hardly type, especially since Ronnie Hyde, realising what had happened, was standing over my shoulder ripping off the pages, paragraph by paragraph, and passing them across to the subs himself.

We just made the last edition, the 'West End Final', and I confess to staying late so that I could carry my first by-line home.

Next morning, there was a letter waiting from Percy Elland. 'My dear Fairley,' it read. 'That was a fine interview you got on the telephone with Miss Sigrist. My warmest congratulations.' I never muttered under my breath at Ronnie Hyde again.

Face to face with the famous

Beaverbrook executives were very good with their letters and telegrams of congratulation. They knew it was a way of motivating staff. And if a reporter was overseas, he always received a cable telling him what had happened to his story the previous day.

Another motivation, of course, was money.

I have kept a note of all my early income and, for the record, it shows that 16 guineas a week in August 1955 became 17 gns. three months later, 18 a year after that, 20 in October 1957 (after Sputnik I went up), £24 in 1958, £26 in 1959 and that in 1960–61, at the age of 30, I earned the princely sum of £3,354.2s.9d., a third of which was reimbursed expenses.

Daily Express reporters, of course, earned much more – at least twice as much – because their paper sold nation-wide. But we on the *Standard* were largely happy with our lot, finishing work in time to enjoy some social life or go to the theatre, instead of tottering home unshaven any time after midnight.

Our work was always varied and at times quite exciting. My contacts book, with its old telephone numbers listed with the first three letters of the exchange name plus a four-figure number, is testimony to the kind of life we led. In amongst organisations such as the Ministry of Fuel and Power, the Clerical and Municipal Workers Union, the Met. Office, Government departments and the regional fire headquarters are entries for Annigoni the painter (WES 3316), Lauren Bacall (BEL 5678), Colonel Bassett (the spy Guy Burgess' stepfather) (REG 2330), the Lords Harewood (BAY 6755) and Hailsham (PUT 4177), Peter Ustinov (FLA 7592), and a host of other showbiz, political and Society names.

I met very few of them. But I did have to phone them, from time to time. And once the number was known, down it went in the little blue Contacts Book – a dossier so precious that it still shows a written offer, inside the front cover, to pay £50 to any finder.

One of those I *did* meet in the flesh was Liberace. I had to interview him after he sued the *Daily Mirror* for libel. I tried to have words with him as he was leaving the High Court but his entourage was too protective. To my surprise, he winked at me over their heads and said 'Come to my hotel.'

'You'd better watch yourself.' Phil Grune teased, when he heard. 'Do you want to take a chaperone?'

Liberace's room was on the first floor of the Ritz and, sure enough, there was a grand piano in it, with one of the famous candelabra on it as well as many bouquets of flowers from well-wishers.

'Come and sit beside me,' he invited from the depths of the capacious sofa. But I sat tight and said, 'Let me finish my tea.' I produced notebook and pen and he started to talk so profusely about his Mom, his fans and his forthcoming appearances before 'the lovely people of Great Britain,' that the sofa never got mentioned again.

As I left, we shook hands and I remember thinking I had never seen such jewellery on a man.

Another face-to-face encounter was with Kim Philby. The previous day, questions about a 'Third Man' being involved with Guy Burgess and Donald Maclean in a Soviet spy ring had been raised in Parliament and the name 'Philby' suggested. So Philby, who had been at Cambridge with the two defectors, called a Press conference in his Chelsea flat to counter the allegations.

I recall sitting on the carpet of his elegant, chintzy apartment with about 14 other reporters huddled around, drinking coffee out of bone china cups while he denied everything. It was a very convincing performance and it fooled everybody. It came as a shock a decade later when he turned up in Moscow, branded as one of the most damaging traitors in the history of Anglo-Soviet espionage.

I also spent several weeks close to Princess Margaret – or rather, to the tail of her car – and that of her equerry, Group Captain Peter Townsend. Along with most of Fleet Street, we tailed the couple everywhere they went while the public thirsted for proof of their love and they agonised in private (insofar as privacy was possible) over their future.

It was not easy work, especially since she often had a police escort and plenty of willing decoys. But I and a sequence of *Standard* cameramen were assigned a Godfrey Davis Armstrong Siddeley with a chauffeur called Bill, who used to be a racing driver, and we managed to stay on the trail most of the time.

Margaret was frosty and not at all helpful. But Peter Townsend, a handsome, sensitive man in an impossible position, earned our respect by behaving courteously, always driving at a safe speed and, in the end, telling us his timetable. In return, he was left in peace for certain routines, such as riding.

I often wonder, in these days of Royal surveillance, whether similar bargains are ever struck. Somehow I doubt it.

The climax to the Margaret–Townsend affair came when the pair spent a weekend at Uckfield House, one of the Marquess of Abergavenny's stately homes in Sussex. Rumour had it that this was to be the make-or-break weekend, resulting in either an engagement or a parting.

The watchdogs moved as a pack in pursuit of the Group Captain as he left his Lowndes Square flat and then took up positions at the front and rear gates of the mansion. Various cars came and went but none of them were the Princess's, nor did any seem to contain her. We wondered if it was yet another red herring.

Then, when it was almost dark, a powerful limousine swept in through the hastily-opened gate, headlights blazing. A figure wrapped in a dark coat was slumped in the back. 'That's her,' someone shouted and most of the pack seemed to agree. As 10 p.m. approached, with no more comings or goings, the verdict was reached that the pair were definitely inside together. But it was not unanimous.

One man steadfastly refused to phone his office with the news because, as he put it, 'I did not see her with my own eyes'. He was John Edwards, an ex-RAF flyer and a veteran reporter for the Press Association. The Press Association (PA) had a reputation for accuracy and authority and John had no intention of jeopardising it.

He refused all Saturday and all Sunday, despite the fact that a couple of *Paris Match* photographers had somehow managed to penetrate the security curtain, lain low in the woods and been rewarded (they swore) by pictures of the couple walking hand-in-hand.

On the Monday morning, as many cars – including Townsend's – were leaving Uckfield House and we evening paper reporters were phoning over our 'think pieces' for the early editions. The *Paris Match* fired John but he did not seem to mind a bit. He knew he had not compromised his standards.

To him, truth was more important than the job. If only there were more like him.

CHAPTER THREE

Crime and Punishment

O ne Spring week-end in 1956, my wife and I bought our first car. We paid just £30 for a 1923 Singer. It rattled a bit but otherwise ran smoothly for two years until I sold it to the 17-year-old office 'boy' for £13, whereupon it broke a half-shaft within a week.

Unfortunately, while we were out buying the car our house-boat, the *Moby Dick*, was burgled. Not much was stolen – money from a piggy-bank, a silver sports trophy and a sheath knife – but we reported it to the police and, a day later, the CID arrived. Much to our delight, because our home was on water, the crime was investigated by the Thames River Police, who arrived by launch.

Life tends to run in cycles and, for the next year, I found my-self sent on a variety of other people's crime stories, as well as enduring several spells at Scotland Yard's Press Bureau.

The Bureau was where each national and London newspaper based a reporter to liaise with the police. It was more like a prison cell, with sparse furniture and a steel door between the Bureau and the rest of Scotland Yard, which was always kept locked, except when the police wished to issue a statement.

Then the key would squeak, the door open and a plain-clothes clerical officer appear, either sitting down at one of the tables to read his statement or standing on a chair. The room was usually littered with the days newspapers or packs of cards and full of cigarette smoke – the 'stench of boredom' I used to call it.

The statements usually raised more questions than they an-swered, to which the spokesman would reply with an infuriating 'No comment' or 'That's all we have to say'. Nevertheless, they were high spots in otherwise tedious days and the Pressmen were as grateful as beggars fed with crumbs off a rich man's table – a fact of which The Bill was only too well aware.

The *Standard, Evening News* and *Star* reporters would scamper to the telephones on the wall, composing stories in their heads as they went: the morning paper hacks would write more considered pieces, or go to public call boxes outside to 'make further enquiries'. If a newspaper office wanted its correspondent to ask the Yard for information or comment, the reporter had to go to the steel door and ring a bell, whereupon a small shutter would open and a *sotto voce* conversation take place.

I hated those stints at Press Bureau, mainly because I found myself smoking more than usual but also because the 'regulars' were a clique and made you feel like an intruder. Victor Toddington, the *Standard*'s Chief Crime Reporter and a great raconteur, craftily stayed away from the place – 'got to meet a copper in a pub, old man' – while it was the physical absence of our permanent Bureau correspondent, Nelson 'Sully' Sullivan, either on holiday or sick leave, which necessitated my being there as stand-in in the first place. His advice was available but not his cheerful, Cockney company.

The crime writers had a jargon all of their own, much of it spoken out of the corner of their mouths, and I never mastered it. But I did achieve a grudging admission into their circle for a time because of three particular stories.

One was the Bodkin Adams Case.

Dr. John Bodkin Adams was a chubby, Pickwick-like GP practising in and around Eastbourne. He had a penchant for Rolls Royces and similarly expensive motor cars and a lucrative private practice made up largely of elderly women, many of them widows. There was no doubt that his patients found his bedside manner charming and his prescription pad effective and he was always at pains to keep visiting them regularly, even if they had gone into a nursing home.

Quite a number of them left him gifts (such as their limousines), some of them adding codicils to long-standing wills to do so.

Everything at Eastbourne seemed to be balmy until the family of one wealthy lady – a Bodkin Adams patient – became suspicious about her death, especially since she had unexpectedly altered her will to leave the good doctor her Rolls.

After initial enquiries, Sussex police decided to call in Scotland Yard and Detective Superintendent Bert Hannam – known as 'The Toff' because of his immaculate suits and hats – arrived on the scene. So did Fleet Street, including me.

We billeted ourselves (expenses paid, of course) in the fashionable Cavendish Hotel on the seafront and spent our days following up rumour after rumour, attending Hannam 'off the record' briefings in the pub opposite Eastbourne police station and our evenings either dining at leisure or investigating the town's night life.

It went on for six weeks, by the end of which even the most depraved of us had become bored, especially when the routine started to include observing 5 a.m. exhumations in misty graveyards. In the end, Hannam believed he had enough evidence to convict Adams – and charged him.

The trial was a sensation. It filled the pages of every newspaper for several days until, unexpectedly, the jury found the cherub-faced doctor not guilty. Those in the know put it down to a failure by the prosecution to call the right evidence. Hannam was shaken and so were we, the murder-hunt veterans long back from Eastbourne, who were convinced of his guilt.

As ever, there was a dissenter. He actually championed the doctor and spread innocent explanations of his behaviour across the feature pages of the *Daily Express* – and thus, via Express Newspapers Syndication Service, across the world – for several days after his acquittal. The dissenter's name was Chapman Pincher.

Chapman Pincher – Harry to his colleagues and friends – was to play an increasing role in my life, not least because I became the nearest thing to his counterpart on the *Standard*, which at that time was part of the Express Group. He was the Express's Man-in-The-Know on science, medical, defence and any other matter in which he had a particular interest. His particular interest in Dr. Adams was their common love of fishing. His decision to tell the doctor's side of the story was exactly in line with the policy of our master, Lord Beaverbrook, who believed that every Left should have a Right and that *all* controversy in newspapers was good 'good for circulation'.

You might have expected sister papers to share at least some of their secrets, if only to co-ordinate coverage and reduce costs. Not so. We were no more privy to the whereabouts of John Bodkin Adams, after each Pincher post-trial disclosure, than the *Express*'s arch rival, the *Daily Mail*. This really infuriated Ronnie Hyde who despatched me to Eastbourne 'to see what you can pick up'.

It was like looking for a needle in a haystack. The bachelor doctor's housekeeper had left him some months previously; he apparently had no close relatives; and the police had washed their hands, if not their memories, of him.

The irritation became unbearable to Ronnie when, on Day Three of the Pincher series, the *Express* carried a large picture of the acquitted GP fishing from a river bank. It looked like any one of a score of river banks in Sussex but I was asked to purchase a map and check them all.

The weather was gorgeous and I thoroughly enjoyed roaming the river banks, stopping for Ploughman's lunches at delightful country pubs and using the phone to check in and report 'Sorry, no luck'. In the end, interest in the Adams story waned and I was called back.

Some years later, I learned that Pincher had not hidden him away in Sussex after all, nor even in Southern England, but in Scotland. And the tantalising picture had been taken beside one of Harry's favourite fly-fishing rivers in Berwickshire.

A devious detective

Bert Hannam believed in being straight with the Press. Rather more devious was Detective Superintendent Jack Capstick, appropriately known as 'Charlie Artful'. I first came into contact with him in 1957 during a murder investigation near Crystal Palace.

A 12-year-old boy had been strangled. It was a sex crime and Capstick, who had set up his murder hunt headquarters in Gipsy Hill Police Station not far from the scene of the crime, was looking for a pervert. Capstick loved his 'elevenses' – the higher the proof the better – and there was a small, rectangular bar opposite the 'nick', where the crime reporters gathered to wait for 'the chief' to slake his thirst before questioning him. They then queued for the privilege of 'buying him one'.

I forget the precise details except that it was a Saturday morning and Capstick had been furious with the latest batch of Press stories. He told everyone present that they had betrayed a confidence – printed something 'on the record' when it was quite definitely 'off'. Then he said he would forgive us if we 'didn't do it again' and came and sat down by me.

'I exclude you from that bollocking,' he told me quietly 'you're the only one, throughout the whole of this case, who's played fair.'

'Perhaps that's because I'm not really a crime reporter,' I said, taken by surprise. 'Listen, lad,' he went on, 'I'm going to give you a break. Don't say a word to anybody but I've promised to go with your colleagues to a club in Streatham at lunch-time – we'll probably spend three or four hours there. I intend to make them pay for letting me down. What they don't know – and only you do – is that we've got hold of a home movie, taken around the time the boy was murdered, of a wedding at the church almost next door to his home. My lads up at the Yard are going to ana-lyse that film this afternoon, frame by frame. It's just possible that the murderer was among the crowd outside the church when it was taken, perhaps already in the company of the boy.'

Charlie Artful added. 'Don't ever let on I told you.'

I didn't. I excused myself from the Streatham party on grounds that my News Desk wanted me to do something else at Gipsy Hill, went to another pub and waited until 1.15 – then phoned over the new development in the murder case. The story led the paper for the rest of the afternoon. The *Star* and the *Evening News* news desks apparently went berserk trying to track down their reporters, who knew nothing of it anyway. And by then, Capstick had left.

The murderer was eventually caught (although not through the movie) and convicted. I am sure Jack Capstick will not mind my breaking his confidence now – for sadly he is dead.

My most embarrassing moment

Crime stories are probably responsible for more alcoholism and cirrhosis of the liver among journalists than any other occupa-tional hazard. This is because they frequently involve a lot of waiting around while the police make their enquiries and because detectives, by and large, enjoy a drink. The pub offers hospital-ity, seclusion and – at the end of a tête-à-tête – a telephone.

But they pose an additional problem for evening newspaper reporters, who have early deadlines to meet.

Much police work does not start before 9 a.m., by which time the first edition of an evening paper may well be closing. Unless you are prepared to stay with the mob, usually drinking until all hours, you have no way of knowing the latest developments in a case until the officer-in-charge starts *his* working day.

So what do you do? Well, I usually bought all the morning newspapers, found a cafe, read the total coverage of the story and tried to decide which version was likely to be closest to the truth. Then I would concoct some innocuous follow-up such as 'Detectives this morning were still hunting a man with a scar down his face'.

This was a disgraceful practice and I am not proud of it. But what else could one do? Space in the paper had to be filled with *something* and, in those days, it was extremely difficult to get any co-operation from the uniformed police at the station (the CID were more approachable but it was still up to the 'guvnor' to talk to the Press and he, if he'd had a late night, might well not appear until mid-morning).

A classic situation was the one which faced me early one Thursday in 1956. It led to the Most Embarrassing Moment of My Life (the squeamish should move on to the next chapter).

The body of a 10-year-old boy had been found under some bushes by a road at Loughton, Essex. He had been sexually assaulted and suffocated in the process. It was a particularly vile crime and every newspaper sent at least one reporter into the area to search for eye-witnesses and monitor police activity. The murder hunt HQ was Woodford Green Police Station.

The search for the murderer looked like going on for several days and most of the other crime reporters moved into an Essex hotel for the duration. But I preferred bed aboard our houseboat and the Singer provided the means for commuting between Chelsea and Loughton, although it meant setting off around 5.30 each morning.

A routine developed: drive to Woodford Green, ask the Station Sergeant what was happening (to which the answer was invariably 'No comment'), buy the newspapers, sit in a cafe to write a first edition 'think piece', phone it to the *Standard* and then return to the police station to await the arrival of the 'guvnor'. It would usually be lunchtime – and several gins later – before I could get any 'hard' news, and the news was usually that detectives were interviewing yet another known sex offender to establish his movements on the day of the crime.

But that Spring morning in 1956 was different. For one thing,

I developed an excruciating pain in my gut during the drive from Chelsea, almost certainly due to a suspect curry eaten the night before. For another, the Station Sergeant, instead of saying 'No comment,' said 'haven't you heard?'

'Heard what?' I asked, in surprise.

In return for a promise not to divulge the source of the information, the sergeant revealed that one of the perverts on the CID list of suspects had been admitted to Whipps Cross Hospital during the night, after being found with his head in a gas oven. Even more amazing – *he lived in a house at the end of the garden owned by the 'guvnor' in charge of the murder hunt.*

It was then 8 a.m. Mindful of my first day at the *Standard*, I knew I must check the facts at the hospital before phoning a story, even though it was a policeman who had given them to me. With the gripes getting worse, I pushed the Singer flat out to Casualty at Whipps Cross and rushed in.

Another 'No comment' greeted me. But a £5 note to a porter produced not only confirmation that a man had been admitted suffering from coal gas poisoning but that a detective inspector was sitting at his bedside *at that very moment.*

It was enough. I ran to a callbox near the hospital gates, frantically trying to compose the story of the prime murder suspect having lived right under the nose of his hunter. As I reached the phone, my bowels went into one final spasm and I was left with a terrible dilemma; return to Casualty, find a 'loo' and miss the first edition? Or dictate the story, catch the edition and probably foul my trousers?

I like to think Lord Beaverbrook would have been proud of his young crime reporter, had he known. But I will never be able to forget the horrible sensation of trying to assemble a coherent story in the head while soiling my underpants below.

Afterwards, I eased myself gingerly out of the underpants and tossed them into a ditch by a hedge outside the phone box, covering them with grass. Then I went back into Casualty, cleaned up and waited for the inspector to come away from the suspect's bedside. By now, my rivals from the *News* and *Star* had arrived, followed soon afterwards by the 'nationals'.

The 'guvnor' emerged at about 11 a.m. and asked us all to go back to Woodford Green, where he would hold a Press conference. At this, he confirmed that his No.1 suspect had indeed attempted suicide but said that he still had 'one or two ends to tidy up'. For one thing, he still had to find various items of the murdered boy's clothing which were not in the gas-filled flat when it was searched. He would be using dogs.

After he had offered to hold another Press conference at 4.30 p.m., we all went to the pub. I remember downing several 'horse's necks' (brandy and dry ginger ale) partly to settle my stomach and partly to raise morale after the embarrassing experience. I had the distinct impression that my colleagues were keeping their distance.

When we all trooped back for the conference, a trestle table with a green baize cloth over it had been set up near the 'guvnor'. On it, there were various items of clothing in plastic bags : and there, near the front, *were what looked suspiciously like my underpants.*

I don't remember much of what the detective said after that – except that his men were going to try to trace laundry marks – because my mind had frozen in shock. What was the best thing to do? Ignore them and hope the trail would go cold before it reached me? Admit to littering a public place? Own up in front of my colleagues and become the laughing stock of Fleet Street? I decided to come clean (excuse the pun) but *after* the Press conference was over.

I hung around until the last reporter had left, then sidled up to the table. 'Er hum,' I coughed, 'you needn't waste your time on those.'

The pants were indeed mine but 'the guvnor' was extremely nice about it. 'Don't worry' he said afterwards. 'We've all got our reasons to remember *this* one (case)'.

CHAPTER FOUR

Heads Science – Tails Transport

L ife at the *Standard* continued apace with more time being spent on stories *outside* the office than in, as trust and confidence built up. The office had an atmosphere all of its own – strip lighting, organised muddle, ringing telephones and shouts of 'boy' on the editorial floor and the all-pervading smell of hot lead and printer's ink on the type-setting floor below. Nine times a day, you felt – and then heard – the thrum of the presses and the squeal of brakes, as the delivery vans with their rubber mud-guards drew level with chutes and men started tossing quire upon quire of papers, bound with string, across the pavement for loading.

It was good to be inside in winter but better away from the office in spring and summer.

After spells of crime reporting, I found myself involved with Circulation Drives and Souvenir Editions. The circulation of the *Standard* was around 750,000 copies at that time, compared with about 1.2 million for the *Evening News*. The *News* great strength lay in the appeal of its early editions to readers (mainly house-wives) in the suburbs and Home Counties. So, every so often, the *Standard* management would decide to have a blitz on a par-ticular area and try to sell more copies. This was done primarily by offering incentives to newsagents and by faster distribution. But a reporter was also posted to the area to find stories which could be headlined on the billboards.

I spent several enjoyable weeks in the Reading, Sevenoaks and Maidstone areas digging out 'overnights' – 'soft' news stories which could be pre-set in early editions and bill-boarded locally, then replaced later in the day as 'hard' news came along. But, more importantly, I got to know the circulation reps.

The *Standard*'s reps. were the salt of the earth – unsung, often un-thanked heroes, tireless in their efforts to persuade news-

agents and street-corner sellers to work harder. Their camaraderie was close – many were Masons – and they possessed a ribald
sense of humour. At the end of each Circulation Drive, they would
hold a dinner, to which I was usually invited. The close understanding of each other's working problems, which developed from
these meetings, proved enormously helpful to my career later.

Souvenir editions were another way by which newspapers built
up circulation. They were often timed to coincide with visits by
royalty and filled with 'soft' stories at the start of the day and then
'hard' coverage of the royal visit later, in the hope that the townsfolk
would like a souvenir of the visit.

My assignments included visits by the Queen to Guildford,
Weymouth, Reading, and Chelmsford. Although they were qualified me for a by-line, they left me with contempt for the obsequi-
ousness shown by some of the local dignitaries and officials who
were due to meet the Queen. I called it 'Queen Fever'.

At times, it came close to madness. On one occasion, when the
temperature was close to freezing, I watched a Scoutmaster call a
troop of young Sea Scouts to rigid attention five whole minutes
before the Queen's train was due to arrive at the platform where
they were drawn up as a guard of honour. Not surprisingly, one
of them fainted and had to be removed with a cut forehead and
bruises.

On another wintry occasion, it transpired that the wife of the
Mayor who was also the Mayoress – had broken her leg the previous day and was confined to a hospital bed and therefore unable to meet Her Majesty. Even a relatively inexperienced 'Royal
watcher' like me could predict what would happen. So, while
Queen and Corporation were lunching, I sped to the hospital
where the Mayoress was in traction and waited. Sure enough, a
telephone call came, informing Matron that the Queen was changing her schedule and coming to the hospital to avoid disappointing the Mayoress.

Pandemonium followed. During the 20 minutes prior to the
Queen's arrival, the Mayoress was physically transported downstairs in her bed, positioned in Matron's office near the front door
and propped up on clean pillows. The carpet in the office was
lifted and a brand new one laid. Orders were given to 'borrow' all
the patients' flowers from the wards and bank them in the foyer
outside Matron's office. Finally, every mobile patient was invited
to leave his or her ward immediately and assemble – many in

pyjamas, on crutches or in wheelchairs – in the car park by the door where the Queen would enter.

They shivered. I shuddered. I wondered how many of them would suffer complications due to having to wait for half an hour in skimpy clothing and near-freezing temperatures. And I vowed to write a book one day, called *Behind the Ballyhoo*, with a whole chapter on Queen Fever.

How nice it was to discover, some 12 years later, when I actually met the Queen, that she, too, disliked such obsequious behaviour.

Royal visits, strikes, crimes, missing persons, coroners' inquests, tribunal hearings, road accidents, train crashes, society scandals, Mansion House speeches – all such items were bread and butter to a general reporter on a London evening newspaper in the 1950s. I found the life stimulating for a while. But in 1956, an incident occurred which profoundly altered the nature of my work and changed my life for ever.

The date was Saturday, October 14, 1956. The time: 12 noon. With Denise Richards, I had gone to the Two Brewers – the pub opposite the *Standard* – for a sandwich lunch. We decided to share a bottle of Macon Villages. It had been a quiet morning and mid-way through the bottle we started to see life very clearly, as one often does with a good bottle of wine.

We were concerned about our future careers on the paper. We realised that we could not expect much advancement it we remained general news reporters . So we analysed what the *Standard* lacked and what it needed.

In those days, there were not many specialist writers in Fleet Street. Two specialities which we pin-pointed as definitely of interest to our paper were Science and Transport.

'Let's flip a coin,' said Denise, taking one from her handbag. 'Heads Science, tails Transport – you first.' I can remember seeing the two bob piece scatter the sawdust on the pub floor before it came to rest heads up.

We decided to crack another bottle of wine while we discussed the implications of her becoming Transport Queen and my having to cover a subject which ranged from Agriculture and The Atom to X-rays and Zoology. Afterwards, as we crossed Shoe Lane, we realised we were late.

The Army had taught me that, if you are holding a piece of paper, you look busy. So, hardly daring to look at the News Desk,

we both grabbed technical magazines from the pile which was
always deposited on the reporters' desk in the hope that someone
might unearth a story. The one I grabbed turned out to be *Municipal Engineering* and was sub-titled *The Muck Shifter*.

Through an alcoholic haze I saw a story, with picture, of a
machine which could dig a slit trench three feet deep at the rate
of three yards a minute. I turned to Denise and said, 'What
wouldn't the Old Contemptibles have given for one of these in
the First World War?'

'Why don't you write it up,' she replied, 'as if we've spent the
lunch hour watching it in action? Go on – it'll give us an excuse
for being late.' So I wrote about 200 words, based on the technical data – under the heading 'God's Gift to the Old Contemptibles
Fifty Years Too Late' – and handed it in to the News Desk.

'I didn't know you were interested in this kind of thing,' re-
torted Phil Grune (for it was he in charge, yet again). 'Didn't
you?' I said with a touch of sarcasm. 'Why, I've got one of the
best technical brains in the office'. His eyes twinkled as he reached
into his desk drawer and pulled out a book. 'Next Tuesday,' he
said, 'the Queen is going to open the world's first commercial
atomic power station at Calder Hall and Features have asked for
1,000 words on atomic energy what it is and what it will mean for
us all – by 11 o'clock on Monday morning. Go on Technical
Brain – you write it.'

I still have the book on my shelves. It is called simply *Calder
Hall* by Kenneth Jay of the Atomic Energy Research Establishment at Harwell. It is one of the most lucid books on a technical
subject that I have ever read and I had no difficulty in understanding atomic energy and producing the 1000 words by that
Monday morning.

When I handed the feature in, Grune passed me a rail ticket to
Seascale in Cumberland (Cumbria) and said, 'You'd better get
up there and cover the Queen's visit.'

Wednesday, October 17, brought plenty of excitement. To fill
the early editions of the paper with some kind of relevant story,
before the Queen pulled the switch to feed some 90,000 kW of
electricity into the National Grid, I had discovered that the man
in charge of this latest example of complex, high-technology lived
in a cottage lit by *oil lamps*! The Atomic Age might have dawned
for him but it certainly hadn't for his wife.

The previous day, we had donned white coats and been shown

around one of the two turbine halls, through the Control Room and over the top of a gas-cooled reactor while Atomic Energy Authority Press officers fed us a stream of facts. They used fine words such as 'ushering in a new age of clean, cheap power' and a 'British world first' and kept stressing the peaceful 'swords-into-ploughshares' significance of the station.

The Queen picked up all these points in her speech, which I duly reported by phone to the *Standard*. It was not until 20 years later that I discovered that Calder Hall *wasn't* the world's first commercial atomic power station (the Russians had been operating one at Obninsk, 55 miles from Moscow, for two years) nor was its prime purpose peaceful. It was to produce plutonium for atomic bombs.

But it made a good story at the time and we all felt proud and optimistic about the Atomic Age. More important, when I returned to the office next day, Phil Grune said sarcastically, 'You'd better start calling yourself the Science Correspondent, Technical Brain!'

Thus, within 96 hours of the flip of that coin, I had actually achieved my objective.

Coming to grips with Science

The word 'Correspondent' had too many letters to it for the liking of a Beaverbrook paper and so, initially, I started to slip the title '*Standard* Science Reporter' on top of those stories relating to science. Nobody stopped me and I kept on doing so until, eventually, the empire had grown so large that I felt bold enough to substitute 'Editor' for 'Reporter'. Again, nobody stopped me and so I have been a Science Editor, on and off, to this day.

All this may sound big-headed and boastful but it was more important as a status symbol to *others* than to me. For one thing, Editors get invited to many more events than Reporters and, besides, it was a title more in tune with being an Expert or Specialist. The only problem was that I quickly had to become an 'expert' in many different disciplines, including Engineering, Technology and Medicine.

It was the decade when science was regarded as wonderful and scientists were looked on with respect – even in awe. Actually, more often than not, it was *technology* that fascinated people, but *scientists* were usually given the credit. We used to have a saying: 'Scientists have the idea – engineers make it work.' As the son of an engineer, who did not like my using any piece of equipment in the home unless I could strip it down, repair it (if broken) and then put it in working order again – including the family car – I was particularly conscious of this misnomer and have often wondered why science received so much recognition in newspapers and engineering so little.

Maybe it was because several of my colleagues in Fleet Street quickly realised, like me, that by becoming the Science Reporter, Science Correspondent or Science Editor, they would be 'onto a good thing'. So they pushed the title as hard as they could without diluting it.

I soon realised that the only way to acquire enough knowledge to write authoritatively about such a broad subject as was to read voraciously and build up a large cadre of genuine experts with whom I could consult and check my copy. So I began taking a briefcase full of work – mainly technical papers and magazines – home at night.

I was also fortunate to attend a medical conference in Edinburgh and spend a 'free' day with Ronnie Bedford, the Science Editor of the *Daily Mirror*, who had been one of the pioneers in the business, despite the handicaps of having no roof to his mouth and such poor eyesight that he could only read print if he held it about two inches in front of his eyes. As we sat for nearly three hours on the banks of the Firth of Forth, he told me about phraseology, contacts, danger areas everything he knew about the job.

One of his pieces of advice was that scientists and engineers enjoy good lunches just as much as the rest of us. So I started to use the *Standard*'s generous expense allowance to good effect. The stories flowed in.

The Atomic Age was quickly followed by the Electronic Age and then the Space Age. There was hardly a night when 'science' did not receive prominent coverage in the paper. Feature series started to appear – five 1,000- word features on consecutive days in a week – with titles such as 'Challenge', 'The Computer Age', 'Moonbound' and 'Breakthrough' which reflected the tremendous pace of discovery and invention at that time.

The individual subjects covered in 'Breakthrough' – the laser, superconductivity in metals, hyperbaric (high-pressure) oxygen in medicine, high pressure physics and the chemical origin of life on Earth – were highly complex. But I felt that I had to *try* to make people aware of their importance.

The pay-off came with another letter from Charles Wintour: '*The Circulation Department reports that your series 'Breakthrough' was a tremendous success with readers, particularly the younger ones.*'

'Science' was actually beginning to help sell the *Standard*. To my delight, my salary was increased again.

'Big Bang' causes a bang

The importance of a friendly relationship with the Circulation reps. was further confirmed by a story which appeared across four whole pages of the paper on February 12, 1962. An astronomer contact had tipped me off over lunch that the team of radio-astronomers at the Mullard Observatory in Cambridge had obtained scientific evidence amounting to proof that the Universe began with one Big Bang.

Up till then, two conflicting theories had been put forward to explain how our world came to be here. One was that a dense clump of matter originally exploded with one Big Bang and that the fragments, in the form of stars and galaxies of stars, had been rushing outwards ever since. The other, known as the Steady-State theory, held that matter in the Universe was continuously evolving, some dying away, some being created afresh, but more or less in the same places all the time. Few of us science-writers ever expected the conflict to be resolved.

I rang Professor Martin Ryle, head of the observatory. 'Is this true?' I asked. 'Are you prepared to put your hands on your hearts and say it began with a Big Bang?'

'It *is* true,' he replied, 'but you put us in a very embarrassing position. We feel it would be wise to carry out one more set of experiments – just to double-check our figures and avoid making asses of ourselves; and I feel duty-bound, with something as important as this, to communicate our findings first through *Nature*. Can you hold off for a while?'

Nature, contrary to popular belief, was not a nudist magazine but the learned journal of the scientific community. My problem was that it was published on a Thursday evening, with a midnight embargo, which meant that national daily newspapers had first crack at it and could run stories from it in their Friday issues Ryle was asking me to hand my scoop on a plate to my rivals.

We struck a bargain. I would suppress the story until he said 'go', providing that when the time was right, I could have full details and a chance to run the story in the final edition of Thursday's *Standard*.

I waited nine months. It was the longest nine months I have ever known and not made any easier by Ronnie Hyde querying regularly why we still could not 'blow' the story. Then, on Monday, February 9, Martin Ryle phoned. 'OK,' he said. 'We're ready.'

Next day, photographer Harry Thompson and I drove to Cambridge, stopping on the way to take pictures of the extraordinary criss-crossed lines of antennae, spread across fields, which gave the Mullard radio-telescope its extraordinary range and sensitivity (it was recording events as they happened 10,000 million years ago across a distance of some 100,000 million million million miles of space. The energy given off by those events had taken that long to reach the Earth).

We took pictures of Ryle's team of young radio-astronomers who had done much of the work – Dr. Anthony Hewish, Paul Scott, Rupert Clarke, Mrs. Pat Leslie and Dr. F Graham Smith (later to direct the radio-telescope at Jodrell Bank). We took pictures of the equipment in the Cavendish Laboratory and of the computer read-outs, which told the whole story in graphs and digital language.

Basically, what they had discovered was that stars were clustered around the edges of the Universe in greater numbers than in nearer space and that the distant stars had quite different characteristics from the closer ones characteristics that were still changing: also, that the most distant were still racing outwards almost at the speed of light.

All those findings fitted the concept of a gigantic explosion – a Big Bang – with the solid matter still travelling away from the centre like pieces of shrapnel from a bomb. It did NOT fit the theory of a 'steady' Universe.

Ryle told me: 'Now that we have some *proof*, we can tackle some of the minor variants to the theory by enlarging the radio-telescope and looking still further back in time. I am looking forward to exploring some of the other unknowns such as why and how some of the matter is changing – but I would like a chance to do some thinking first. At times, this work can be very hectic.'

The next two days certainly were so. The team invited the world's Press to a conference in the underground cinema at Mullard House in Torrington Place, Bloomsbury, on Thursday, February 12. The Press conference was timed for 4.30 p.m. with a midnight embargo on the news. That meant that my rivals, the *Evening News* and *The Star*, were excluded. I was given permission to run the story in our 4 p.m. edition. The paper did it proud, with huge headlines and a graphic diagram of an exploding Universe on the front page and three other pages of pictures and text, inside and on the back.

I had the personal satisfaction of watching 160 of my colleagues from Fleet Street troop into the cinema past a white-coated newspaper seller, clutching a sheaf of *Standards* to his chest, shouting 'Universe began with Big Bang, say scientists'. The story ricocheted around the world for 96 hours, with TV, radio and foreign newspapers joining in the coverage.

In the next issue of the current affairs journal *Time and Tide*, the columnist Pertinax devoted a whole page to the affair. His report began:

> When Professor Martin Ryle left the historic Press conference at Mullard House last week, he met an irate journalist waving the *Evening Standard*. The front page story, under the headline 'SCIENTISTS GRASP CLUE TO RIDDLE OF UNIVERSE' was by Peter Fairley. The journalist barked out an expletive and asked the Mullard Press officer what had happened. He was told: 'He followed up a hint that a big story was coming.'

Pertinax went on.

> Fairley's story was one of the most intelligent. It is clear he had time to prepare it.

Nine months, in fact. Martin went on to become Astronomer Royal and a knight, but finally suffered a stroke and died. My reward came sooner – next day, in fact – when I received another of those Wintour letters. It read:

> Dear Fairley, Warmest congratulations on your very fine scoop on Prof. Ryle's discoveries. Your reputation is expanding as fast as the Universe. The circulation department reckon that they sold

an extra 10,000 copies on your story alone. This was a fine effort. I hope you enjoy your holiday. I have told the News Desk to leave you alone to enjoy it in peace.

Ha ha. Funny joke!

The World of Science

As soon as it was noticed that the *Standard* had appointed a Science specialist, a large volume of technical and semi-technical information started to pour in — news-releases from firms and research laboratories, Government departments and professional institutions, scientific papers and journals from the learned societies. It would not be exaggeration to say that, if I was away from the office for a fortnight, a pile of paper one foot high and two feet wide would be waiting on return. Every item *might* have contained a story. It all had to be sifted. Often, even if not dynamic, it proved interesting. So I decided to start writing some of the stories in a weekly science column which we called *The World of Science*.

The World of Science appeared every Friday, 52 weeks of every year between 1958 and 1968. When it first appeared, it filled one column. By the time I had written my last, it had spread across two, sometimes three columns and included pictures.

It was not easy filling so much space, without fail, with stories which would 'keep' for a week without their appearing in another newspaper. But I stuck to the task because Beaverbrook Newspapers were quick to see the column's syndication potential and because the *Standard*, with nine editions to fill, was always needing 'overnight' material.

The policy paid off. Not only did it earn money for the Group but the suppliers of the information were usually so pleased to see their stories used that, when they had an item of really important news, they were inclined to give it to the *Standard* first.

Much of what appeared in *The World of Science* was less than memorable. But some stories had interesting sequels and a few I shall never forget.

One concerned a column published in July 1959. A technical Press release came in from a multi-national company, Cyanamid, about a substance called AM 9 Chemical Grout. The chemical had been developed to stabilise shifting soil. What interested me about it was that it had a delayed reaction which could be remotely controlled – it would set at a precise time underground according to the number of scoopfuls used: one measure per minute of delay needed, as I recall. This meant that it would stay liquid until it had permeated all the pores in the soil – or penetrated all the underground nooks and crannies – and then suddenly set rock-hard. And the reaction-time was so accurate that a builder could set his watch by it.

It was not the most earth-shattering of stories (excuse the pun) and I only gave it a couple of paragraphs in the column. But three days later the phone rang and a voice said words to the effect of 'This is so-and-so of the Atomic Energy Authority – where can we get hold of some AM 9 Chemical Grout?'

It transpired that the construction team building the Dragon nuclear reactor at Winfrith Heath in Dorset had hit a problem – underground springs. Everything the construction workers had tried, as a way of keeping out water and firming up the ground before foundations were laid, had failed. Then a local newspaper published my *World of Science*.

I put the AEA man in touch with the UK manager of Cyanamid, supplies were rushed to Winfrith, the chemical reaction worked and, to this day, Dragon still stands firm (although now de-commissioned) on a bed of AM9 grout.

The science of bull-fighting

Using the title *World of Science* as the excuse and the column as the outlet, I used to get a lot of pleasure out of finding scientific 'angles' in unexpected subject areas. One such was bullfighting.

I had been sent to Madrid to cover a conference and, as a matter of courtesy, made contact with the paper's local 'stringers' in order to pick up advice about restaurants, transport, phone links to London and so forth. Our Spanish correspondents were Christopher Morris (later to join the BBC) and Tim Brown, two of the most efficient and likeable journalists I have ever met.

In their office, they were employing a chauffeur-cum-general factotum named Henry Higgins and the four of us went out, on the first night, for a gourmet dinner in a restaurant opposite the front gates of the Patio de Caballos, the larger of Madrid's two

Peter with his grandfather, Thomas Fairley.

Peter on his pony in India.

A toy soldier in India!

Peter boarding train for evacuation to Betws-y-Coed in 1939.

Peter at the Royal Oak Hotel, Betws-y-Coed after evacuation.

Peter with his parents Frank and Ethel Fairley, at Sutton Valence School.

As a young man.

Evening Standard

The world's greatest adventure begins

HE'S UP and BACK
MAN REACHES FOR
THE STARS

Soviet major is Spaceman No. 1 — for 108 minutes

The man whose name will live in history

By PETER FAIRLEY

MAN HAS BEEN INTO SPACE and come back alive. He zoomed gloriously into orbit atop a mighty Russian rocket. Buffeted. Deafened. Comforted—but safe.

Just one orbit

'For this exploit...'

Evening Standard

After a day of agony the moment of glory

AND THIS WAS THE MESSAGE THAT WILL GO INTO THE HISTORY BOOKS

GLENN
Once, twice and again

ORBITS

London mystery of the naked men

Ban-the-bomb six sentenced

Evening Standard

'Britain's future in danger'

BRAIN DRAIN:
STAGGERING
FACTS

LONDON MP DIES IN ROOM OF GAS

By PETER FAIRLEY

SIX THOUSAND TWO HUNDRED scientists, engineers and technologists are leaving Britain EVERY year for better paid jobs in other countries, says a Government-sponsored report out today. This is double the number leaving six years ago—and most are aged 25-30.

● TWO out of every five young engineers are quitting.

● IN the United States—main magnet for Brain Drainers—a young scientist can get THREE TIMES as much as he could earn in Britain and keep more of it from the taxman.

● IT costs Britain between £6000-£16,000 to train these men. On arrival in the U.S. they are worth about £78,000 to America.

● BRITAIN, the report adds, will HAVE to pay these men more as a deliberate national policy if the Drain is to be stopped.

● UNLESS it is, the report concludes, 'the future well-being of Britain will be in danger.'

TAYLOR'S PORT
everything a fine port should be

Evening Standard

'A flash and that was it...'

DEATH TRAP
RIDDLE OF THE
MOON MEN

Soccer's biggest day since World Cup

WIFE DIES IN HOUSE BLAST

Police shoot girl, 'SHE WAS LOOTING'

By PETER FAIRLEY

A selection of Peter's lead articles for the Evening Standard.

A meeting with Russian cosmonaut Lt.-Col. Valery Bykovsky.

Peter, at a conference, talks to Dr Wernher von Braun.

Paul Haney, Alastair Burnet and Peter.

ITN Newsroom: (left to right) Peter Cole, Peter Sissons, Don Horobin, Michael Nicholson and George Ffitch.

ITN Newsroom: (left to right) David Nicholas, Alastair Burnet, Andrew Gardner and George Ffitch.

bullrings. 'You must have a steak.' urged Chris. 'You'll never eat fresher beef anywhere.'

The steak virtually fell apart in the mouth. More importantly, we all got on famously and I quickly grew to like Henry who, despite being English, was actually a novice matador, working in the newspaper office merely to supplement his income.

Next day, he showed me his bejewelled matador's waistcoat, crimson cape and black hat and offered to take me to a bullfight.

The following Saturday saw us sitting in two of the best seats, along with 20,000 roaring Spaniards and a few fainting tourists, watching the legendary El Cordobes in action, while Henry quietly explained the finer points of bullfighting. 'The first thing a matador does on the morning of a fight,' Henry began, 'is to listen to the weather forecast.'

From that moment I was hooked.

He explained that it was not red that made a bull charge but movement. Unexpected gusts of wind, rippling an outstretched cape just as the matador was poised for the *coup de grâce*, posed the biggest danger of all and, if breezes were forecast, the bullfighter modified his technique accordingly. He also told me how carefully bullfighters study bovine anatomy, even to the point of attending university lectures on the subject.

I decided to devote the whole of a *World of Science* column to bullfighting and, after six gripping fights in the ring, Henry took me to the Bullfighting Museum by the Plaza de Toros de Ventas, containing some of the strangest surgical instruments that I had ever seen, many of them shaped to deal with wounds caused by horns. Outside the museum, stood a huge statue to Sir Alexander Fleming, discoverer of penicillin.

'He's our hero,' explained Henry. 'Bullfighters owe more to him than any other man in history. Penicillin has completely transformed bullfighting.'

Henry went on to describe how previously, if a matador was gored, he was usually a 'gonner' – 'Even if he didn't bleed to death, infection would set in and kill him,' he added, 'but antibiotics now enable most fighters to recover.'

Henry Higgins went on to become one of Spain's most celebrated bull-fighters and a very rich man. Ironically, he was not killed in the ring but in a hang-glider accident. He now lies buried in the cemetery of the seaside town of Mojacar, where fans maintain a continuous tribute to him with flowers.

The science of jazz

I found another bizarre subject for *The World of Science* in Orlando, Florida. We had spent several weeks waiting for John Glenn – the first American to orbit the world – to lift off at Cape Canaveral. While I was there, Dave Brubeck and his Quartet were billed to give a one-night 'gig' in Orlando University. Being a lover of jazz and 'easy listening' music – and a bit of a Brubeck fan – I leaped at the chance to spend $10 and hear him play 'live'.

After a seafood supper and several frozen daiquiris, I turned up in excellent spirits at the lecture theatre, where the group was performing.

The warm glow lasted throughout the three hour session, during which Big Questions and Great Truths began to form in my mind, as they had after the bottle of Macon in the Two Brewers three years earlier.

Brubeck's group had just scored a hit with *Take Five*, which had an uneven 5:4 beat. Somebody had once told me that the reason why so many people love popular music is because its rhythmic beat reminds them, subconsciously, of the lub-a-dub of their mother's heartbeat. If this was so, why had *Take Five* – which, in heartbeat terms might have equated to a hole-in-the-heart condition – been such a hit? Had Brubeck ever thought about that? What was *his* explanation?

I was also struck by the animation of the audience. What accounted for the extra impact of a 'live' performance over a recording? Had Brubeck ever thought about that?

After the session, I plucked up courage to ask. There were others waiting to have 'words' with Brubeck and so I decided to chat first to Joe Morello, the quartet's drummer. Joe told me that Brubeck was indeed interested in such things and that I should persevere. In the meantime, he filled me in with a colourful description of the group's life on the road, including the fact that every booking contract had to include a female escort for Paul Desmond, the saxophonist.

By the time I got to Brubeck's dressing room, it was midnight. Despite the late hour, the interview continued for three hours, during which he described scientifically-controlled experiments which he had carried out in a New York hospital, to investigate the 'live' performance phenomenon.

He also said he listened regularly to heartbeat recordings (including some from hole-in-the-heart patients) in search of new rhythms.

The 'live' tests had involved a ward-full of catatonic patients – comatose men and women with little more brain response than vegetables – wired up to electro-encephalographs (brain-wave recorders, or ECGs). First, tape recordings of the Brubeck Quartet were played from behind screens at one end of the ward: the ECGs registered nothing. Next, the quartet itself took up positions behind the screens and played the same tunes: this time, the needles clearly moved on the tracing paper. Finally, the screens were removed, the group played once more – and the ECG needles peaked and troughed all over the place.

'At least it proved conclusively,' commented Brubeck, 'that a "live" performance is a powerful stimulant. It's something you have to be careful about if you are to avoid audience hysteria- perhaps alternating relaxing music with arousing music is the best safeguard.'

The bandleader had recently toured the world in search of interesting rhythms, as well as having listened to many recordings of different heartbeats. 'I've heard this theory about the mother's heartbeat,' he said, 'and I wondered about *Take Five* too. But I've come to the conclusion that rhythm is far less important to a person's appreciation of music than repetition.'

'On the Indian sub-continent,' he went on, 'we heard many unusual rhythms – 9:4, 5:2, for example. They became enjoyable to Western ears – and sometimes quite haunting – if the rhythm was repeated over and over again. In fact, I would say that composers need not worry about new melodies for the next hundred years – there are enough unusual rhythms to keep us going.'

Science and the Greyhound Derby

The final *World of Science* column worth mentioning was the one which forecast the result of the 1960 Greyhound Derby.

I had been interested for some time in the application of scientific techniques to gambling – such as the use of computers to forecast the results of races (or at least improve the odds on winning). The Greyhound Derby seemed to offer a suitable opportunity to put theory to the test.

Willie Wicks and the rest of the dog-racing department at the *Standard* agreed to help and worked for four whole days to provide the data we needed. The beauty of the Derby was that there were a number of measurable factors in it. To have reached the final, the six dogs must have run on the White City track at least twice before. They were timed to half way as well as over the full course. They came either from Irish or from English kennels. The pedigree records were available as well as the records of the trainers – and so on.

We fed all the data into an Elliott Automation computer at 8 p.m on the Thursday of Derby Week. The machine literally gurgled for five minutes. Then a punched tape came chattering out of the printer with the winner's name in code. Deciphered, it read 'TRIP TO DUBLIN'.

Next day, I wrote the whole of the science column about how and why an Irish dog named Trip to Dublin was about to win the Greyhound Derby. Not surprisingly, we all put money on the dog (Bill Roland put £50) and I even went to the track to watch the race on the Saturday night.

On Monday morning, there were some sheepish looks – both at Elliott Automation and at the *Standard*. Trip to Dublin had come in last!

Why? Why, had a dog with a faultless pedigree, running in Trap No.1 (the inside trap) renowned for its quick start, never beaten if it did make a quick getaway – how could such a 'dead cert' come in last?

Analysis of a film afterwards showed that Trip to Dublin, notoriously quick out of the trap, had been last out that night. His records had shown that, if he was in the lead at the first bend, he never lost. That night, he was fourth at the bend. I remember Willie Wicks, a cheerful Cockney with years of track 'know how' – who had, of course backed the winner – almost dancing with glee.

'I told you so,' he said. 'I told you there were things about dogs which you could never program into a bloody computer.'

Willie explained that there were two factors about dogs which did not present themselves until Derby night itself. One was the individual dog's reaction to music (on Derby nights, at the White City, a brass band played between races). The other was that the crowd, in their excitement, shouted 'They're off' so loudly that the crescendo of voices drowned the hum of the electric hare as it neared the starting traps. Some dogs, like some athletes who swear they can hear the click of the hammer on the detonator before the starting pistol fires, would start leaping forwards the moment they heard the hare.

Which if either of those factors affected Trip to Dublin we shall never know. I had a hard job fighting off colleagues who wanted *me* to reimburse them for the money they had lost and it brought home to me the limitations of computers as a means of forecasting race results – limitations which can only be worse in horse-racing, where there are so many more variables.

Much to my surprise, I recently discovered several computer bureaux specialising in such forecasting – not only with dogs but horses too – although none of them would disclose how many clients they had on their files, nor their success rate!

The first 'Flying Saucer'

The late '50s and early '60s were notable for some remarkable inventions and technical developments. Each commanded large areas of newsprint and allowed science and technology writers to establish reputations.

A prime example was the hovercraft. My office had received a tip from a yachtsman who had seen a strange machine being worked on behind the half-open doors of the Saunders-Roe hangar beside Cowes Harbour. Ronnie Hyde called Bill Roland, the Shipping Reporter, over. 'But this can't be a *ship*,' protested Bill.

Next he called James Stuart, the Air Correspondent over. 'If it's at Cowes, it won't be an aircraft these days,' was his comment. Finally, he turned to me. 'Is this scientific enough for you, Peter?' he asked, handing me the tip.

'I don't care whether it is or isn't,' I said, 'it sounds an interesting story.' That night found me asking questions in the bars of both East and West Cowes. The whiff of news was strong.

June that year (1959) began, in the Isle of Wight, with a mini-heat wave. White-hulled yachts swung gently at their moorings and the water sparkled as, on three successive days, the roar of a powerful aero-engine burst from behind hessian screens shielding Saunders-Roe's slipway at East Cowes.

It was tantalising. What sort of a vehicle was it? Why the tremendous engine noise? How fast could it go? Were there *military*

implications? There were many questions but few answers and
Saunders-Roe were saying nothing. However, the tightness of
the security was an obvious measure of the importance of the
story.

Eventually, in a bar in East Cowes, I found someone who had
not only heard about 'the contraption in the hangar' but had actually seen some intriguing experiments with small skimming
models – he called them 'flying saucers' – in the grounds of a
house further up the hill. For a fiver, he showed me where, The
house belonged to a Mr. Cockerell. But there was no one in.

Next day, June 7, I had a stroke of luck – I spotted Gavin
Cochrane, a former *Exchange Telegraph* reporter and an old friend
from my news agency days. He had switched to public relations
and was in Cowes to advise a client – the National Research Development Corporation (NRDC). 'Anything to do with what's
going on across the harbour?' I asked.

Gavin then offered a deal. In exchange for my promise not to
publish anything before June 11, he gave me the full, accurate
facts about the research and development of the hovercraft and
the exciting possibilities it offered for high-speed land-sea travel.

The information, given in advance, enabled me to find and
interview Christopher Cockerell (later knighted for his services
to engineering) and his wife Margaret, obtain plans, sketches and
diagrams, fine up vantage points for cameramen and fully brief
the *Standard*.

June 11 saw marquees on the lawns of the Saunders-Roe works
in East Cowes. Caterers fussed around a massive buffet lunch
as coach-loads of journalists arrived from the Solent ferry to
hear the principles of hovercraft explained in public for the very
first time. Dick Stanton-Jones, Saunders-Roe's chief designer,
used lantern slides to illustrate how a whole range of hovercraft
from 3 to 10 to 100 and even up to 10,000 tons – already seemed
feasible because the air-cushion principle implied that the bigger they grew the more efficient and comfortable they would
become.

Afterwards, five model hovercraft, buzzing like angry wasps,
were allowed to skim freely among the guests drinking sherry and
wine on the lawn.

By now, the *Standard* was carrying the whole story. But at 4
p.m. it replaced it with an update which began like this:

Up she goes. Forward she goes – and backwards and sideways. 'She' is the world's first true flying saucer, the ferry of the future, opening up a new era in travel.

British-invented. British-designed, British-built (this was good Beaverbrook stuff) the world's first hovercraft made her debut today before 300 Pressmen and holidaymakers – and she was piloted by a Briton, too. At 3.20 came the historic moment etc., etc., etc.

The story was accompanied by a marvellous picture, taken by Vic Drees, which the *Standard* and then international picture agencies made the most of – the hovercraft passing in front of the SS *Queen Mary* on the Solent, the old saluting the new. Next day, when we returned home after a lively night in Cowes, we both found telegrams from the Editor waiting for us.

I found myself covering all sorts of hovercraft stories after that – the first Channel crossing, the first military hovercraft, hover-ferries, hover-lorries, the hover-bed, the hover-train – even the hover-kiln. Many have gone into routine use, others have yet to realise their full potential.

I also had many dealings with the NRDC, for whom I eventually wrote a book (see Ch.11) and frequent meetings with Sir Christopher, who probably saw in me a means to jerk Authority into action as well as a rare species – a journalist prepared to 'sit' on a story.

Every time I crossed the Channel aboard *The Princess Anne* or *The Princess Margaret*, Hoverspeed's two 400-ton SRN 4 hovercraft, I used to send him a congratulatory postcard.

The world below the waves

In the early 1960s, I had a great deal of contact with the Royal Navy and the underwater world. The development of the Polaris submarine – with its nuclear power reactor and 16 nuclear rockets – gave the subject of life under the sea a new importance. I developed a close working relationship with the British Sub-Aqua Club – and with one of its founder members in particular – a science-writer called Peter Small.

Peter firmly believed that Man had once been a sea creature – possibly the sea-ape postulated by Sir Alister Hardy, Professor of

Zoology and Comparative Anatomy at Oxford, in a public lecture in1960 – and that more and more of his activities would require the ability to live and work for long periods underwater.

As well as writing about it, Peter was a diver himself – keen to go deeper and deeper into the oceans, breathing novel mixtures of gases. At that time, a Swiss mathematician called Hannes Keller (a disciple of J.B.S. Haldane, the inventor of staged decompression for divers) had published a set of tables setting out levels of oxygen, nitrogen and helium to breathe for different periods under different pressures at different depths, including after the diver had returned to the surface. These were designed to avoid the diver getting 'the bends'. Helium was the novelty in the mixture.

Dr Keller organised a diving expedition from a ship off Catalina Island, California, to prove the safety of his gas tables and he agreed to take Peter with him. Peter wanted to reach – and do some work as a frogman –1000 ft. down, thereby setting a new world record for ocean-diving. He hoped that this would give him the necessary stature to act as a consultant, both to the Royal Navy and to manufacturers of underwater equipment and to attract interest in the whole subject. 'If Britain can't make it in space,' he told me, 'at least we can lead the world in undersea exploration.'

I promised Peter extensive coverage in the *Standard* – which would then get syndicated – if he kept the news story exclusive to us. The two of us hatched a plan.

Mary, his lovely wife, whom I had first met at their wedding three months previously was to ring me in London when Peter returned safely to the diving capsule, after his work stint at 1000 ft. on the seabed.

Pictures of Peter, Mary, Keller, the diving ship and the capsule were either taken or acquired by the *Standard* before they left for California. All was set for a 'world exclusive' – for once, I even pre-wrote the story.

I remember the phone ringing by my bed a few days later just before 6 a.m. It was Mary, although I could hardly recognise her voice.

'Peter's dead,' she sobbed. I couldn't take it in at first but she went on to explain that Keller had left the capsule first and planted a Swiss flag on the seabed. But just as Peter was getting out, he had collapsed – she did not know why and one of his frogman fins had become jammed in the hatch as Keller tried to close it. I can't tell you more,' she added. 'I'm coming back to London as soon as this is sorted out.'

Despite the tragic circumstances, Mary had kept her promise. 'Do you still want me to go ahead and write the story?' I asked her. 'Please do,' she said, 'I want people to know what a brave man he was.'

At 9 a.m. that morning, the first edition of the *Standard* came out reporting that a new world diving record had been set up but that one of the divers had perished. Re-writing my story was one of the hardest tasks I have ever had to handle but that was not all. News came a few hours later that Christopher Whittaker, a young support diver, had failed to surface after going down to help close the hatch (his body was never recovered).

There was worse to come. Before the year was out Mary, inconsolable at the loss of her husband, committed suicide. I asked my colleague Bill Roland to write the obituary – it was too much for me.

The case of the vanishing frogman

Peter's death served as a salutary reminder of the dangers to individuals operating below the waves, as Commander Lionel 'Buster' Crabb found out.

Crabb had had a distinguished wartime career as a frogman and had carried out a number of operations as a civilian diver for the Secret Intelligence Service (SIS) during the so-called Cold War which followed.

Although the facts are still an Official Secret, Crabb had either been hired or had volunteered to swim down into Portsmouth Harbour to inspect the propeller and rudder of the Russian cruiser *Ordzhonikidze*, which had brought the Soviet leaders Nikolai Bulganin and Nikita Kruschev on an official visit to Britain. The Admiralty was very interested in the *Ordzhonikidze's* propulsion and steering system because the vessel was unusually fast for a cruiser.

It now seems that Crabb dived, surfaced near the cruiser for a minute or so, re-submerged and swam ashore for some adjustments to his breathing apparatus, dived again – and vanished.

I was covering the 'B and K' visit in London – involving long spells of 'door-stepping' outside Claridge's and, when they finally appeared, getting the answer '*Niet*', or a shake of the head, to every question – and I knew nothing of the drama in Portsmouth Harbour until after the Kremlin leaders had returned home.

Then the Admiralty announced briefly that Cdr Crabb was 'presumed dead as a result of trials with certain underwater equipment'. Nothing about Portsmouth. Nothing about Soviet cruisers.

The whiff of news almost reached gale force as I drove to Portsmouth with Ronnie Hyde's drawl in my ears, 'Find Crabb, dear boy', was all he said.

I remember drinking a beer and sitting in the pub garden overlooking the entrance to Portsmouth Harbour, gazing at the blue-black water and expecting, somehow, the body of a frogman to float to the surface. I spent many hours driving to points along the shore and walking the beaches, in the same hope.

The pub by the harbour became 'base' for half a dozen Fleet Street reporters on the same hunt but there were few discoveries to share (or not share). However, with the aid of a few pound notes, we did manage to find the small hotel where Crabb and another man – later identified as Bernard Smith of the SIS – had stayed for the night before the dive, although the page from the guest's register had been torn out and the manager told to say nothing.

The barman was more talkative and he told us that the man who was called 'Buster' by his companion had drunk five double whiskies during the evening. If it was Crabb – and it now seems certain that it was – he broke one of the prime rules in diving because at least some of the alcohol would certainly remain in his bloodstream and affect the breathing of gas underwater.

There were rumours of a James Bond-like fight with Soviet divers under the hull of the cruiser, of a lethal underwater shock sent out by anti-submarine equipment – even of capture and transportation to the Soviet Union (Crabb was reported to have been seen in Moscow two years later). But without a corpse and with the MoD still keeping mum, interest waned and we were all, eventually, recalled.

Months later, a body was washed ashore near Havant . It had no head, no hands and no feet, but it was identified by *somebody* as Crabb. Still the MoD remained silent.

One explanation for what had happened appeared in a letter to the *Daily Mail* on March 20, 1995. It was from a Mr. C. Worby of Hampshire who wrote:

> The son of the man who trained Commander Crabb – one of the last to see him alive – assures me his death had nothing to do with the Russians. He had been out of training when he offered to dive. He was unfit and ill-prepared for the long, bitterly-cold swim, in full dry-suit and aqualung, in darkness.
>
> When his body was picked up, he was found to have exhausted himself and drowned. The watertight seals at neck, wrists and ankles of his dry suit were intact. The suit had preserved the flesh inside, but exposed parts had rotted away or had been devoured by marine fauna.

Skull and bones too, Mr. Worby? I still wonder.

Life in a confined space

Peter Small's death was only a temporary blip on the progress chart of underwater exploration. Other divers went to 600 ft. and returned safely. Jacques Cousteau organised expeditions in which his French divers lived – first for hours, then for days – on the seabed in the Mediterranean.

America set up a Man-in-Sea programme, using a succession of underwater 'habitats' called Sealabs.

One story I wrote for the *Standard* was about two Royal Navy divers, Lieut. Cyril Lafferty and Petty Officer Derek Clark being invited to join a team of 33 'aquanauts' and live for a while in Sealab 3.

The aim of the Sealab programme was, officially, to extend knowledge of the problems of divers living and working for long periods on the seabed. There was romantic talk of aquanauts 'fish farming' and scouring the seabed for minerals and helping to prospect for oil. But the real motivation was the awesome possibility of a Polaris submarine sinking, with its nuclear arsenal and more than 100 sailors aboard, and the need to recover it.

Sealab 3 was basically a cylinder, 57 ft. long and only 12 ft. in diameter, with a changing and shower room attached on one side and an observation room on the other. The divers were expected to spend up to 15 days at a time in it, 600 ft. down off San Clemente Island, California. A bottle-nosed dolphin, a sea-lion and two seals were to be trained as 'messenger boys', carrying mail and other small supplies from the surface.

The men would stay down for the whole fortnight, breathing Keller-type gas mixtures, instead of surfacing regularly and having to 'de-compress' each time – a procedure which could take days if they were not to suffer 'the bends'. Once their bodies had become saturated with the gas, a lot of extra working time on the seabed could be won. They were set a heavy programme of work to test not only their physical strength and stamina but their mental alertness, too. It looked like another fascinating tale of Man's effort to push forward the frontiers of knowledge in difficult circumstances. I was all set to fly to California when the project was postponed indefinitely.

During the preparation of Sealab 3 for the mass-dive, a US Navy diver had been killed, while another was recovered exhausted.

But the concept fascinated me, as did the psychological problems of living in confined spaces for up to a year – something which might well be required of a Polaris crew member.

I was at that age and in that mood of senseless bravado that made me want to experience human challenges before writing about them. I had already been whirled around in an RAF centrifuge to experience the 'g' forces that would be felt by an astronaut riding a rocket into space, sailed in a glider to get the feel of thermal air currents, spent an hour in a hyperbaric (high-pressure) oxygen chamber (it had potential for treating heart and arterial disease and was already saving the lives of victims of coal gas or barbiturate poisoning and the limbs of patients faced with amputation).

I had breathed helium gas to make me talk like Donald Duck (for a radio programme on the problems of diver communication) and even survived being fired at in a glass coffin to test the strength of the bullet-proof glass used in sheikhs' motor cars. Now I wanted to go to sea in a submarine.

The Navy were willing but cautious. I agreed to undergo the standard Navy physical examination (which revealed a 40 per cent hearing loss in my right ear 'probably due to rifle-shooting without earplugs when you were a schoolboy' according to the naval doctor) – and I accepted an offer to practise underwater escape, using the Navy's 90ft tall submarine escape tank at Gosport (the secret was not to hold your breath but to breathe out slowly and under control as you rose).

All that produced useful 'I was there'-style copy for the *World of Science* and other overnight pages of the *Standard*. Then the day came for me to join a hunter-killer submarine at Gosport and put to sea for a day.

Admiralty regulations forbade a submarine to dive until it was (I think) 12 miles from shore. The weather was wild − fierce, gusty winds and huge, undulating waves which the sub. dipped in and out of with great clouds of spray. I spent the first hour 'up top' with the First Lieutenant, gripping the rail around the conning tower for dear life, the salt stinging our faces and eyes (it was impossible to see anything through spectacles). It was ironic to be aboard a vessel built for a smooth ride yet forced to endure discomfort.

Eventually, Number One said, 'Time to go below and have some cocoa.' But the boat was still rolling and the warm air, coupled with the smell of diesel oil, made me wish I was still on the conning tower. At least the air up top was fresh. I looked at my mug of steaming cocoa and thought, 'Hold on, Fairley − don't disgrace yourself'.

The final straw came when the sub. started to dive. The whole wood panelled wardroom seemed to change shape, turning from a rectangle to a square and from a mahogany-brown colour to pea-green (but that may have been my face). I lurched for the door, ran for the 'heads' and was terribly sick.

'You OK, old boy?' one of the junior officers asked, sliding my mug of cocoa across the polished mess table towards me, with a hint of a smirk. 'Well . . .' I started. But the Captain chipped in kindly, 'Don't worry, old chap, it happens to all of us.'

Then he added, 'As a matter of fact, the conditions are so bad today that we wouldn't, normally, put to sea. But we knew you were coming and we didn't want to disappoint you.'

Treasure under the seabed

On July 29, 1959, a giant drill belonging to the NAM Company of Holland bit through hard rock 7300 ft. underground near the Dutch town of Groningen and released a jet of gas. It was colourless and odourless − mostly 'marsh gas', or methane − a natural gas formed by the decay of forests and other vegetation which had become buried with time.

Scientists had suspected it. Engineers had searched for it for years, But it lay deeper than anticipated.

Other bore-holes were drilled. The Groningen discovery turned out to be one of the largest gas fields in the world, capable of meeting the Netherlands' need for gas well into the 21st century.

One man who foresaw that the Groningen 'find' might bring benefits far beyond the shores of Holland was a British oceanographer, Dr Tom Gaskell, Scientific Adviser to British Petroleum. After meeting at an international conference in 1960, he and I found we were definitely on the same wavelength and it was he who opened my eyes to the whole subject of exploring for oil and gas under water.

Aware that BP had been drilling in Eastern England and had found similar rock to that below Groningen, he put two and two together and concluded that the field might stretch all the way across to Britain, under the North Sea. Oil would probably be found with the gas.

Over a long lunch, he painted a picture of a fleet of mobile, semi-submersible rigs drilling bore-holes along the geological strata, with permanent production platforms and pipelines following to bring the gas and oil ashore. It would make Britain one of the richest nations in the world, he predicted.

Tom, despite his joviality and love for 'a drop of the hard stuff', was a serious scientist. After writing up the interview for the *Standard* I told ITN about him and they decided to hire a rowing boat, and take him offshore and interview him bobbing about on the waves. I went with them.

Just as he started to speak from the bow, there was an explosion several hundred yards behind him and a plume of water shot up and splattered down again. The cameraman just managed to get it 'in frame'.

The great North Sea exploration had begun and, by a stroke of good luck, we were in at the start. More seismic surveying followed. An aerial, electromagnetic reconnaissance was carried out. It all looked encouraging and so drilling began. But the first 'strike' – natural gas lying in what is known as the West Sole field – did not come until 1965.

Much of what went on in the North Sea was 'under wraps' for years, for reasons of commercial secrecy. But Tom did manage to get me aboard a small BP rig in Weymouth Bay, to get a feel for the atmosphere of drilling at sea. The prospectors were hoping to strike oil at any moment and you could feel the tension rising as each new core sample was brought into the geologist's hut on deck for analysis.

I had to leave before the verdict was reached, in order to phone about 1000 words to the *Standard* from Weymouth station. By the time the train arrived, two editions had carried the story and I wished I owned some BP shares. Apparently on the strength of my (literally) breathless prose, the share price had risen sixpence. However, when BP announced a week later that Weymouth Bay was a 'no go', it fell back sharply again.

CHAPTER FIVE

The Medicine Men

The popularity of *The World of Science* eventually grew to the point that I decided to try writing a medical column as well. For some time, I had been scouring the medical journals, as well as scientific publications, for news. It seemed a fertile area, only covered thoroughly in those days by *The Times*, *The Daily Telegraph*, *News Chronicle* and *Daily Mirror*.

I remember taking home my first *Lancet* and *British Medical Journal* and, with the aid of a small medical dictionary, spending the weekend trying to assess the meaning and importance of the different, highly-technical reports in them. By the Monday, I was convinced that I had cancer, heart disease, rheumatoid arthritis, needed a colostomy, was developing gout and might well be going down with a condition called 'cold weather itch'. Fortunately, nothing seemed to get worse and, before long, I realised that I had fallen into the trap of jumping to alarming conclusions on the basis of a few mild symptoms, a syndrome which GPs recognise only too well. I read more and more medical journals, attended more British Medical Association conferences and built up contacts among physicians and surgeons until I felt confident enough to tread the medical minefield and emerge with *The World of Medicine*. It ran three issues before I received a letter from the Editor which read as follows:

Dear Fairley,

I am delighted to see that we have a medical column under way. It has some interesting material in it this week. But, at the same time, it is all very impersonal. Wouldn't it be possible for the doctor to have patients coming to him with questions about their children's health and for him to give sensible advice about it, in line with up-to-date knowledge? For example, what is the latest form concerning a child getting pneumonia? I believe it is not all that serious, thanks to modern drugs, but undoubtedly people worry about it tremendously. Is it possible to give details of the new operations being performed? And anything that applies to the health of the aged would also be of interest.

I think that the column got away to a very good start but, at the same time, we must try and humanise it if possible. I think that Polio, for example, is a first-class subject but an intro which starts '*The Government is pressing ahead with . . .* ' lacks the human element to some degree.

Yours sincerely etc.

He was right, of course, and it was the first of many pieces of wisdom and encouragement from a man whose vision and judgement I came to respect increasingly during the rest of my days in Fleet Street. His letter made me look at news in a different way and I developed a discipline which I follow to this day: ask yourself 'What is it the reader or listener or viewer *really* wants to know?' and then report accordingly.

It also made me define my 'target audience'.

At whom should the Science/Medical Reporter on a London evening newspaper be aiming his stories, in terms of subject interest and complexity of language? Although the *Standard* was an influential newspaper, read in the corridors of power, science and medicine were complex subjects and I wanted them to be understood by every reader.

So I decided to aim each story at an imaginary figure – a woman in a brown dress, married to a lorry driver and living (curiously enough) in Wapping in East London. I visualised her greeting her husband with a peck on the cheek, then taking from his hands that night's *Evening Standard* and, while he went upstairs to change out of his overalls, sitting on a small, chintz-covered chair with castors, reading my contribution and reacting in one of two ways – either, 'Wow, isn't that interesting!' or, 'Gosh, I never knew that before'.

I reckoned that, if I could get that sort of response, I had 'got it about right'.

When, years later, I started working in television and radio, I simply substituted Birmingham, Manchester, Newcastle and Glasgow for Wapping. But I continued to try to communicate with the woman in the brown dress (who, I realise now, was based on my grandmother).

Charles Wintour's letter, dated October 20, 1959, turned *The*

World of Medicine into *Tell Me, Doctor* in a week. One of the contacts I had made through attending a medical conference was a London GP, Dr. Gerald Breen. He agreed to be my medical mentor – the expert to whom I put patients' questions – but only if I was prepared to conduct the weekly consultation over lunch at the Chelsea Arts Club (for which he would pay). No problem!

Gerald was a *bon viveur* as well as a confidant of most of the great painters and sculptors in London and our Wednesday lunches became a highlight every week. They usually began with an introduction to all present over sherry, incessant anecdotes from the artists across the table and a *sotto voce* question-and-answer session about medical matters over a brandy in the coffee lounge.

As with *The World of Science, Tell Me, Doctor* not only allowed me to off-load a lot of 'soft' news but also attracted people with 'hard' news to contact the *Standard* in preference to other newspapers in Fleet Street.

From time to time, I used to get calls from the commissionnaire on the front desk at the *Standard* saying 'a gentleman's here to see you who says it's important but won't say what it's about.' With sinking heart, I would go down in the lift and, almost invariably, find a little man in a shabby mackintosh, with unkempt hair and a battered briefcase, who insisted on showing me – or telling me about his invention.

Almost invariably, he was a 'nutter'. I would listen patiently for a while (just in case), then interrupt by saying, 'Look, I appreciate your telling me this first but the *Standard* can't really do justice to something as important as this – there's a man at the *Daily Mirror* just up the road who specialises in inventions. I suggest you tell him right away.'

Whether Arthur Smith, then the *Mirror*'s Deputy Science Editor, ever realised where his string of 'nutters' came from I do not know – but it usually worked.

'Come and see my cockroaches'

On one particular morning, however, the commissionnaire's call produced a distinguished-looking man in a grey overcoat and trilby, who said simply, 'Hello. I know this sounds strange but I would like you to come and see my cockroaches.' He turned out to be Peter Greening, Senior Thoracic Surgeon at Charing Cross Hospital (the original one, located just opposite Southern Region Station). The cockroaches were running around his operating theatre, which was supposed to be sterile.

'I'm desperate,' he explained, as we took a cab to the hospital. 'I've tried every method I know to persuade the Hospital Management Committee to do something about it but I get nowhere. They still expect me to operate in conditions which expose seriously-ill patients to infection. I had dinner last night with Harvey Flack and he recommended you as someone who would expose the scandal without revealing where you got your information from.'

Dr Harvey Flack, at that time, was Editor of Family Doctor Publications and a pillar of respectability in the British Medical Association. Through many dealings over lunch, he had become a personal friend. 'OK, tell me all,' I said to my visitor, 'and I promise never to say it was you.'

A senior surgeon's word was enough to get me past the reception desk at Charing Cross Hospital and we rode the lift to the fifth floor unchallenged. There were actually two operating theatres, one of which had been ripped apart by builders prior to refurbishment. The other was empty but still functional. But it was separated from the building work simply by a plastic sheet which was torn and flapping.

'Look,' said Peter Greening, running a finger across the lampshades over the operating table. They were thick with grey dust. 'I'm supposed to do a heart operation in here this afternoon.' He pointed to a crack between one of the walls and the Victorian marble floor. 'Look there!' Sure enough, two cockroaches scuttled away.

In the pub opposite, he spelled out the long, frustrating story of his (and other surgeons') attempts to persuade the Hospital Management Committee either to insulate the theatre and re-sterilise it properly or close it altogether and transfer patients to other hospitals for surgery.

It was a scandal: there was no other word for it. Peter Greening agreed to escort one of our photographers up to the operating theatre and we waited, discussing how the story might develop once the first news was out, until he had finished.

At 2 p.m., just as Mr. Greening was getting ready to operate, the *Standard* hit the streets. Somebody must have telephoned the

Hospital Secretary within minutes and read the story over to him for Peter told me afterwards that the man burst into the changing room, just as the surgeons were gowning up, and gasped, 'Stop. The operation's off.'

However, the respite was temporary. The team were told to resume operating next day, with only the torn plastic sheeting having been replaced.

That prompted another call from Mr. Greening. 'I've got my anaesthetist here with me – he'd like to tell you a thing or two,' he said. And so, on Day Two, the *Standard* carried the story about the problems of administering gas safely to patients using obsolete – and at times faulty – equipment.

The Ministry of Health then stirred itself, setting up a Committee of Inquiry at Charing Cross Hospital to consider the various complaints and possible remedies. The chair was taken by no less a figure than the Minister himself, Kenneth Robinson. Unfortunately (for him) he made the mistake of co-opting Peter Greening onto the committee with the result that, after each meeting, the surgeon would slip away and phone me a report of what had been said. At one point, Peter told me, the Minister had banged the table and shouted, 'I think it's time we closed the *Evening Standard* news desk inside this hospital.'

The operating theatres were shut down. Work on refurbishment was accelerated. New procedures for anaesthesia and for general hygiene were introduced and, whilst I do not believe we were instrumental in bringing forward the building plans for a new Charing Cross Hospital (later built in Fulham Palace Road), our exposé certainly did nothing to delay them.

The scandal rumbled on for weeks, supported not only by fresh developments at Charing Cross but also by several other hospitals ringing me up with their particular items of shocking news. I remember the Matron at one hospital in South Wales saying, 'Mr. Fairley – we want you to come and see our rats.'

Ethics and the Royal Society of Medicine

A similar example of high-level collusion concerned a medical paper read to the august Royal Society of Medicine.

Harvey Flack, by then a firm friend, invited me to lunch at Au Savarin in Gerard Street, adding mysteriously, 'I want to tell you something in the strictest confidence.' Over the meal, he told me that he had become impotent. However, he had found a genuine cure. 'After we've finished here, I want you to come with me to Cavendish Street and meet a man called 'Tibby'.' He went on, 'Don't be put off by his appearance or by his middle-European accent – he's a super chap.'

Hungarian-born Dr. Tiberius 'Tibby' Reiter was a short-sighted hunchback with a limp. His consulting rooms looked like something out of the last century and his surgery was untidy, to put it mildly. But the tale he told was lucid and scientifically sound.

Tibby, who was in his 60s, had fallen in love with a beautiful woman half his age but had found that he too was impotent. He had seen specialists and undergone treatments but none had worked. So he had started to research the whole subject of impotence himself.

He had identified what he called the 'IDUT syndrome' – Impotence, Depression, Urinary symptoms and Thyroid disorder. They all went together, often resulting not only in loss of sexual prowess but in loss of ambition and business drive – and occasionally, in suicide. Further research had shown that the syndrome was caused by a low level of the male sex hormone, testosterone.

That was not surprising – in fact, some Harley Street consultants had been making fortunes out of giving quick 'fixes' of testosterone to 'sugar daddies' about to go on dates with young women. But they rarely worked – the hormone was rapidly excreted on the first visit to the 'loo' (which usually preceded sex anyway).

Tibby realised that the challenge lay in somehow maintaining a consistently high level of testosterone in the bloodstream. He started to experiment on himself.

He decided that the hormone needed to be natural, not synthetic, and should be produced as a solid which would only dissolve very slowly in the bloodstream. A pharmaceutical company made some samples for him, fusing the crystals of testosterone together at a very high temperature. They looked like short lengths of white crayon.

Using a thick needle, Tibby cut a hole at the top of his right rump and pushed three of the implants in. There was a little soreness for a few days – then his mood became brighter and his young wife (for they had married by then) openly appreciative.

The improvement lasted three months, after which he repeated the procedure. Harvey Flack was his first volunteer patient. Others followed until the point was reached where a scientific report could be prepared for the *British Medical Journal* or *The Lancet*, giving the results of the small-scale clinical trial.

Both rejected it. He tried other learned journals. They all rejected it.

Harvey Flack recognised the importance of Reiter's work but, as he explained, the problem was to communicate its efficacy to others. 'Very few men are willing to admit openly that they are impotent,' he added. And, as an ethical practitioner, Tibby could not advertise.

The best hope lay in a promise he had extracted from the Royal Society of Medicine that he would be allowed to ask the first question during a symposium on fertility problems due to be held the following month. Five minutes was the traditional 'slot' for that first question. The proceedings of the meeting would be published in the Society's *Journal*.

The three of us sat down to hatch a plot.

Before asking his question, Tibby would declare the results of the trial and describe his method. Harvey would sit by the door of the conference room and, as soon as Tibby had finished speaking, would head for the telephone. I would have a full story set in print and waiting. In that way, everybody's ethical code would remain unbreached.

It worked like a charm.

'NEW SEX HOPE FOR MEN' screamed the *Standard*, although not until there had been some nail-biting: Harvey's call came only four minutes before the last edition went to press. But again, Charles Wintour had seen the potential and we had the front and back page pre-set with the story.

Next day, all the national dailies carried the story. My phone scarcely stopped ringing: 'How can I contact Dr. Reiter?' Newspaper ethics allowed us to give that information and, within a fortnight, Tibby's appointments diary was full for months ahead.

I like to think that I helped to improve life for many men that afternoon but the reaction from the Royal Society of Medicine was typically stuffy. . . its President threatened to report me to the Press Council. A hand-written letter delivered to my Editor claimed that I had broken the Society's rule that no member of the public was allowed to be present at a meeting.

Charles Wintour was always extremely supportive of his writers unless they committed *real* sin and his reply was short and sharp: 'Fairley wasn't present but had obtained the story by other methods which he was not prepared to divulge.' End of matter.

But the incident was exceptional because, by then, many in the medical profession were coming round to the idea that patients had a right to know and were prepared to be more open with journalists, especially if they were members of the newly-formed Medical Journalists Association.

The need for such a body, with aims of improving the standards of medical journalists and persuading institutions to adopt more of an 'open skies' policy, had become apparent after thalidomide.

The lesson of thalidomide

We had all read an early warning printed in the letters' column of the *British Medical Journal* to the effect that the drug was being withdrawn from the market, pending further research and testing. But we had also seen an announcement that another widely-used drug, previously withdrawn as a precaution, had just been given the 'all clear' and was to become available again.

To raise an alarm over thalidomide – a drug designed to prevent morning sickness in hundreds of thousands of pregnant women – would immediately become an emotional issue and could well lead to accusations of irresponsible 'scare-mongering', if, as we suspected, it was eventually cleared.

I remember very clearly a meeting of seven of us medical writers, from national and London evening newspapers, in a Fleet Street pub, where we debated what to do. Almost desperate to show ourselves 'ethical', we decided, out of a sense of responsibility, to do nothing.

The self-imposed silence lasted for 13 weeks until John Stevenson of the *Daily Sketch* could stand the strain no longer and 'blew' the story of the birth defects which the drug was believed to have caused. We all immediately followed.

I often wonder, had we reported the story when it was first available, how many tragedies might have been avoided.

The boy with no arms

Virtually every journalist that I know, who came into contact with thalidomide victims when they were children, was impressed by their intelligence and by their loving ways. It seemed as if God had, to some degree, compensated them for their misfortune.

We humans found it less easy to dispense compensation. The manufacturers of the drug wriggled, lawyers argued, some of the parents grew embittered and the hypersensitive in the community averted their eyes.

It was not just a matter of designing prostheses and administering physiotherapy when they were infants. As they matured, other factors needed to be taken into account before fair damages could be awarded.

Should a thalidomide victim receive more for being without arms or legs? Are two 'flippers' worth more than one? What price do you put on the emotional suffering of a thalidomide boy who finds that he cannot dance with his girl because he has no arms to hold her as, in those days, dancing involved arms. Such questions vexed both doctors and lawyers.

Around the 10th anniversary of the first case of thalidomide in Europe, I was sent to Heidelberg to interview a professor of psychology at a special clinic, set up on the banks of the Necker to help equip thalidomide children for living life to the full. By then I was working mainly for ITN and I met a German TV crew at the clinic next morning.

It was one of the most moving days of my life. The professor led us immediately to his office and introduced us to an eight-year-old called Thomas, who had two stunted 'flippers' for arms. He spoke briefly to Thomas in German and then said, 'Watch'.

The boy was wearing a short-sleeved shirt, shorts held up by a belt, a pair of socks and slip-on shoes. He began by squatting on the floor and, raising his right foot over his head and shoulders, pulled off his shirt. Shoes and socks followed, levered one against the other. Only the shorts remained, but the belt had a buckle.

Thomas walked to the office wall and I noticed a screw projecting at (his) waist height. After a few tries, he managed to press a notch in the leather belt over the screwhead, wiggled his hips and – hey *presto* – the buckle was undone and the shorts were on the floor.

'Do you think Thomas could do all that again, but just a bit faster?' I asked the professor. 'I'd like to film it.'

There was another brief conversation in German, Thomas nodded and we readied the camera. This time he did it faultlessly – in just 57 seconds. I shall never forget the impish grin on his face as, using 'flippers' and feet, he dressed himself again, against the stopwatch, in 1 min. 20 secs. We filmed that, too.

We filmed an incredible variety of remarkable feats before I left children without legs swimming, others 'dog-paddling' without arms, wheelchair races and a game of 'flipper football'. I can hear the laughter and obvious happiness of both children and staff still to this day.

When I returned to ITN, the *News at Ten* Output Editor – who decides the content and timing of items for the bulletin – asked me, 'How much do you think it makes?'

'Five minutes,' I said. He looked aghast. He was not one to be impressed by scientific or medical news, believing that the viewer preferred political, labour relations or industrial stories and the longest time he had ever allocated for one of my contributions was two minutes.

'All right,' I conceded. 'Let me edit it as tightly as possible and then come and watch it.'

That night, *News at Ten* transmitted six minutes of Thomas and his thalidomide pals – the longest item I ever had on the routine news bulletins.

Eye-witness at operations

Some time previously, I had been offered the chance to witness (and report exclusively) one of the first operations to transplant frozen corneas into the eyes of patients who needed them. Until then, only 'fresh' corneas, from the eyes of newly-expired people, had been available and there had always been a problem in finding a donor and a recipient together in the right place at the right time.

The research on freezing corneas and the operation to graft them into the eye had been devised at Westminster Hospital by a small team led by Patrick Trevor-Roper, an ophthalmologist of international repute. His team included a young Irish eye surgeon named Tom Casey, who subsequently became a personal friend.

'I think the best way to explain this is for you to watch a transplant operation,' said Tom. 'I'm doing one tomorrow.'

Next morning found me gowned and masked, just a few feet from the operating table, while Tom – microscope strapped to his forehead – performed an amazing feat of needlework on the eyes of a 60-year-old woman. What shook me was to listen, throughout the delicate operation, to a running discussion between Tom and the theatre sister about a movie shown on TV the previous evening. It was as if they were chatting over coffee.

This was followed by an invitation to see a very different type of surgery in close-up.

After the Charing Cross scandal, the whole subject of infection and cross-infection in operating theatres kept cropping up in the medical journals. Then an orthopaedic surgeon named John Charnley published a report in *The Lancet* describing experiments carried out at the Wrightington Hospital, Wigan, which offered an ingenious way to reduce infection at relatively low cost.

Charnley's solution was to encase the whole operating table, its attachments and the surgical instruments in a plastic tent, in which sterile air was kept at 'positive pressure' – in other words, at a pressure higher than that of the air in the rest of the operating theatre. This 'pressure barrier' would prevent germs from reaching open wounds during surgery.

Charnley was reporting a 10,000:1 drop in the germ count inside his tent and a big reduction in the number of patients developing infections after their operations. It was a technique similar to that used to keep spacecraft 'clean' and uncontaminated before they were launched on journeys to the planets and I was very interested.

'I think the best way to explain it,' said Charnley over the phone, 'is for you to come and see an operation.'

With some foreboding, I drove up the M6 to the Wrightington Hospital. John Charnley was already operating on a male patient, but he had left instructions for a nurse to gown, mask and glove me. I shall never forget the sight that greeted me as I pulled aside a flap and entered his plastic tent.

There was quite a lot of blood. The patient's hip was wide open and a cut extended down the thigh. The surgeon was using a massive brace and bit to gouge out eroded bone from the hip socket. Various sharp saws and a mallet and chisel lay on a stainless steel trolley beside the patient.

'Morning,' said Charnley, without looking up. I was unable to reply. I was struggling to stop myself fainting. I remember thanking God for a cold tent pole which I found behind my back and gripping it for the rest of the operation.

It was all such a contrast from the miracle of micro-surgery which I had seen at the Westminster. I had not known what type of surgery I would see when I accepted the invitation but I realised, at that point, that this was one of the early hip replacement operations and it required brute force. Had it not been for the dazzling reflections off the stainless steel instruments and all the blood, I might have believed I was in my father's carpentry workshop.

Afterwards, Mr Charnley explained the whole operation in detail – how his tent worked, how the germ count was done and why it was so important, with such massive wounds, to keep it as low as possible. He showed me the 'Charnley Prosthesis' – a plastic-lined socket and stainless steel ball with a spike on it – which formed the artificial hip and demonstrated, on a dangling skeleton, how the spike was pressed down the centre of the femur and cemented in position to help take the patient's weight and the sideways strain of walking. He introduced me to patients in various stages of recovery and several said the operation had 'given them new life'.

I decided to write not only a news report about the germ-free operating tent but to devote the whole of the following week's *World of Science* column to the new operation and the benefits which it would bring.

What I did not know was that Charnley had a rival. Another surgeon in a different hospital was also doing hip operations but using a steel-on-steel ball and socket joint. He believed his prosthesis was the correct one and was furious to see such publicity given to the Wigan team. So he made an official complaint to the General Medical Council about John Charnley and, to my Editor, about me.

Fortunately, both were rejected. John Charnley went on to become Sir John and bring relief from pain and a new mobility to thousands of patients – his prosthesis is still in use – and I learned a valuable lesson: jealousy can run deep among medical men.

The kidney transplant that succeeded

I don't think it was jealousy but vanity that brought the wrath of another leading surgeon down on my head on November 2, 1960. – my thirtieth birthday.

A fortnight previously, through a mutual friend, I had been tipped off that John Hopewell, a young urologist and surgeon at the Royal Free Hospital was about to perform the first kidney transplant operation ever to be tried between two brothers who were not identical twins. Were it to work, it would be a major breakthrough in medicine.

The *Standard* broke the story and, as a result, I had a phone call ten days later from a woman in Southwark who said that her two sons were about to take part in a similar exchange of organs at Hammersmith Hospital. Son Tommy desperately needed the kidney. Son Jimmy, two years his elder, had volunteered to donate one of his and had flown from Cyprus for the operation. The family was proud of them both. Was I interested?

I took a taxi to Southwark, interviewed the parents and sister, collected pictures of Tommy and Jimmy and raced back to the office. The story was so obviously true that, apart from checking with the hospital that the two brothers were indeed patients, I did not feel that further confirmation was needed. However, out of courtesy, I warned the hospital Administrator that the story would be appearing in the 3 p.m. edition.

Next morning the phone rang. 'This is Professor Shackman at the Royal Postgraduate Medical School,' an angry voice said. 'How dare you write about my patients without asking my permission. Come down here right away.'

According to an unwritten code of newspaper ethics, I had done nothing wrong. The story was true. It had been checked. I had not invaded family privacy and I was not obliged to ask permission from anybody to print it. I was tempted to tell Shackman to go to hell.

However, I took the tube to Hammersmith and absorbed 10 minutes of the Professor's ranting and raving before he calmed down. We then discussed the situation rationally. It was not clear whether I was in the wrong for unjustifiably raising the hopes of other kidney patients, or for being pessimistic about the whole state of kidney transplant surgery. One thing was clear

– in my report I should have mentioned Ralph Shackman.

We struck a bargain. I would not write another story about kidney transplants at Hammersmith until he had contacted me to say he had a success (John Hopewell's patient had died). In return, he promised he would definitely contact me.

Nearly a year went by, during which I checked twice that he had not forgotten. Then, one Tuesday, the phone rang. 'Ralph Shackman here – come on down, we've got a good one.' He introduced me to Djemal Ali, a greengrocer from Hampstead, who had received his younger brother's kidney six weeks previously. Dejemal had spent the time since in a room sterilised by ultraviolet lamps and would be allowed to return home that afternoon. 'We're really proud of him,' said the Professor. 'Go on – he's all yours.'

I sat on Djemal's bed and scribbled the facts in my notebook – age, address, wife's name, brother's name (he, too, had flown in from Cyprus for the op.) details of the surgery, attitude to the future, etc, etc. Then I asked him, 'How did you come to be a patient in Hammersmith when you live near the Royal Free?'

He explained that his GP had given him 'about three months' to live. His wife had become almost hysterical at the news. On the way home, they had bought a newspaper and read that two nonidentical brothers were about to undergo a kidney transplant operation at Hammersmith. Back home, his wife had rung the hospital and insisted on speaking to the surgeon in charge – one Professor Shackman.

'Do you remember which newspaper you bought?' I asked.

'Yes – it was the *Evening Standard*.'

The last I heard of Djemal Ali was in 1986. He was still alive and in good health – the longest-surviving 'non-identical' kidney transplant patient in the world. Sadly, Ralph Shackman has died. But if ever it was worth putting up with a little bad temper and remaining patient, the Djemal Ali case was a classic.

From kidneys to hearts

It was an exciting time to be reporting medicine. Medical research was uncovering new and often surprising facts about diseases, science was producing remarkable new instruments and surgical techniques and hardly a month went by without the pharmaceutical industry announcing some new 'wonder drug'. However, we soon learned to ignore cancer 'cures' – especially when they were announced by privately-funded US research institutes and hospitals in the pages of their annual reports to shareholders – and we grew to use the word 'breakthrough' sparingly for fear of debasing it.

Every new development seemed to bring in its wake an ethical dilemma.

'Should the doctor tell the patient if he or she has cancer?', 'When is a doctor or surgeon justified in letting a patient die?', 'To what extent should patients be used as 'guinea pigs', 'Should doctors tell parents if they put young girls on The Pill?', 'Does health screening justify its cost?', 'Should rules restricting abortion be relaxed?' – these are just a few of the ethical questions over which doctors were beginning to agonise in the early '60s, usually in the full glare of publicity.

The relationship between the medical profession and the Media became a question in itself, with some doctors and surgeons actively seeking publicity while most of their colleagues continued to shun it. The dilemma was not eased by the need to 'get noticed' in order to attract research funding.

Nowhere was the debate hotter than in the field of transplant surgery and, in particular, heart transplants.

First there was Louis Washkansky, the 55 year-old South African who became the world's first heart transplant case in 1967 but who died after only 16 days. Then Dr Philip Blaiberg, another South African patient of Professor Christian Barnard at the Groote Schuur Hospital in Cape Town, who survived more than two years – and then Frederick West, a 45-year-old building contracts manager from Leigh-on-Sea, Essex, who had his new heart grafted into place at the National Heart Hospital in London by Mr Donald Ross and survived 46 days. They really set the headlines screaming.

I remember interviewing the tall, good-looking Barnard in his hotel room at the Savoy, just after the West operation, when he was en route for a lecture tour of America. I formed the impression, on first acquaintance, that he was a modest man. He even asked me whether he should ring up his old colleague, Donald Ross, and ask if he could see West, or wait for an invitation.

'The problem is,' he added, 'that I don't know if my advice would be of help.'

When I interviewed him again, three years later, he was at the centre of a furore over publicity-seeking . He had even brought with him an LP gramophone record about heart transplants which was about to go on sale to the public.

He had become much more self-confident and there were rumours of his involvement in sexual scandal, but I still formed the impression that he was more concerned to help patients than in acquiring glory. Others did not agree.

I was more surprised by the antics of his old friend Donald Ross who, on May 4, 1968, had carried out a four-hour operation to remove Frederick West's diseased heart and replace it with the healthy heart of a 26-year-old Irish labourer, who had just died from a fall at a building site.

After weeks of secrecy and speculation, he suddenly called a TV and Press conference to announce details of the operation. Not only did the entire operating theatre team (13 of them, including all the nurses and two other surgeons – his unrelated namesake, Eric Ross, and Mr. Donald Longmore) – pose for the cameras but they all produced, on cue, miniature Union Jack flags.

'Unseemly' was the word used by many colleagues in other hospitals. But it showed how far senior and respected medical figures were prepared to go to 'bend' the ethical rules about self-publicity and advertising when it suited them.

Whether with PR advice or not, they saw a wonderful opportunity to raise their hospital – and heart research in general – in the pecking order of charity donations. And it worked.

CHAPTER SIX

Crossed Artichokes and Gold Braid

Perhaps because I was born in Malaya and lived for a while in India, perhaps because of some in-built wanderlust, I have always craved foreign travel. Work has taken me to 52 different countries, to date.

The first opportunity came in 1958, when it looked as though de Gaulle might return to power and some very militant generals were threatening to repossess French North Africa.

Because I spoke French, I was despatched to Paris by the *Standard* to help out Sam White, its legendary foreign correspondent cover the political crisis. At that time, Sam was the only staff man allowed to live permanently away from the office (it was rumoured that he would never be recalled because he knew too much about the private lives of Max Aitken and senior Beaverbrook executives and the fun times they had in Paris – having arranged most of them).

Sam was a gruff, hook-nosed, heavyweight who spoke with an appalling French accent, which he never bothered to improve. As predicted, I found him holding court with the other Paris correspondents in the bar of Le Crillon Hotel at 11 a.m. (when the hotel was refurbished in the 1960s, the management gave him the bar as a souvenir for his apartment).

Over a Pernod, Sam explained what he wanted me to do – interview a wily old political lawyer and clandestine agitator called Maitre Tixier-Vignancour.

Sam did not expect me to get the interview but I did, returning to the Paris office to phone it to London after he had vetted it. 'This is dynamite,' he said, without explaining why. 'You must leave France before they come and question you.'

Mark Wilson, in his pre-golf days the *Standard*'s best reporter, and Denise Richards, who also spoke French, were due to join us and I was looking forward to a great evening in Paris over a gourmet meal. I had set my heart on artichokes vinaigrette as a starter. Instead, I was put in a taxi to the airport with my few possessions, told to pick up a ticket to Tunis and stay in the North African capital until further notice.

It was cool in Paris and I had brought only a Harris tweed sports coat. It was 90 in the shade in Tunis and I had no money to buy clothing. Furthermore, the entire Express Group had over-spent its Bank of England foreign exchange allowance, so it would be another 10 days before I could get any.

The whole English Press corps had taken up residence in the Tunisia Palace Hotel, a white marble palace of a place with a courtyard shaded by tall, gently-waving palms. More importantly, it was willing to allow us 'tick' and many cool drinks were sipped under those palms while the day's events were analysed.

The situation in Tunisia was tense. The Tunisian Army had encircled every French garrison in the country in the sweet hope of containing a take-over by the Foreign Legion if de Gaulle re-sumed as Head of State and decided to re-colonise.

'Brushes' between the warring factions had already occurred in several distant desert locations. Would things escalate? Would the Tunisians throw the French out? Would the Legion break out of its forts and topple President Bourgiba? Each of us had Opinions and Views, but no Inside Knowledge.

In the middle of all the hot gossip, permanently chair-bound under the tallest palm, sat Alan Dick, a veteran feature-writer from the *Daily Herald*. Not for him all this boring political stuff: the feature he was cabling was about a British bee, which had somehow stowed away inside his suitcase in London and emerged in Tunis only to find its honey impounded by Tunisian customs. It was hilarious stuff. My admiration for Alan was soon replaced by gratitude for he, like Alan Whicker two years previously, heard about my financial plight and acted.

He lent me enough money to buy a fly-swat (for mosquitoes), a bathing costume and a haircut.

Although there was political tension, with marches in the even-ings by mobs shouting the Arabic equivalent of 'Out with the French', the situation during the day was calm, normal and even a little farcical.

We found that we could take a taxi to the Foreign Office, knock and push open the Minister's brass-studded, leather-bound door and say, 'Hello Mr Mokkadem, what is happening?' He would invite us to sit down, offer us sweet tea and proceed to describe the latest incidents and the Government's view of them.

We would then take a taxi to the French headquarters at Salammbo, 25 miles away on the coast, and put the same question to the French Commandant, General Fernand Gambiez. He would give us his version.

Although a lot of it was light-hearted, we did feel the hair on our necks rising each time the Arab taxi dropped us at the Tunisian trenches. We would smile nonchalantly at the soldiers, then set out to walk 100 yards across the desert with their guns pointing at our backs until the giant wooden gates of the Beau Geste-style fort opened to admit us.

Our identities were carefully checked before we were led along cool, arched corridors to the general's office, where a bottle of wine always seemed to be waiting. The general himself – a calm, dignified man looking over pince-nez spectacles – seemed the exact opposite of the belligerent warmonger which the Tunisian officials made him out to be.

It was extremely difficult to judge who was telling the truth. So, on May 27, after a passionate but unreliable briefing by M. Mokkadem, Robin Stafford of the *Express*, Noel Clark of the *Daily Mail* and I decided to find out once and for all.

There had been some kind of battle 250 miles south in the Sahara desert at a town called Gafsa. The French claimed that Tunisian troops had attacked them at their base outside the town. Mokkadem claimed that French aircraft had bombed the 15,000 strong civilian population, causing scores of casualties. Whoever was right, it sounded serious.

The three of us walked out of the Foreign Office and hailed a taxi. 'Would you take us to Gafsa?' Robin asked. The driver didn't bat an eyelid. 'Of course,' he said. 'Jump in.' And so began one of the most memorable journeys of my life.

I realised that the reason for my being allowed to accompany the two correspondents from the national dailies was simply to defray the taxi fare: communication links from Tunis to London were, at the best of times, bad – little better than using two cans joined by a length of string: add in the remoteness of Gafsa and they would be impossible. Robin and Noel would be able to gather the facts, write their stories and return to Tunis to use the phone. Whatever I wrote could not reach London until their copy had appeared in print.

Or so they thought.

The night was warm. A full moon turned the desert into a silvery sea, with camel trains sailing smoothly across the surface as we sped past. Every so often, a swinging lantern blocked our path, forcing us to halt while a soldier in Arab head dress thrust his gun into the taxi and demanded to see our papers.

'*Nous sommes journalistes anglais,*' we cried, holding out our passports. Every time, we were waived through without further questions.

Dawn broke just as we reached two escarpments two miles outside Gafsa.

The daylight revealed a French tricolour on one side and a Tunisian flag on the other, with our road running between and below both. Unfortunately, somebody chose our arrival to start firing tracers at the opposite side.

We reasoned that, if there had been a lot of casualties from an air attack, the place where we would find them would be the town's hospital. We drove there and asked if we could look in the wards. We found just two patients – both Tunisian infantrymen.

Further enquiries failed to reveal any civilian casualties. It was propaganda.

Robin and Noel decided that they would seek out the French commandant for some supplementary facts. I decided I had enough and would try to phone London. 'You must be joking,' said Robin as the taxi dropped me off at Gafsa Post Office. Their smirks grew broader as, suddenly, some tribesman with long rifles appeared and prodded me up the wooden steps. My last view of them was through the taxi's rear window, roaring with laughter, as they sped off to the French camp.

I had never been arrested before and my '*Je suis journalist anglais,*' sounded pathetic. But I was taken in front of the postmaster, an Arab who spoke excellent English and was charm and courtesy itself.

I explained who I was, why we had come to Gafsa (leaving out the checking the truth bit) and why I needed a line to London.

'We have no links with London,' he answered. 'How about a priority line to Paris?' He invited me to sit at his desk, brought me a glass of ice-cold goat's milk on a silver salver and withdrew while I scribbled my story. After 15 minutes, the phone on the desk rang and I was through to Sam White. 'Could you relay this to London if I dictate it?' I asked. 'No, but Lilianne (his secretary) will – I'm due at Le Crillon.'

The line was clearer than if I had been phoning from across Fleet Street. The postmaster refused any payment (which was a relief) and we passed the time eating bread and cheese until Robin and Noel reappeared with the taxi. 'You all right, old boy?' they asked with false concern. They did not even bother to ask if I had got through to London.

I decided to let them wallow in their ignorance until we were speeding back along the desert road to Tunis. Then I said quietly, 'The first edition should be going to press about now. I wonder if they've given me a by-line.'

'WHAT?' they both yelled. 'You don't mean you got a story out?'

The rest of the ride was taken in silence. Eventually, they were informed that their reports were used in a fairly low-key way on page 2, the *Standard* having run the story front-page the previous evening.

They never spoke more than a few words to me again but I did not care: the call had come for me to quit Tunis and return to Paris. Unfortunately, the Tunis Air Dakota developed an engine fault over Marseilles and we landed late, with most of the Arab passengers fiddling with their worry-beads and the emergency services chasing us down the tarmac.

When I reached Sam's office, they had all gone out to lunch. But a notice told me where and, fastened above with string, there were two globe artichokes crossed one upon the other . . .

Bloodshed in Jerusalem

Among the accounts which Gavin Cochrane, my PR friend, had to look after were Middle East Airlines in the Lebanon and the Jordanian Tourism Authority. He was constantly thinking up ideas to get more tourists to go to both countries. I suggested one novel way.

Scouring the technical journals had turned up an article in the proceedings of the Soviet Academy of Sciences, written by a reputable Soviet astronomer, postulating that the ruins of the Temple of Jupiter at Baalbeck in the Lebanon were actually relics of an ancient rocket firing pad, built by technically-advanced visitors from another planet. How else, he argued, could the temple's massive blocks of stone, geometrically-cut and assembled with precision, have been quarried several miles away and then moved to their present site unless it was with the aid of huge cranes and a sophisticated transport system?

Would not a feature in the *Standard* attract tourists, I suggested?

As far as Jordan was concerned, I had long been interested in the discovery and analysis of the Dead Sea Scrolls. Would not a feature on those also attract tourists to Jerusalem?

Gavin came up with two tickets – one for my wife – and we flew MEA to Beirut. Beirut, in those days, was a delightful city, busy with money dealers and entrepreneurs, offering several luxury hotels and some excellent restaurants. We started by re-laxing on the clean, sandy beaches.

A hired car took us to Baalbeck. En route, we passed the quarry where most of the temple's stone originated. One of the giant blocks still lay there, askew in the sand. It must have been 15 feet long, five feet wide and six feet high. How indeed could the ancient Lebanese have handled stones like it, much less trans-ported them a mile to the temple site?

The temple itself, adjacent to a smaller temple honouring Bacchus, was in poor nick with only six of its 58 columns still standing. But the main court, measuring 343 by 338 feet and created out of the solid blocks, was still in good condition. This was supposed to be the alien visitor's firing pad, around which the Romans later built their temple.

A staircase of 60 steps led up to it and, from a distance, it did look a little like a rocket launch pad. But as we reached some of the blocks, I noticed holes about the size of soup cans at either end. An archaeologist on site laughed when I related the Rus-sian's theory. 'No,' he said, 'you can see similar holes in blocks which make up the Egyptian Pyramids. They're where the slaves inserted stout poles to push the blocks over wooden rollers from the quarry to the site.'

But it made a good feature, which I cabled to the *Standard* before flying on to Jerusalem.

While in Beirut, we had looked up an old friend, Arthur Cook, then Middle East Correspondent of the *Daily Mail*. 'If you're only going to Jerusalem for a few days,' he said, 'I'll get a friend of mine to take you around – it'll save a lot of time.'

The friend turned out to be the Sheikh of Bethany, Mahmoud

Abu Reesh, a proud Christian Arab with one wife and nine healthy young children – a fact which he ascribed to a daily tablespoonful of olive oil (the whole family had to line up before breakfast each day to swallow it with Mahmoud taking a double dose at the end).

Mahmoud owned a battered old car, which transported us not only around the tourist attractions of the Holy City but to Hebron, Nablus and the Dead Sea as well, where we did the traditional thing by bathing, floating on top of the salt-rich water reading a book.

That night, Mahmoud laid on a candle-lit banquet for us, at which a whole lamb, baked in clay, was served. As I feared, I was given the eye, which I managed to swallow whole but which nevertheless took away my appetite for the rest of the evening.

A fellow guest was Joseph Saad, a tall, serious Arab who was then Director of the Palestine Archaeological Museum, where much of the piecing together of fragments of the Dead Sea scrolls was being carried out. We arranged to meet at the museum the following morning.

The fragments of papyrus – some white, some grey, some stained dark brown – were laid out under glass on trestle tables in a cool room known as 'The Scrollery'. Others, wrapped in lavatory paper (that was how the Bedouin who found them delivered them to the museum) were stacked, awaiting examination.

Many had been rescued from the nests of rats. They were stained with urine and tended to crumble to the touch. These were placed in a humidifier, then gently stretched between the fingers of a researcher. I watched how a sliver of what looked like tree bark was photographed under infra-red cameras. Suddenly, Hebrew words leaped, clearly visible.

Joseph was excited because, a few days prior to my visit, a scroll had been deciphered revealing the text not of 150 psalms, as in the Anglican Bible, but of 151. 'That piece of evidence alone is priceless,' he said. 'I paid the Bedouin £50,000 for that scroll and bits of a few others. It is always a gamble – sometimes the papyrus is blank.'

We drove back to the Dead Sea past the ruins of the monastery where the scrolls – texts from the Old Testament dating back to 300 BC – were carefully scripted by a breakaway Jewish sect called the Essenes (the pure ones). Then on to Qumran, where many of the pieces of scroll had been found in large terracotta jars in caves, hidden by the Essenes as they fled from an advancing Roman army. The first had been found by a goatherd, searching for a missing kid, who threw a stone into the cliff-face cave and heard it hit a jar.

On the way, we passed a cluster of black tents with a shining Cadillac parked outside.

'They are some of my suppliers,' Joseph explained. 'We pay the Bedouin for what they find. They usually do three things with the money – take a fresh wife, buy new clothes and a car and have a big party with anything left over.'

Qumran was the start of a wilderness – 150 miles of white sand, fringed by 100 ft. high sandstone cliffs, dotted with thousands of caves. Only 11, at that point, had yielded scrolls and I realised what a gargantuan task lay ahead of the researchers.

But Joseph insisted: 'My Bedouin, the Taamreh tribe, have vowed to uncover every one. As Lawrence of Arabia said, "they have patience as deep as the sea". They'll need it.'

My last thought that night was, 'Gavin is going to be really pleased about this one'.

Our sleep was interrupted around 6 a.m by some chanting outside our hotel. I looked out and a small gang of youths, sticks and stones in hand, was jogging down the street. I went back to bed. Fifteen minutes later, the chanting was louder and the gang larger – and so it went on until, by 9 a.m., it was a mob and the yells could be heard all over the city.

Mahmoud had another engagement and so we were due to meet a policeman guide at the tourist office close by, in order to visit the Garden of Gethsemane and the Wailing Wall. As we reached the corner, the mob – now some 200 strong – came towards us.

The policemen explained that political agitators were at work, demonstrating against King Hussein's Government because they wanted Jordan to join the United Arab Republic. He led us upstairs and, just as we reached an office, a stone smashed the window. More followed. Next, one of the crowd climbed on another's back and tore the Jordanian flag from the pole outside the window, tying in its place a UAR flag with four stars (the fourth for Jordan).

As soon as the mob moved on in search of more flags, we slipped back to our hotel. Sightseeing was out of the question – the whiff of news was overpowering and I wanted to telephone London. But as we neared the National Hotel, the mob reappeared from one alleyway and the Jordanian army from another.

The army started firing.

We hurled ourselves up the hotel steps and through the swing doors just as bullets began to fly. Outside our bedroom door, we found the maid in hysterics. I asked Vivienne to take care of her and entered the room – just as a bullet smashed the window glass. I pulled both mattresses off the twin beds, the telephone from the table and lay in the gap between them. I asked the Jerusalem operator for a line to London.

As with Gagarin's launch, there was no time to write down words: they had to come straight from the head. But the adrenaline slowed when the operator rang back and said that there were no lines free to London. I tried again and again.

Each time the answer was the same until, eventually, a man's voice came on and said, 'Mr Fairley. We want you to stop trying to communicate with London.'

It was a bit eerie. Who were 'we'? How did they know my name? And why did they not want me to contact London?

I'm a cussed s★★ and it only made me more determined. Then I remembered Arthur Cook in Beirut. The operator put me through. 'Quick Arthur, grab a pencil,' I said. 'Can you relay this to London?'

'I'm crouching behind mattresses in our five-guinea-a-day suite in the National Hotel, Jerusalem, bullets spitting all around us and a howling, pro-Nasser mob fleeing down the street . . .'

It was as far as I got. The line went dead – and stayed dead.

My wife was drinking tea with the maid and I told her what had happened. I went to Reception to protest. The clerks simply shrugged their shoulders and said there was nothing they could do – I suspect they were part of the 'we'. I approached several American tourists but they, too, did not want to know. But as I moved away I heard a quiet 'pssst' from the cashier who said, 'Sir, I think I can help.'

He indicated that we should meet in the 'loo'. We did. He explained that he used to work for Associated Press and knew how frustrated I must feel. 'Did you know,' he went on, 'that there's an English air hostess in Room 203 who is flying to Cyprus this afternoon?'

I slipped him an English £5 note and went to her room. She was packing. She was one of those charming, intelligent, attractive English women who, although suspicious at first, quickly grasps the situation and enters into the spirit of things. She said her name was Yvonne and she was crewing a charter flight to Cyprus via Damascus, leaving in three hours.

'Sure,' she said, 'I'll phone your story from Cyprus. I'll send you a telegram to say it went through.' I hugged her, then went off to write the story.

Before Vivienne and I dined that Saturday night, I was summoned to police headquarters, thanked for halting the phone calls and asked to guarantee that I would not try again for a further 48 hours. 'This is very sensitive,' the superintendent added (it was indeed – it was the first time that Arab had fired on Arab since King Abdullah was assassinated in 1951). I gladly gave my promise.

On the Monday morning, Gavin Cochrane was walking to his office in Fleet Street when he saw, to his horror, the newspaper sellers fixing *Standard* billboards which read 'I WATCH JERUSALEM TERROR – STANDARD REPORTER SEES BLOODSHED IN THE HOLY CITY.'

Happily, Gavin has forgiven me and remains a good friend, although he later lost the Jordanian Tourism account..

I have a telegram as a souvenir. It reads simply: 'Everything arranged,' and is signed 'Yvonne.'

Eskimos and Indians

In the late 1950s, the US Air Force started to build a chain of giant radar tracking stations known as BMEWS – the Ballistic Missile Early Warning System – to keep watch for Soviet nuclear missiles coming over the North Pole. It was to provide a 4-minute warning of an attack so that a counter-strike of US nuclear bombers and missiles could be launched to devastate cities in the Soviet Union. BMEWS was part of the West's Great Deterrent.

By 1961, two stations had been built – at Thule in Greenland and at Clear, Alaska and a third had been started on Fylingdales Moor, Yorkshire. It was to be protected against the weather by three huge screens, shaped like golf balls, which would be visible for miles around.

Yorkshire folk did not like it. Stories started to circulate about people who had walked in front of the other radars being fried alive, or suffering from radiation sickness. So the US Air Force decided to take a party of 15 British defence writers to Greenland and Alaska to report at first-hand how safe the stations were. I was one of the party.

We reported on June 12 to the US base at Mildenhall in Cambridgeshire and the send-off party was on a scale that made us feel like heroes. I remember consuming a vast quantity of alcohol in close company with the base commander. Next morning, heads throbbing, we flew to Thule.

We filed colourful little stories about the landing strip (although the base stood on thick permafrost, refrigeration plant had to be imported to keep the runway from melting); about the hut known as 'Las Vegas' where the airmen gambled night and day; about the Eskimo community and what they thought of the Yanks; and, of course, about the radars themselves and their safety. We left next day, after another party.

We landed at Elmendorf Air Force Base in Anchorage, Alaska and as we swept in, I noticed two Lockheed U-2s parked in open-ended, semi-circular hangars beside the runway.

The U-2s were high-altitude reconnaissance planes and, some 18 months earlier, a U-2 pilot named Gary Powers had been shot down over Russia by a heat-seeking missile, captured, put on trial as a spy and imprisoned. The US Government had then halted all such reconnaissance and nothing had been heard of the spy-planes since.

I had a whiff of news but could do little about it because, after checking in at the Officer's Club, we were each taken into the bosom of an Anchorage family and whisked away for the day. My family decided to show me the beautiful Alaskan Mountains by car and ski-lift . I learned with deep regret, many years later, that they all perished in the severe earthquake which devastated Anchorage.

Next day, it was the US Air Force's turn to play host and they took us to Fairbanks, the shanty-town capital, to board a paddle-steamer and go up-river to see a 'traditional' Indian village. We padded through the fir trees for a few hundred yards until we came to a circle of wigwams, smoke rising through the top of one, with squaws sitting cross-legged stitching moccasins, braves honing spears and dyeing feathers and children playing checkers with little tufts of walrus hair.

We all bought some souvenirs and then headed back to the steamer, where drinks were served before getting under way. As we chugged back along the muddy river to Fairbanks, we were overtaken by two large, painted canoes with powerful outboard motors. Each was packed with Indians.

When the chief stood up and raised his hand in salute, we realised that they were the same Indians from whom we had bought our souvenirs half an hour previously. We found out that they lived in modern dwellings in Fairbanks and only manned the 'traditional' village when there were tourists around.

'The U-2s are flying again . . . '

It was time to visit our second BMEWS station and, to do so, we had to fly by CA 35 transport plane from Anchorage to a short airstrip at Clear. As before, I noted the U-2s in their hangars.

Once again, we were impressed by the efficiency and safety of the radar and returned to Elmendorf to file stories, before attending another party in the Officers' Club. I decided to buttonhole the base commander and ask the question: 'What do you use the U-2s for nowadays?'

'U-2s?' he answered. 'What are they?'

I asked a major the same question. 'We haven't got any U-2s here,' was his answer. 'But I've seen two,' I persisted, 'in hangars beside the runway.'

'Then you must have been mistaken.'

Since wartime boyhood, I had made a hobby of aircraft-spotting and I knew perfectly well what a U-2 looked like – long, narrow, drooping wings, tiny wheels under the belly, a high tail and a fuselage like a powered glider. The whiff of news grew stronger but I said nothing more until we flew off next day. The U-2s were still there.

Copies of the *Anchorage Times* were circulated after take-off and, by an extraordinary coincidence, I read a short syndicated report, datelined Edwards Air Force Base, California which stated that U-2s were being used to test sophisticated radar and other equipment for use in their successors – 'spy' satellites. It did not say where.

Now I knew what those U-2s were doing.

I reckoned that they were flying out from Anchorage over the Bering Straits and doing sideways tests on the Soviet defences along the eastern seaboard. From a height of 80,000 ft., with instruments pointed at a slant, they need not over-fly Soviet territory to get data.

Our US Air Force escort was Major Sam West, who went everywhere with a worried frown (no surprise in view of us 15 journalists) and I put my theories to him before writing a word. 'Peter,' he said, 'you're not expecting me to confirm all this, are you?' And then, before I could reply, adding, 'Of course, I can't stop you writing it.'

Our plane was due to refuel at an Alaskan town called Smuggler's Cove, which gave a nice atmospheric dateline to the story which I cabled to London. It began:

> The U-2s are flying again. They are testing instruments for use in their successors, the 'spy' satellites. They are flying over the Bering Straits which, at their narrowest, are only 36 miles from the Soviet Union. By using sideways-looking devices, they have no need to overfly to get their information. . . .

The *Standard* splashed the story. It appeared on Fleet Street just as I and my 14 fellow-travellers were preparing to go to bed in Los Angeles, our next destination. I was not exactly popular at breakfast next morning. Their phones had been ringing all night.

Promotion – to General

Before we left Mildenhall on that BMEWS tour, we had each been given a typed piece of US Government notepaper. 'These are your Orders' explained Major West. 'If you get separated from the group and run into any trouble, just produce them and they'll explain who you are and what your assignment is.'

I had last seen Orders in the British Army. They were usually issued to soldiers posted to a unit or on official travel. There were about seven items on these US Orders, one of which read 'The following are appointed Temporary Acting GS 16 (without honours).' This was followed by all the journalists' names in alphabetical order. We stowed them away safely, as requested.

Among the 'extras' to our trip, which the USAF had laid on, were briefings from West Coast missile and radar manufacturers, two more cocktail parties and a show at The Moulin Rouge in Los Angeles.

I enjoyed the briefings and the first cocktail party – and the show – but the final cocktail party was too much. I fled through the kitchen and hailed a cab. 'Seventy-seven Sunset Strip' I told the driver.

A detective series with that title, featuring Ephraim Zimbalist Jr and a character called 'Cookie', was running on British television at that time and I was hooked on it. I also wanted to see the famous Coconut Grove night club.

The cabbie was amused. 'There's no No.77 on Sunset Boulevard,' he explained 'but I know where you mean.' Soon we arrived at a restaurant called Dino's, with a signboard bearing the crooner Dean Martin's face. Everything looked exactly as it was in the TV series, which was not surprising since it was the location for most of the filming. The same quartet was even playing as I walked in.

Dino's manager had been a USAF bomber pilot based at Bentwaters, Suffolk, during the war and he was an Anglophile. He was obviously pleased to see a British journalist, refused to let me pay for two margueritas and pressed a souvenir cigarette lighter and ashtray, both bearing Dino's logo, into my hand before I left.

I hailed another cab to the Grove and spent a dreamy two hours listening to Primo Rivera and Keely Smith, for just the price of a drink. Our motel was not far away and so I walked back in the moonlight, humming and very happy.

With my room key, the desk clerk handed me a message from London. It read: 'Kennedy has announced America to land men on Moon. Find out soonest how intend to do it.'

At breakfast, I showed Sam the message and explained that I would need to stay an extra week to visit the key research centres which would be involved in a Moon programme. 'No problem,' he replied. 'When you're ready, just report back to Andrews Air Force Base near Washington and produce your Orders and they'll get you home.'

The group and I parted company an hour later, they to return to England while I visited San Antonio in Texas, Huntsville, Alabama, Cape Canaveral in Florida and finally NASA headquarters in Washington, to hear briefings from top scientists and engineers including Dr Werner von Braun, General Don Flickinger (in charge of setting fitness standards for astronauts) Dr Robert Jastrow (lunar science expert) and James Webb (the head of NASA). It was marvellous copy and I remained pretty breathless throughout.

Finally, I reported to the Transportation Office at Andrews AFB.

It was the end of a holiday weekend and the lounges were full of airmen and their wives, scuffling children and crying babies, all waiting for a Transatlantic flight to Britain or Germany.

'Yup,' said a clerk, 'what can I do for you?' I explained that I needed to return to England as soon as possible. 'Yeah,' he said, 'you and all those thousands out there. You'll be lucky if you're away in less than 48 hours.'

As he spoke, he unfolded my Orders. Suddenly his manner changed. 'Oh gee, sir, I'm sorry. . . . listen, will you just take a seat over there for a moment. . . .' Twenty minutes later, I was in a Military Air Transportation System (MATS) turboprop airliner, strapping myself into a canvas seat. I thought, 'Good old US Air Force, they sure do think highly of British journalists.'

We had to land and re-fuel at Goose Bay in Labrador. As the plane came to a halt, a sergeant-steward called over the passenger address system: 'Is there a Mr Fairley aboard? Will all passengers please remain seated until Mr. Fairley has left the aircraft.'

I went down the aisle to find a uniformed Captain on the runway steps. He saluted. 'Where would you like to go, sir? Officers' Club? PX (military equivalent of duty free)? You'll be about an hour on the ground.' A Jeep drove us to the Officers' Club, which was typical of most, in that daylight never penetrated it, no matter the hour.

The Captain bought me a whiskey sour and started to ask questions. 'Would you mind my asking what mission you've been on in the States? How long have you been over there?' A warning buzzer told me to be vague. 'Oh I've been looking at certain radar installations and I've got to report back to the Ministry of Defence in London,' I fibbed.

'I thought it must have been something like that when we got the signal that a VIP was aboard the plane.' VIP? It was getting better and better.

'What did the signal actually say?' I asked.

'Well, it simply stated that a GS 16 (without honours) was aboard.'

'What is this "without honours" business?' I queried, 'I saw that on my Orders.'

'It means we don't need to roll out the red carpet or have the band ready on the apron,' the Captain replied. 'That's normal procedure with a GS 16.'

'And what rank is a GS 16?'

'That's a Major-General, sir. Hey, can I get you another drink?'

I made some vague remark about, 'Oh, we don't have those procedures in our Air Force', savoured the second whiskey sour and was Jeeped back to the plane. All the other passengers – men, women and children – were strapped in, I had intended starting to write my feature series (to be called 'Moonbound') but I thought I would be lynched if I disclosed my true identity. So I heeled the typewriter even further under the seat and slept until we reached Prestwick.

The formalities were repeated – first off the aircraft, saluted on the steps (this time by a Major) and whisked off to the Officer's Club for a quick breakfast – then a short hop to Mildenhall.

This time it was a Colonel who greeted me on the steps – but not just any old colonel. He was the Base Commander – the very man with whom I had made such whoopee on the eve of our departure.

'Wait a minute.' he said, withdrawing the salute, 'It's YOU. Doggon it, I wondered who on earth this VIP was, making me get up at 5 a.m.'

'Sorry,' I said, 'I didn't ask for it.'

He didn't offer the Officers' Club, nor the PX. He asked if I had bought a transistor radio (it was the latest status symbol) in one of the other PXs.

I said I had. 'OK, I'll get you through Customs with that,' he went on. While the Customs officer cleared the radio, I asked the Colonel why we had all had to be appointed Temporary Acting GS 16 (without honours). He explained that it was to allow us to have our own, large executive aircraft (a Constellation airliner, upholstered in green serge and grey leather, with seats for four grouped around tables) so that we could travel around America in comfort, as one party. Only GS 16 or above were allowed to use such aircraft.

Then he said, 'I'm going to put you in a staff car, send you back to London and I never want to see you again, buddy boy . . .'

I was finally down to Earth. But at least I can tell my grandchildren, when they ask, 'What did you do when you were young, Grandpa?', that for three glorious weeks I was a General in the U.S. Air Force!

CHAPTER SEVEN

The Wheel of Fortune Turns

Every visit abroad meant that a huge pile of Press releases, technical journals and mail had to be dealt with on return.

On this particular occasion, it was the *British Medical Journal* which prompted action. It contained a letter from one Dr John Barker, a consultant psychiatrist at the Shelton Hospital, Shrewsbury appealing for reliable information from fortune-tellers about their methods. It was unusual for a well-qualified doctor to be dabbling in such matters and so I rang him out of curiosity.

He explained that he wanted to find out whether clairvoyants, astrologers, palmists and the like warned their clients if they saw premature death ahead in their 'readings' or horoscopes. Or did they suppress the information, out of concern that they might be causing unnecessary anxiety or possibly even planting a subconscious 'death wish'?

I was intrigued and offered to organise a dinner, during which he could come face to face with some fortune-tellers and question them. But, I added, I would only do so if I could report what happened in the *Standard*. He agreed.

An astrologer called Katina was then writing the horoscopes for the *Standard* and she agreed to take part, putting me in touch also with Tom Corbett, a clairvoyant operating from consulting rooms in Chelsea, Frank King – then regarded as the 'daddy' of British clairvoyants – and Mir Bashir, a palmist. John Barker asked if he could bring along another psychiatrist, who wished to conduct a test.

I laid on a dinner in a private suite at the Charing Cross Hotel and we drank expensive wine. It was just as well because you could have cut the atmosphere with a knife for the first half hour. Both sides looked at each other with frosty suspicion. Then the wine got to work and the evening became almost boisterous. As coffee was served, each psychiatrist took one fortune-teller at a

time into an adjoining room for an interview, using a tape recorder. I tip-toed between them, making notes.

Kay, the woman psychiatrist, produced a gold bracelet and
asked Tom Corbett if he could tell her anything about the owner.
I watched as Tom took the bracelet and rubbed it between his
fingers, saying with eyes closed: 'This is the bracelet of a woman,
a woman of low morals . . . a woman who has just had an operation – but she didn't need the operation – and it's not the first
operation which she's had and didn't need. She's gone away –
she's in Leicester.'

Kay had become wide-eyed as he spoke but at the mention of
Leicester her jaw literally dropped.

'Yes,' she said, 'but where in Leicester?'

Tom rubbed the bracelet again, 'Her mother is looking for her
– no, I can't tell you any more.'

It transpired that the bracelet belonged to a prostitute who suffered from a rare mental disorder known as Munchhausen's syndrome. Baron Karl von Munchhausen was a notorious German
officer who grossly exaggerated his wartime exploits in order to
excite the admiration of ladies. The syndrome named after him
was characterised by patients who faked symptoms in order to
'collect' operations – or, more importantly, the scars from operations – on their bodies.

The prostitute had been referred to Kay as a psychiatric patient in need of help but had discharged herself from Shelton
Hospital. She had been traced to Leicester and her mother was
trying to find her in that city.

I watched and listened in astonishment. I knew that Tom had
never met Kay before, had never seen the bracelet, knew nothing
of the owner, her profession or her exit from hospital. Yet he
answered as immediately and fluently as you can read the words
in this book.

How? Tom himself described it as 'psychometry' (perceiving
facts by touching an object) and 'a perfectly normal part of clairvoyance'. He said he had done it many times – indeed the police
called him in occasionally on cases of missing persons. Whatever
the explanation, it was a remarkable performance and I respected
Tom as a person with unusual talents from then on.

I have thought about the incident many times since and concluded that, actually, it was an example of telepathy or 'mind
reading' and not true clairvoyance that Tom was simply 'read-

ing' facts already in the psychiatrist's mind. Tom denies this. But the fact that he was only able to tell her things about the bracelet which she already knew makes me wish that I had produced a different object (with a background of which Kay knew nothing), asked her to offer it to Tom, retired from the room myself (to avoid any possible 'mind reading') and left a tape recorder running to record his comments.

Instead, the three of us returned to the dinner table where John Barker summarised what the evening had revealed – which was, that if any of the fortune-tellers saw premature death in their clients' future, they did not tell the client. Instead, where appropriate, they confided in the client's relatives.

The psychiatrists caught the last train back to Shrewsbury and I left the hotel with a hefty bill for the *Standard* but enough material to fill two whole pages. Whether I was a convert to fortune-telling or not does not matter – it made a good story.

Setting up a Premonitions Bureau

A few months later, I heard again from Dr John Barker. He wanted to appeal, through the columns of the *Standard* and its syndicated regional papers, for anyone who had had forewarning of the 'Aberfan disaster' to contact him.

Aberfan is a Welsh mining village in Glamorgan. On the morning of Friday, 21 October 1966, a huge mound of coal waste, loosened by days of non-stop rain, slid down one side of the valley and enveloped Pantglas Junior School, killing 28 adults and 116 children.

For days, the event filled TV news bulletins and the pages of every national newspaper and it became apparent that a number of people felt that they had had warning of the tragedy. Dr Barker, who was fascinated by the subject of premonition, wanted to contact them while their memories were still fresh.

We received 60 replies. Barker went to Aberfan and interviewed them all, concluding that 22 were of real interest (having spoken of their premonition before the event to at least one other person).

A dozen or so of these were invited to appear with the doctor and myself on the Frost programme on Rediffusion TV. We gathered in the hospitality suite and I was dismayed by the strange appearance and facial 'look' of some of them. 'Weirdoes' would be too strong a description, but they were certainly 'different'.

David Frost interviewed John Betjeman, the Poet Laureate, in Part 1 of the programme: we were all supposed to go into the studio during the commercial break and contribute to a discussion in Part 2.

The break came but David did not appear. We watched him, on a monitor, talking to the programme researcher. Then Part 2 started, with Betjeman still in the 'hot seat'. 'Oh, he's just finishing discussing a point with Betjeman that came up before the break,' a production assistant told us. But I had a sinking feeling – and when the final five minutes of programme time was reached without a call, I knew for sure that none of us was going into the studio.

Some of the other guests were furious. Most had come at least 150 miles to appear and reimbursed expenses – even if generous – were no sop. David, perhaps wisely, did not appear in the hospitality suite to explain his decision but I learned later that he, too, had seen the motley collection of 'visionaries' through a crack in the door and decided to play safe.

The incident did nothing to dispel my concerns about premonition. 'The world is full of people who claim to have seen something coming but they always speak out after the event,' I pointed out to John Barker, who was keen to write a book about Aberfan. 'If they do tell anyone, then we still hear from that person afterwards. What we need is a register of premonitions in advance of the events they foretell.'

I spoke to Charles Wintour who agreed that we should set up the *Evening Standard* Premonitions Bureau. We created a special report form on which the name and address of the person reporting in would be logged, together with details of the premonition and the time we received the report. I had a date stamp made. In this way, we would be able to testify independently to what the person saw or felt and when they saw or felt it.

I had no wish to get involved in some World Premonition Early Warning system and so we held on to our 'evidence', merely running routine appeals for more premonitions and keeping newspaper cuttings about major disasters which, if there was such a phenomenon as premonition, should have involved people who had foreseen them. In the first year, we received more than 1000 reports.

We monitored these closely and, after a year, decided to do an analysis. We allocated points to each report – a maximum total of 15 – five for accuracy, five for 'unusualness', and five for timing.

It began to emerge that there were two people – a rather jolly ballet teacher in North London and a night switchboard operator in the East End – who seemed to be scoring above chance.

For example, on November 8, ballet instructor Lorna Middleton 'saw' a building site 'with tons of concrete falling everywhere and men scattering'; five days later, a workman was killed under tons of concrete when 16 flights of stairs in a partially-built block of flats collapsed at Isleworth.

On December 30, she had an overpowering feeling that there was about to be a serious crash involving a lorry with 'an exceptionally heavy load'; a week later, 12 people were killed when an express train hit a low loader carrying a giant transformer.

On July 9, she had a vision of a plane crash in a swamp; 10 days later, there was just such a crash – in Madagascar. And so on.

Four months earlier, telephonist Alan Hencher had predicted, in considerable detail, an early morning plane crash in mountains in which 123 or 124 people would be involved: within a month, a Britannia airliner had crashed into a hill in Cyprus killing 124 passengers and crew.

On April 22, he had foreseen a train accident involving a narrow gauge railway with flat-sided wooden coaches and wooden seats for passengers: within a month, a 'Tom Thumb' miniature train had crashed at Scarborough, injuring seven.

Then, on May 1, he had predicted an 'impending' air disaster in which more than 60 would die – including children – but from which there would be several miraculous escapes. He made a particular point about the airliner's tail fin.

Within a month, such a crash had occurred at Stockport, in which 72 – 16 of them children – had perished but from which there had been some amazing escapes. In pictures of the crash, the tail fin stood out vividly from the wreckage.

These fell far short of conclusive evidence of premonition but we decided to interview Hencher and Miss Middleton. That was a big mistake.

Immediately they began to feel that they were good at it, they lost completely whatever 'power' they might have possessed. That fitted in later with other research which I did in a laboratory at St

Mary's Hospital, in which we used an electro-encephalograph (brain-wave recorder). Alpha rhythms in the brain only become strong when a person's brain is 'idling'. In the same way, 'visions', 'overpowering feelings', 'premonitions', that match the facts only seem to occur when the person is thinking of nothing in particular. I have since wondered if premonitions ride on the back of alpha rhythms. But I have never had the time nor the resources to research further.

When I left the *Standard*, I took the bureau (which we re-named the British Premonitions Bureau) with me and my secretary, Jennifer Preston, carried on logging the phoned-in 'premonitions' and analysing them for three more years. In the end, I concluded that, if there is such a thing as premonition – and I believe that there is – it resides in the non-conscious part of the human mind.

It seems to be, literally a flash of intuition' – instantaneous, overpowering. The person knows that something is going to happen. But the moment conscious thought is applied – for example in answer to a question – it vanishes.

Are you on my frequency?

The quest for truth about telepathy set me wondering why some people 'get on like a house on fire', while others 'can't stand the sight of each other'.

In 1971, I was invited to give the Richard Spriggs Memorial Lecture at Loughborough College School. Richard Spriggs had been a sound recordist working for Rediffusion but had died tragically from seasickness, at the age of 23, during the TV coverage of Sir Francis Chichester's epic round-the-world voyage in the yacht Gipsy Moth in 1967. Four ITV companies had set up a Trust to provide his old school with its own TV studio, two annual prizes and a memorial lecture, which was required to 'excite curiosity, stimulate discussion and arouse the imagination' of the young audience.

I decided to make 'personal communication' the main point of the lecture.

I went in search of facts and theories among psychologists, psychiatrists and medical experimenters but found few. Research had been done into the role of smells in human communication but nothing into 'brain broadcasting', as I called it.

'Bodies radiate heat.' I pointed out. 'Why shouldn't brains radiate messages? If we could prove they do, it might be possible to
remove a lot of tension from the world today by keeping incom-
patible couples apart and allowing only compatible politicians to
negotiate.'

I offered a theory that it all depended on which frequency your
brain was on as to whether you would get on well with other
people. Most of our brains were on roughly the same frequency
band but, every so often, you met somebody who was on exactly
the same frequency, in which case the two of you would 'click',
knowing what the other was thinking without a word being spoken, or feeling intensely close.

'It's rather like a ham radio operator sitting at home, twiddling
knobs,' I went on. 'At one moment, the room is silent. But as
soon as he switches on his radio, he can hear voices. The voices
must have been there – the information must have been travelling
through the room – all the time. As soon as he switches to the
right frequency band, he can hear a lot of voices fairly well. But
when he fine-tunes moving from, say, 162 kilocycles to 162.1 –
he can hear one voice loud and clear, communication is perfect. I
believe it's the same with humans.'

Nobody laughed. Nobody has since disproved the theory. For
me it remains a neat explanation for a disturbing question – is it
possible to find true love more than once?

Answer: yes – if there is more than one person on your frequency.

The man who dreamed the winner of the Grand National

I became infected by the premonition bug myself for a while.

I had never been a betting man – except on Derby and Grand
National days but in 1967, the Bureau received a telephone call
from a young Australian called George Cranmer. 'Look,' he said,
'this probably means nothing but I had a very powerful dream
last night in which I saw the colours of the jockey winning the
Grand National. Do dreams count as premonitions?'

I said they did. We recorded details and time–date stamped the
form.

George said that he had checked the colours and they were

those of a jockey due to ride a horse called Foinavon in the National next day. I duly filed the form but did nothing more about it because Foinavon was a rank outsider.

Next day, I watched TV in frustration as horse after horse fell and more than a score of jockeys tumbled, leaving Foinavon to pick his way through the casualties and win at 100–1.

Two months later, Cranmer rang again. This time he had dreamed of a horse carrying the colours of Ribocco parading in the winner's enclosure after the Derby. Another premonition? At first it seemed not because Ribocco came in second at Epsom although at a fair price – 22–1. But he went on to win the Irish Derby a week later (at 5–2).

Then I opened a letter from a reader named Pia shortly after reading a story about Pia Lindstrom, Ingrid Bergman's daughter. I had never, until that day, heard the name Pia. It was Oaks day.

The midday edition of the *Standard* dropped onto my desk, back page uppermost, and I noticed that among the runners listed for the Oaks was a filly called Pia. I shot down to Joe Coral's betting shop in Fleet Street and just managed to scramble £1 on before the 'off'.

Pia won at 100–7.

Despite this, I did no more betting until the Derby of 1969.

On the morning of that race, I heard the name 'Blakeney' four times – none of them in connection with a horse. At lunch, I found there was a Derby entry called Blakeney. I put £1 on with Joe Coral – and the horse came in at 15–2.

Next, I was lunching at L'Escargot restaurant in Soho and, while waiting for my guest, read that there was a horse running called L'Escargot. I shot out to the nearby betting shop, put £2 each way on and heard, after lunch, that it had won at 33–1.

It was around that time that I had an idea for a TV documentary on the science of gambling and started to get unscientific 'feelings' about gee-gees. I could look at a list of runners in the newspaper and know which horse was going to win. Each time it happened, I placed a bet.

In the space of three weeks, I made almost £400. But I began to laugh and joke about it with my colleagues and they would come up to me with a 'Got anything for the 3.30 Peter?' – and, as suddenly as it had started, the 'gift' went.

Why? Was it because I was in a cycle of luck which eventually turned? Or was it because I started to apply conscious thought to the selection? I am still no wiser.

However, the research for the documentary continued and moved from horses to fruit machines, blackjack, football pools, craps and, finally, to roulette.

I made a lot of money from roulette, the biggest win coming on the 1970 Election night. By then, I was working almost full-time for ITN and, because there was no possible reporting role for a Science Editor on Election night, I was put in charge of the 'Green Room' – the hospitality suite in which politicians and other pundits were entertained, prior to being taken into the studio to be interviewed.

At 6 p.m. after checking the bar, I decided to pop into the nearby Sportsman Club and while away two hours before guests started arriving.

In those two hours, I won £700, almost without thinking. And that may have been precisely why I won; I was not consciously thinking as I spread the chips around. Or it may have been the cycle of fortune again.

Harold Wilson lost the election and immediately afterwards my luck ran out too, and I started to lose heavily. I ended the 'research' about £2,000 down but with three clear conclusions.

The first was that, of all forms of gambling, roulette offers the best chance of winning, providing you play Odd-Even, Red-Black, or Low-High, The odds are then almost evens (34–35) in what is equivalent to a two-horse race – far, far better than the odds a bookie would offer and infinitely better than a fruit machine. I also decided that fruit machines were, literally, a waste of time: if you won, it took a long time to win an amount which you could win in a few seconds at roulette.

The second was that luck does run in cycles and that the only way to test whether you are 'on the up' is to try a bet or two – but to stop immediately if you do not get clear results.

The third was that gambling is a mug's game. For the one successful gambler, there are tens of thousands of failures, some whose lives are ruined. By then, late nights were damaging my family life and it was not difficult to give up.

I have never gambled since – except £1 a week, for amusement, on the National Lottery . . .

Encounters with politicians

Science and politics are usually poles apart, but being put in charge of ITN's Green Room on Election nights did bring me face to face with several MPs and an occasional Minister. I was amazed to see how totally wrapped up in themselves they were.

Ted Heath was a classic example. It was traditional for Reggie Bosanquet to report the outcome of the voting in his Bexley constituency and then bring him to ITN to be interviewed by Alastair Burnet in the studio. On the night Margaret Thatcher was re-elected Prime Minister for the first time, we had arranged for every MP entering the Green Room to be handed an up-to-the-minute print-out of all the constituency results while they relaxed with a drink and some 'nibbles' before going on air.

Reggie arrived with Ted around 10 p.m. A programme researcher took his coat, another gave him a glass of wine and a plate of canapés and I appeared with the print-out, which he took without a word or a glance. His eyes were riveted to a TV monitor.

I stood there for a minute or so until Reggie said, 'Ted, I don't think you know our Science Editor, Peter Fairley.'

Without taking his eyes from the monitor, he popped another canapé intact into his mouth and boomed, 'A *science* man – what's he doing here?' – and went on eating, drinking and watching TV.

Jeremy Thorpe was similarly dismissive. I once had the misfortune, when the Green Room was packed with guests, to splash a little white wine down his navy blue overcoat hanging on the coat-stand. 'Clumsy boy,' he said loudly, despite my apology, as he stepped forward with a handkerchief to dab at it. I was 52.

Others came and went, leaving the impression that they had no time to bother to converse with anybody outside their world at Westminster.

The exceptions were Tony Benn and Harold Wilson. When the former turned up in the Green Room, he refused a drink but spent the time asking questions about space and my visits to America. He seemed genuinely interested. Subsequently, after he had become Minister for Technology, I met him on many occasions at functions and his office at Millbank.

I admired the way that he put major advances in technology

and transport into historical context, using huge graphs around the walls of his office to show the speed at which they had evolved. It indicated the rate of invention in any one subject area at a glance. At the same time, in his desk drawer, he kept one of those ornate and colourful flags from trade union workers' marches of the '30s.

'From time to time, I unfold it and look at it – just to remind me of my origins,' explained the man who had renounced the peerage to become plain Anthony Wedgwood Benn.

One summer, long before 'phone-ins', he sounded off in public about the BBC being too dictatorial and not allowing the public enough airtime to express views on issues of the day. He also accused the Corporation of bias.

I offered to hold a series of private lunches with a psephologist and a senior computer engineer from ICL at which the four of us could explore ways of helping the public to feel that they had more influence over important issues than a vote in an Election once every five years or so.

After three of these, we arrived at a range of options and a scale of costs, starting with the creation of an independent institute of Public Opinion, through regular postal balloting to a scheme which we called 'Friday Night is Voting Night'.

'Friday Night is Voting Night' would involve assigning a TV channel on Friday nights to broadcasting short, factual programmes explaining the current issues of the day in simple terms. At the end of each item, viewers would vote from their own homes. The voting would be done either by switching the household lights on and off – to cause measurable fluctuations in demand at the power stations – or by an electronic voting box with buttons, held on the lap.

The audience would get their satisfaction by watching a 'Swingometer' on the TV screen.

None of the proposals, carefully minuted, saw the light of day in the form we envisaged, although elements of the ideas have since appeared. I still think that they would help to reduce disillusionment with Parliament and whoever is in Government but there are some politicians, of course, who believe that the less opportunity the public gets to affect administrative decisions the better it will be for the efficiency of the country.

Eyes on No. 10

The next time I saw Tony Benn was on a programme called *Face The Press*, broadcast by Tyne Tees Television. He was the 'victim' and I was one of a panel of three journalists, with Peregrine Worsthorne in the chair.

These programmes were transmitted at 7.30 p.m. from Newcastle and afterwards Tyne Tees entertained us to dinner at The Windmill restaurant, finally escorting those based in London onto the overnight sleeper to King's Cross.

Before I even had time to remove my tie, there was a knock on the door. The sleeping car attendant said simply: 'Mr Benn wonders if you would care to join him for a drink in his compartment.'

I was a little surprised, as I knew that he did not drink but he immediately offered me a cognac, with a soda water for himself. Then began one of the most bizarre experiences of my life, which continued with the pair of us sitting on his bunk until 3.30 a.m. as the train rattled through the night.

Respect for confidentiality precludes me from describing in detail the conversation but what he basically wanted was a sounding board to help him reach a decision: should he make a bid to become Prime Minister?

Harold Wilson had been in office for almost two years but jockeying was beginning within the Labour Party over a successor and Tony Benn wanted people's private opinions over whether he should present himself openly as a challenger.

I cannot remember the logic but I advised 'No – wait'. I suspect others said the same. He did wait – and Jim Callaghan got the job.

Social gaffe at No. 10

I had met Harold Wilson a few months earlier at No. 10.

After tickertape parades in New York and scores of speaking engagements in U.S. cities, the crew of Apollo 11 went on a world tour and Harold Wilson threw a party for them in Downing Street.

He invited a mixture of politicians, scientists, stage folk and media people and I was impressed by the homework that he must have done on his guest list. He knew each of our names and had some little comment or other to make as he introduced us to the three astronauts.

When it came to turn, I was amazed to hear him say, 'The only reason why Peter is here is because he had less sleep that night than you (the Apollo crew) did.' This was a reference to ITN's marathon Moon landing coverage (see Ch. 10).

A total of 215 guests had been invited – that total being dictated (we were told later) by the bearing strength of the floors of No. 10. Never having been inside No. 10 before, I got there early. I was given a glass of champagne and steered through to the third of the ornate State rooms, where an elderly man and a beautiful woman were deep in conversation.

They turned and I found myself face to face with Nyree Dawn Porter, who had starred in the BBC TV series *The Forsyth Saga* and with whom I was inconsolably in love. We shook hands and she said she had enjoyed the Moon walk programme. Then the portly, greying man introduced himself. 'I'm Armstrong,' he said, 'William Armstrong.'

'Oh really,' I said. 'Are you by any chance related to Neil?'

'No,' he replied. 'He's one of the Irish Armstrongs, whereas we come from Northumberland.'

'What do you do?' I asked.

'I'm a civil servant,' he replied, 'Oh really.' I blundered on. 'What branch of the Civil Service?'

There was a moment's pause – then he said quietly, 'Well, actually I'm the head of it.' Suddenly, I realised he was Sir William.

Nyree by now was laughing. It was at that moment that I wished the bearing strength of the floors had been 214 and that I could have fallen through.

CHAPTER EIGHT

Behind the Iron Curtain

On October 4, 1957, the world learned with astonishment that the Soviet Union had launched the first artificial satellite – Sputnik 1. The Space Age was born.

I was sitting at the long reporters' desk in the *Standard* when the newsflash came and I was promptly despatched to the BBC Overseas monitoring station at Tatsfield in Surrey, where the new sound – beep-beep . . . beep-beep could be heard through the earphones of the engineers.

That night, the *Standard* devoted four whole pages to what, by any standards, was sensational news. What was particularly astonishing was the size of the satellite – no mere 'grapefruit' (as the Americans launched six months later) but a veritable basketball 22.8 ins. in diameter and weighing 184 lbs.

Sputnik I was followed only a month later by a further sensation – Sputnik 2 containing a dog named Laika. Laika, a bitch, lay breathing in a sealed cabin alongside a food store, air conditioner and equipment for recording pulse, respiration, blood pressure as well as an electrocardiogram for monitoring the behaviour of her heart. The whole capsule and its electrical supply weighed half a ton, showing that the Russians had very powerful rockets indeed.

Space, with its whole new vocabulary of words, quite frankly excited me. I realised that very few people in Britain knew anything about the subject and that, if I made an in-depth study of it, I could become as good as any 'expert' and perhaps better than some. Because the subject fascinated me, it was no burden to take home a briefcase full of 'homework' each night.

I read every relevant book, kept file upon file of cuttings and got to know the saner members of the British Interplanetary Society who, until then, were virtually the only people in the country with any expertise. The *Standard* gave me every encouragement because, pretty soon, the Circulation Department was reporting that space stories were definitely helping to sell the newspaper.

The Sputniks were followed by a whole string of Cosmos satellites from the Soviet Union, Explorer satellites from the US and research probes, from both sides, aimed at the Moon. I became a frequent visitor to Jodrell Bank, waiting with colleagues – often through the night – for news of the progress of Pioneer space probes which the giant radio-telescope tracked for several days at a time, until the signals suddenly stopped, indicating that the probe had crashed into the Moon dust.

Much of the early space programmes of both the Soviet Union and the United States were intertwined with military research and defence weapons. Apart from my Army background in tanks, I knew little about the modern defence scene but it somehow became my bailiwick with the exception of the RAF which had always been my colleague James Stuart's responsibility as Air Correspondent. So it was a huge relief when the Standard decided to appoint a Defence Correspondent in his own right.

Actually, the decision was taken at a higher level – for the man appointed was a personal friend of Max Aitken who had felt unhappy in his role as part of the *Express* group management team and requested a change of direction. He was Group Captain Hugh 'Cocky' Dundas, and, like Max, a Battle of Britain fighter ace and holder of a DSO and bar and a DFC – clearly the ideal Defence Correspondent. His arrival at the *Standard* caused something of a stir, but for the wrong reasons.

'Cocky' was a charming, courteous man with a nice sense of humour and the very last person to wish to upset anybody. He may not even know now what happened.

The *Standard* editorial floor was open-plan. Only the Editor and his Deputy had offices with doors. The problem was: where should a person with such a distinguished war record and 'connections' to the son of his Lordship sit? Clearly he could not be plonked at the Reporters' desk nor at any of the other nests of desks used by other specialists. There was, however, one other possibility – the Night Reporter's room.

This was a small, glass-partitioned office, with a door, beside the editorial floor. It was normally used for interviews by day and by the duty reporter at night. It was where he scoured the national dailies and arranged any follow-ups which required an early start. It had a torn, upholstered chair, a desk and a typewriter. The day before 'Cocky' arrived, a cushioned, swivelling executive chair was substituted and a carpet laid. The duty reporter was told to work at night, outside on the editorial floor.

All this would have been accepted with equanimity had it not been decided that 'Cocky' should also be given a key to the Executive 'loo'. There were only three – held by the Editor, his Deputy and the News Editor, Ronnie Hyde.

Ronnie Hyde, despite having served in the post for two decades, was asked to hand over his key. I shall never forget his face, nor the thunderous look which he bore for several days – until a fourth key was cut.

'Cocky' stayed in the post for about a year, after which he headed off to Rediffusion, the chairmanship of BET plc and a knighthood. Defence came back into my bailiwick until finally Tom Pocock joined the paper and made it his speciality.

In the interim, Space and Defence required me, more and more, to go abroad. Although I made many unsuccessful applications to visit the Soviet Union, to see something of their space activities at first-hand, the Americans welcomed specialists like me with open arms, laying on visits, briefings and interviews with top officials without demur.

Brunettes and bribes

One of the most fruitful sources of space news was the annual conference of the International Astronautical Federation, at which key figures in both the Soviet and the US space programmes would appear, either to hear scientific papers read or plans announced for future projects. It took me, in turn, to Paris, Athens, Belgrade, Washington and Warsaw but, most memorably, to the Bulgarian seaside resort of Golden Sands, on the Black Sea.

Our plane landed on a tiny airfield near the fishing port of Varna, about five miles from Golden Sands. We all trooped into a wooden hut where Bulgarian immigration officials took – and kept – our passports. As a Brit., I had been taught never to be parted from my passport but it quickly became clear that, unless I agreed, I would not be allowed in.

Night fell during the coach ride to the hotel (which also happened to be the IAF conference hotel) and we arrived to find a power failure. The hotel restaurant and lounge were lit by candles and packed with noisy delegates, flushed with vodka. I checked in and my bag was carried upstairs by a man bearing a candle in a saucer. As he opened the door for me, I was pleased to see a black, pedestal telephone by the bed and thought, 'This should be a cinch – attend the sessions and come upstairs to phone copy to London.'

A moment later the door opened and the hotel official, in a state of agitation, indicated that I was in the wrong room. I followed him upstairs to another room but, this time, his candle revealed a bedside table without telephone. 'Oh well,' I thought, 'when the lights come on I'll ask for a different room – one which does have a phone.' I went downstairs, helped myself to vodka and caviar and located some American scientists whom I knew.

The lights came on. I went to Reception and asked if I could change my room to one with a phone. 'There are no telephones in rooms – only this one (on the Reception desk).'

'But I have seen one.' I protested. 'No,' the clerk insisted, 'there are no telephones.' The argument was repeated three times. I felt as if I was in a scene from the spy film *The Lady Vanishes* where the hero is told, again and again, that a lady whom he had definitely seen come aboard had never been on the train. In the end, the clerk had his way but the whiff of news was never stronger.

At breakfast, I met fellow science-writer Robert Chapman, my opposite number on the *Evening News* and he was bemoaning the fact that our only telephone link with London would be via the one phone on the Reception desk, in full earshot of everybody.

We were joined by two attractive brunettes, who introduced themselves as Viva and Vanya. They said they worked for Intourist, the Eastern bloc travel agency and had been assigned to us as guide-interpreters. 'Anything you want,' they promised, 'let us know and we will try to arrange it.'

'A room with a telephone,' I started, going on to recount my experience. 'Wait here,' they said, 'and we will see what we can do.'

They returned after a few minutes. 'We are sorry – there is only one telephone in this hotel and that is at Reception. You must have been mistaken.' I gave up.

However, Viva and Vanya discovered that there were six public telephones at the Continental Hotel, a mile away and they led us along the sand to them. We placed a call to London and settled down to wait. By then four other Fleet Street science reporters had joined us, all seeking a communications link with their offices.

We drank coffee. We ate a snack lunch. We had tea. Eventually, London's working hours ended – but with no contact. That evening, we had an enjoyable supper with Viva and Vanya, who introduced us to the delights of Bulgarian hock then it was a quick kiss on the cheek and away they went as suddenly as they had appeared.

Golden Sands is a good name for the holiday resort for the sand is pure and it stretches for miles, edged by a low escarpment covered with fir trees, in which white-concrete hotels were dotted about at different levels. It was September and the holidaymakers had mostly gone home, to be replaced by parties of East German factory workers on cheap package tours. Each group was in the charge of a tourist guide, usually a large, muscular blonde.

As we walked back along the beach to our hotel, after dark, we could see these women sitting at the head of long refectory tables, flanked by men and women in their shabby best, all desperately trying to have a good time in low-wattage lighting conditions. Their menus were pathetically simple and usually began with a large, raw tomato.

We decided to take it in turns to cover the actual space conference, while all the other British journalists took up vigil by the phone booths at the Continental Hotel. It was Wednesday afternoon before any of us contacted London and then only by a fluke.

We discovered that a Telex bureau had been set up in the hotel to allow journalists from all over the world to report a chess congress being held nearby. The White Russian Telex operator had a notebook containing the names of all those accredited to use the machine and, for some unaccountable reason, our names were among them. What is more, all accredited reporters were allowed to reverse the charges – the bill would be sent to their London offices.

Life took on a different hue. I filed a 1,000-word feature about Bulgaria, which I called 'topsy-turvy land' and then walked to the Telex each lunchtime, having actually listened to some of the Conference.

I had brought with me some gifts to use either as bribes or 'thank you's'. Bear Brand nylons in sizes 8 to 11, bars of 'Fabu-

lous Pink' Camay soap and half-pound slabs of Cadbury's Dairy
Milk chocolate . . . the Telex operator got razor blades. All the
rest went to a woman whom I met each evening at the so-called
Night Club.

I saw her first, sitting with a small group of East Germans,
close to the oval dance floor. I spoke no German beyond '*Achtung
Spitfire*' but she agreed to dance and we communicated. She was
short, buxom and game to learn The Twist, which I had repeatedly danced (to no less than Chubby Checker's band) at Cape
Canaveral. She told me her name was Ilse.

The top cabaret act was a Russian woman gymnast. After she
had flexed her muscles, we danced some more until it was time
for me to walk Ilse back to her hotel. We cuddled a little, during
which I produced some of my 'gifts' – a size 9 pair of Bear Brand
nylon stockings, one bar of soap and a bar of Cadbury's Dairy
Milk. We agreed to meet next evening at the club.

I saw Ilse every night after that, drinking schnapps at the table,
gyrating to more of The Twist and smooching to slower Western
music. During the cheek-to-cheek moments, she told me that she
worked in an East Berlin chemical factory but was desperate to
escape to the West. Could I possibly help her?

If there is one act of folly which no legitimate journalist should
even consider, it is getting mixed up in a political escape – no
matter how sympathetic one might feel – and I certainly had no
intention of doing so. But it did not spoil our friendship and, over
the next three nights, I parted with three more sizes of nylons and
most of my supply of soap and chocolate.

Friday night – and the last tryst in the club: I went armed with
the largest (size 10) stockings and the last bar of Dairy Milk.

To my surprise, she was not at her usual table. In fact, she was
not at any table. I waited 20 minutes and was just about to leave
when one of the muscular blonde guides came up to my table
and said simply, 'Mr Fairley, we know what you have been doing.'

Mr Fairley? How did she know my name? Been doing – doing
what? As if to answer my question, she placed on the table all the
packets of nylons, all the bars of soap and all the bars of Dairy
Milk, with the exception of four squares from one bar. 'Please do
not try this sort of thing again.'

I was dumbfounded, so much so that I could not find words
for questions as she walked away. I realised that Ilse must have

been closely watched and hoped that the observation did not include the cuddles behind her hotel. I never saw her again and can only hope that loss of a few luxuries was regarded as sufficient punishment for fraternising with a British journalist. I had an eerie feeling as I walked back to my hotel.

The following morning was brilliant and very hot. I decided to bathe in the sea. Afterwards, I fell asleep on the sand, waking with a parched mouth. I remembered some grapes and returned to my room to get them.

As I climbed the central staircase of the hotel, I passed the bedroom into which I had been misdirected on the night I arrived. The door burst open and out popped one of the Soviet scientists whose reports on space missions I had listened to during the week. He bounded downstairs, leaving his door open.

As he did so, I heard a telephone ring. I pushed the door fully open – and there it was, by the bed. Exactly as I had remembered . . .

'Bugged' in Poland

I was reminded of the incident a year later when the conference venue switched to Warsaw. Before I left Golden Sands, I made inquiries and discovered that all the senior Russian delegates to the Bulgarian conference had been accommodated in rooms on the central staircase, one above the other. Telephones had been supplied, branching off a vertical cable, stretching from ground to roof.

In Warsaw, all the British science reporters were booked into the Bristol Hotel and we soon discovered that our rooms, too, were in a vertical column, one above the other, regardless of the fact that there were plenty of spare rooms on either side – in fact, we could all have been accommodated on the first floor, had the management wished.

I thought, 'Bet we're being bugged.'

It was a week after a microphone had been discovered hidden in the eagle positioned over the US Ambassador's desk in Warsaw and 'bugging' was still a hot topic. We dispersed to search our bedrooms thoroughly, arranging to meet in the bar at 6 p.m.

Each of us came in with the same story – one electronic 'bug' behind the wallpaper, another in the 'loo', connected by wires to a vertical cable outside the window. We decided to have some fun.

After the conference closed each day, we met in a different bedroom, facing one of the 'bugs' and discussed the day's news. But into the discussion we wove references to Britain's space activities (very limited), laser weapons, faster-than-sound bombers and high-speed nuclear submarines, It was hard not to laugh.

We poured out so much bogus information that I like to think it took a team of little men, with earphones and tape playback machines, at least a year to make sense of it all – or, at least, try to.

The other amusing incident in Warsaw occurred on the day of arrival. In his conference pigeon-hole, every US delegate received an instruction to attend the US Embassy the following evening to receive a warning about careless talk. Every British delegate received an invitation, too, to the British Embassy. But it had nothing to do with 'bugging'.

It was to celebrate the Queen's birthday – with a tea party.

A visa at last

Nowhere was the Iron Curtain more impenetrable than around Soviet space establishments. The cosmodromes were out of bounds. The launch pads were secret. The Soviet Academy of Sciences admitted only scientists of international repute and then only under close escort. I made 17 applications to go to the Soviet Union before I was finally granted a visa – to do a TV report from Moscow to mark the 21st birthday of Sputnik 1. The Russians could see no significance in the request since their culture does not recognise 21 as 'coming-of-age' and I suspect that was why they granted the visa.

They put up a scientist for interview – the head of the Soviet interplanetary programme – we grabbed the opportunity.

I flew from Heathrow in an Ilyushin airliner whose interior resembled Queen Victoria's railway coach – red plush upholstery, brass curtain rails and mahogany tables. The pilot flew it like a fighter plane, virtually doing a victory roll as we reached Moscow, where no amount of persuasion would get the immigration officer to stamp my passport (they feared copies) and where I was met by a young man from the Soviet Foreign Office who drove me to my hotel. He said his name was Alexei.

It was a Friday afternoon and Alexei's wife had just had a baby. He was obviously keen to get back to her and so we struck a bargain – he would leave me alone in Moscow if I promised to behave myself – until 9 a.m. on Monday, when a Soviet film director would collect me from the hotel. I handed over all my English newspapers and current affairs magazines and he went away happy.

The first thing I did was check the room for 'bugs'. I soon gave up because the ceiling and ornate candelabra were too high to reach – anything could have been hidden there.

Then the phone rang.

'Harry?' queried a husky feminine voice. 'No,' I said, 'I'm not Harry.'

'But you must be Harry,' she persisted. 'You said ring at six.'

'I'm sorry – I'm not Harry and I didn't arrange to be called at six.' I replied.

'What is your name?' 'My name is Peter,' I said, after a pause.

'Well, Peter, shall I come up?' By now the alarm bells were ringing full strength and I remembered my promise to Alexei. 'No, I don't think that would be a good idea,' I said and put the phone down.

She rang again four times before I finally convinced her that I wasn't Harry and didn't want her company. That night, I had a quiet dinner in the hotel and retired early, double-locking my door. It was just as well because I was woken twice by the sound of somebody trying to get into my room. Whether it was Harry or 'husky voice' – or the old harridan of a supervisor who sat by the stairs all night I shall never know, but it all helped to build up suspicion and distrust to a point that, when I left the hotel next morning to explore Moscow, I was convinced I was being followed.

I was. I spotted him in GUM, the department store beside Red Square which the Russians claimed was the equivalent of Selfridges but which looked more like the old floral hall of Covent Garden, with bridges across at first-floor level. He was a caricature of an undercover man – trilby hat, frowsy mackintosh and a copy of *Pravda* which he kept pulling up in front of his face whenever he saw me looking at him.

There was nothing worth buying in GUM – what little there was attracted large crowds, who pushed and jostled, roubles held skywards as if they were bidding at an auction. I decided to try to dodge him in the Metro.

Moscow's Metro is unique – chandeliers over the escalators and each station an architectural delight with a decor different from the others. I bought a rover ticket and studied the map. Comrade Mac studied *Pravda*. It only took one change of train to lose him. I waited until the doors were closing before stepping out. As the train moved off, the newspaper was still in front of his face.

Thereafter I had the Soviet capital to myself – a call at the Intourist office to buy a book of dinner tickets, then Lenin's tomb in Red Square and the Museum of Space Technology (where I saw most of the spacecraft and satellites, that I had been writing about for years, 'in the flesh') and finally the Red Army Museum.

That was the real eye-opener. The central staircase was flanked with dummy soldiers, standing in front of a long line of captured German regimental flags: but these only led the eye to the largest photo I have ever seen.

It stretched from floor to ceiling and around the walls of a hall and showed Red Army troops holding literally hundreds more of the captured battle flags, dipped in the dust of Red Square, in front of the Soviet leaders lined up on the balcony of the Kremlin.

The scale of the Red Army's victory over the Germans was finally brought home to the visitor by a glass display case filled with Iron Crosses. The case was 20 yards long, a yard high and a yard wide and must have contained 20–30,000 Iron Crosses.

That night, I helped to celebrate a victory of a different kind. I used one of the meal tickets to eat at a Georgian restaurant and was directed by the *maitre d'* to sit at a table set for four but this was already occupied by three boisterous young men. They clearly did not like the fourth seat being occupied by a stranger and I soon found out why; the fourth member of the group arrived and the *maitre d'* was obliged to provide a fifth chair.

After that, all was smiles again. Part of the meal ticket included a small carafe of vodka and a bottle of *roda* – red wine. The group were onto their second bottle of *roda* when my vodka arrived, so we shared the drink and toasted each other.

It was the first of many toasts – for they turned out to be the centre forward, centre half and goalkeeper of the Kiev Dynamo soccer club, who had that day beaten the crack Moscow Dynamo side. The fourth man was the chairman of their supporters club.

Georgian tradition requires food to be taken as a long series of small but delicious courses, each course being washed down by alcohol. With two carafes of vodka and three more *rodas* in the kitty, the evening grew merrier and merrier despite the fact that the only method of communication was drawing on the restaurant's paper napkins.

The players knew the English clubs by name and I remembered many from having filled in the weekly pools. So we toasted one club after another. By the time we had reached Alloa Athletic in the Scottish League, it was 1 a.m. and I was almost incoherent. They then started to sing – in English – 'Here we go . . .'

Missing out in Moscow

'You English?' I nodded.

'You like sex?' I nodded.

'You like group sex?' I didn't bat an eyelid.

She was short, a touch buxom and the lamplight outside the Ukraine (pronounced 'Oo-cry-eena') Hotel in Moscow revealed that the roots of her dyed-blonde hair needed attention. But she was pretty.

'How many in the group?' I asked.

'Three,' she replied – then added, ' Thirty English pounds.'

It was said hesitantly, almost as a question. But my answer was quick.

'Sorry. I don't have thirty English pounds. This is my last night in Moscow . . .' I began. But her eyes were already back on the revolving door of the hotel exit.

I walked to a waiting taxi, whose driver merely wanted to exchange my remaining pounds, illegally, into roubles. 'National Hotel, *po-zhaista*.'

I had told the woman the truth. I didn't have time to explain that I had spent most of my meagre foreign allowance in bars and restaurants in the company of other ladies who had seemed only too keen to practise their English on a lonely Westerner whose Russian was limited to '*Da*', '*Niet*', '*po-zhaista*' (please) and '*spassiba*' (thank you).

One, Irena, had actually invited me home ' for coffee'.

The fraternisation had all taken place in the plush bar of the National Hotel, meeting point for diplomats, journalists, businessmen, single ladies and, I suspect, KGB agents. The problem for three nights had been what to do when the voices became huskier and the caresses began.

It was futile thinking of taking anyone back to your room for, positioned like a rottweiller at the top of each staircase or lift-shaft, a muscular concierge kept vigil, 24 hours a day, suspicious of any sign of hanky-panky. But the problem usually solved itself when your 'friend', downing one more whisky, announced that it was late and she had to return to her husband and children.

Not in Irena's case.

She said she had no husband, no children and would love to give me coffee back at her place. Curious to the eyebrows and always in search of new book material, I accepted.

I might not have been so keen had I known that 'her place' was a 20-minute taxi ride from the National in Red Square, with the fare – an English £5 note – down to me.

It turned out to be a small apartment in a three-storey block set, with others, in a birch wood. Her furniture was cheap and modern, except for a huge Victorian sofa, covered with a Romany shawl, on which she indicated I should sit while she went to make the coffee.

At that time, the Cold War was still a bit chilly and Greville Wynn, the British businessman, was in Lubianka prison after being arrested as a spy. I gave the room a quick eye-search for hidden cameras and felt around the sofa for microphones but found nothing suspicious.

It was then that I heard voices – Irena's and a man's. I decided to put my remaining banknotes under the inner sole of my shoe and had hardly done so when she reappeared – without coffee.

She sat down close to me and put a hand on my knee 'My mother . . .,' she started, '. . . she says you must pay first.'

'Pay?' I queried. 'I thought we were having coffee.'

She smiled coquettishly. 'I am vary good for you.' she purred. 'Don't worry – we have wonderful time. But money first.'

I did not even ask how much. The man's voice did not sound like 'mother' and Irena's face, seeing my reaction, had already begun to harden.

I sprang for the half-open door, fled out of the apartment and took the communal stairs two at a time. On the way, I passed the kitchen and caught a quick glimpse of a burly, fair-haired man buckling on a broad, leather belt. There was no aroma of coffee.

I ran through the woods and out onto the highway. I was lucky enough to flag down a motorist who spoke a little French and gave me a lift back to the Hotel Ukraine. In bed, I counted blessings instead of sheep.

Recently, I went back to Moscow. A fellow writer, based in the capital, up-dated me. 'Coffee' he said, 'back at "her place" would now cost at least £50, group sex – if available – more like £300.

'And you would never make it past the kitchen,' he added. 'The Moscow Mafia would grab you and not only take your banknotes from your shoes but probably take your shoes and socks as well.'

I also noticed that the surly old harridans who used to guard every hotel floor had been replaced by attractive, much younger women with seductive smiles. Why?

I had no chance to investigate because with me, this time, was my wife.

CHAPTER NINE

Beaverbrook and Blindness

Journalists on the *Standard* and the *Daily Express* were always conscious that they were being watched. No matter where Lord Beaverbrook was in the world, he cast a critical eye over his newspapers. When he was abroad, he had copies flown out to him: when he was at home at his mansion – Cherkley Court, near Leatherhead – or his flat in Arlington House, Piccadilly, he was frequently on the phone.

On many mornings at the *Standard*, between 9 a.m. and 9.20, the Editor's morning conference would be interrupted by his secretary buzzing through. 'Lord Beaverbrook on the line.' Everybody would have to leave the office while the conversation took place. Sometimes Charles Wintour would disclose the topics discussed: at other times, he kept mum. But we were all aware for the rest of the day that 'the Beaver' had his finger on our pulse.

I met his Lordship twice. The first time was after I had written a feature entitled *On the Horns of a Dilemma* after interviewing Sir Solly Zuckerman. Solly had just been appointed Chief Scientific Adviser to the Ministry of Defence and his dilemma was how to recommend a successor to the 'ultimate' weapon – the Polaris submarine missile. It was only just going into service and had taken 10 years to evolve from the drawing board to operational use. Its life expectancy was ten years, so the 'go ahead' for a successor was needed *pronto*.

I was summoned to Arlington House and ushered into the Beaver's library by his butler, who invited me to sit in a high-backed chair, positioned directly in a shaft of sunlight. A few minutes later, his Lordship arrived, shook hands, drew up a matching chair and sat so close that our knees were almost touching. The next five minutes are a blur in my memory.

He asked quick-fire questions about Solly, about Polaris, about possible new nuclear deterrents and about the whole UK defence scene – perhaps 75 in the space of five minutes. Sitting in that shaft of sunlight, it felt like a rehearsal for *Mastermind*. The grilling ended when the butler knocked (presumably by pre-arrangement) and announced, 'Your hairdresser, m'lord.'

As m'lord walked me to the door, he asked two further questions. 'How much do we pay you, Mr Fairley?' I told him. Then, 'Do you drive a car?' 'Yes,' I said, ' a small one.'

Quick as a flash, he came back, 'In these days of London's traffic, better a small one than a big one.' Whether due to m'lord or not, my salary was increased again the following month.

The second meeting with Beaverbrook came after the BMEWS tour. This time, I was summoned to Cherkley in Surrey. I drove down and parked in the courtyard. This time, the butler escorted me into the ballroom.

A table had been set for two in the middle of the large, beech-wood dance floor, a cold lunch on the sideboard. The Beaver hobbled in on a stick. 'Well, Fairley,' he growled, 'what have you been up to?'

I told him that I had been on a tour of BMEWS and had been impressed by the determination of the US to survive a nuclear attack – there were shelters everywhere, clear instructions and every serviceman knew what to do. I suddenly had an idea and suggested that it might make a good feature series, in either the *Standard* or the *Express*, to publish guidance for ordinary British civilians on how to survive nuclear attack – how they could convert the old air raid shelter in the garden, or the basement, into a bomb-proof 'survival room'.

'Nonsense,' his Lordship said abruptly, 'the only sensible thing to do, if you survive a nuclear attack, is to commit suicide. All your friends would have died, the whole country would have been devastated – no, suicide is the only thing that would make sense.'

The lunch had not been going well – in fact, I had heard a still, small voice in my ear whispering, 'You're making a cock-up of this occasion.' Suddenly, I felt bold.

'But sir' I protested, 'I'm amazed to hear you of all people talking like that. If you and your son, Max, had taken that attitude during the Battle of Britain, you and I would not be sitting here lunching today.'

I wished I had not said it. His reaction was to push back his chair and hobble up and down, giving me a lecture about the folly of nuclear war, especially if it was a war over Germany.

There had been talk of a second Berlin Airlift and he went on and on about Germany and how we should never trust – or help – the Germans again. The discussion went on in his study, where coffee was frequently interrupted by his Lordship grabbing a microphone and dictating various memos into a recorder. Eventually, around 4.30 p.m he said: 'Mr. Fairley, it's time to go. I'm getting tired. I'll walk you to your car.'

Out in the courtyard, he said, 'I've enjoyed our lunch. I found our conversation stimulating.' But a few yards later, he saw the car: 'What car is that, Mr Fairley?'

'It's a Volkswagen, sir.'

'That's a German car,' he thundered.

'Yes sir,' I said meekly.

'How much did you pay for it?' I told him. Despite his disability, he went all the way round the VW, even climbing half into the driving seat.

'How much did you say you paid for it?' I repeated the figure. 'Huh,' he said thoughtfully, 'you wouldn't get an English car as good as this for that price.'

My salary was not increased after that meeting.

The man who smashed up computers

When I first joined the *Standard*, it was regarded by journalists as a 'subs paper' – all news copy was tinkered with, if not completely rewritten by sub-editors, who wielded incredible power. They moulded it into the *Standard* style (whatever that was) and either added '*Evening Standard* Reporter' on top or printed it without any attribution at all. Usually, they completed their hatchet job without reference to the reporter concerned. Any attempt to introduce colour or individual style into reporting was invariably 'subbed out'.

When Charles Wintour took over, it became a writer's rather than a subs paper and there was real incentive to work hard. He quickly recognised the existence of a huge reservoir of suppressed talent among the reporters and allowed them to write imaginatively, rewarding any piece of good writing with a by-line.

Vocabulary was appreciated and *Roget's Thesaurus* became bedside reading. I took it as a tremendous professional compliment when, years later, Geoffrey Cox – then Editor of ITN – told me, 'Peter, you are the only man I know who uses the word "extrapolate" in the same sentence as the word "plonk".'

Stories, major and minor, continued to pour in.

I kept a particular eye on the development of atomic energy. The UK Atomic Energy Authority invited us to every power station project, held many Press conferences and even offered us a three-day instruction course at Harwell. When the hydrogen-fusion machine called ZETA apparently produced exciting results, they held a Press Day and Fleet Street faithfully opened its front pages and claimed a British breakthrough. Unfortunately ZETA did not live up to expectations, but the flags flew for several days and morale soared.

It is interesting to look back and see how good news was allowed to become bad news, until eventually public confidence turned into fear of everything nuclear. This was primarily due to the efforts of Green Peace and Friends of the Earth, who targeted certain journalists and persistently circulated scare stories.

The Central Electricity Generating Board, which took over responsibility for nuclear power from the UKAEA, did little to counter these stories. Recently I found out why. In the 1957 Electricity Act, there was no requirement to communicate information to the public and no budget to do so either. So the Board chose to ignore the growing public alarm. When, towards the end of the 1970s, it switched to an 'open skies' policy, it was too late. By and large, the public had become 'anti'.

Automation was another subject area rarely out of the news. The development of the transistor made a whole range of computers obsolete before their time and then the silicon chip triggered a further revolution in size, capacity and speed.

I remember attending a Press conference to hear about a new, compact but powerful IBM computer. I asked what was to happen to the perfectly adequate, valve-driven machines known as the '1600 series'. 'They will all be broken up,' replied the chairman.

'Do you mean literally,' I persisted.

'See me afterwards,' he said.

Over a drink, he explained that they would be destroyed because that was the best way to get rid of them. Couldn't they be given to charities? I asked. No, they needed maintenance and charities could not afford the maintenance. Couldn't they be given to universities or schools? No, because America's anti-trust laws

prohibited any manufacturer from making gifts which might influence an educational establishment to buy its products in the
future. Couldn't they be stored and their parts cannibalised for
spares? No, storage space in north London was at a premium,
costing 7s 6d (40p) per cubic foot.

One by one, possible alternatives were ruled out. I asked if the
Standard could take a picture of the demolition work. Sure, no
problem.

Next day, I visited the warehouse at Southgate and met the
man who had the job of breaking up these sophisticated marvels
of technology. He used a sledgehammer and his name was Harry.

'Harry,' I said, 'what thoughts go through your head when
you're smashing up these machines?'

His answer was simple. ' I think of my wife.'

Trust in the computer

Just as distrust of nuclear energy grew, so distrust of computers
grew among a large section of the British public. Leader-writers
would make snide comments; broadcasters like Jack de Manio on
the BBC breakfast programme, would constantly winge about
computers making mistakes (mostly, in his case, in his bank statement).

This used to irritate me. I believed that Britain was in danger
of becoming two nations – one which understood and used computers, the other which did not. Our national prosperity was at
risk. So I tried to rationalise the problem and came to the conclusion that the opinion-formers were attacking computers in order
to hide their ignorance: they were part of a generation which had
never even been taught binary arithmetic.

At that time, one of my friends in PR was Cedric Dickens,
great-grandson of Charles. Despite his literary heritage, he had
become head of Public Affairs for ICL, Britain's largest computer manufacturer. I persuaded Cedric to offer individual newspapers and groups of radio and TV presenters *Computer Days*, at
which simple explanations of how computers worked, what they
could do, their limitations etc., would be followed by lunch and
an opportunity to try a little 'hands on' practice with a machine.

The *Standard* sent its Deputy Editor, Features Editor, Deputy
News Editor, Education and Property Correspondents, Editor of

the *Londoner's Diary* and me to the first of these briefing days and it proved a great success. Other groups followed. Whether Jack de Manio attended, I never asked. But it was noticeable that a lot of the open sneering died away and I like to think that I played a tiny part in gaining wider respect for one of the greatest examples of Man's genius.

Into orbit and into television

The Space Race – as it quickly became – was hotting up. In the three and a half years between the launch of the first sputnik and the orbiting of the first man, America launched 24 satellites against Russia's ten. But the Soviets had a huge advantage in rocket power and the weights of the payloads reflected it.

While the US satellites rarely exceeded 2–3 cwt., the Soviets measured theirs in tons.

The Americans released plenty of information about theirs, the Russians very little about theirs. Reporting the Soviet space programme required a lot of reading, a little deducing and a huge amount of guesswork. In trying to keep pace with – and, if possible, forecast ahead of – events, I was greatly helped by Geoffrey Perry, the rotund Head of Physics at Kettering Grammar School, Northampton who, with his boys, had built their own tracking station to monitor Soviet activities in space.

By listening to satellite signals and plotting orbits, they were able to deduce which were military and which were 'peaceful' satellites and, often, the purpose of their missions.

It soon became clear that, while the US was primarily interested in exploring the physical properties of space and possible applications of satellites to day-to-day living, the Russians were concentrating on putting men into space, with an occasional pot-shot at Venus.

Laika was followed by more dogs – first Belka and Strelka, then Chernuska and finally Zverdoska. By then, the Soviets were testing their Vostok spaceship and so the dogs were safely recovered and the cries of the animal lovers muted.

The events surrounding the launch of Yuri Gagarin on April 12, 1961 have already been described in the Introduction to this book. Suffice to say that the brouhaha went on for several days.

On the day itself, under the headline 'SPACE AND BACK –

MAN ALIVE -OH!', the *Standard* devoted not only its front and back pages but pages 15, 16 and 17 as well. Next day, I worked out from articles in back issues of *Soviet Weekly* that, to lift the four-ton Vostok spaceship, Gagarin's rocket must have weighed about 450 tons – equal to 375 Ferguson tractors or eight Chieftain tanks. Geoffrey Pardoe, a rocket engineer who subsequently became a leading figure in Britain's space programme and then Europe's, helped me to work out the colossal thrust needed (a few years later, cosmonaut Gherman Titov confirmed the accuracy of our figures). It was another sensation and the *Standard* treated it so.

Features followed in which, embarrassingly, I kept on being referred to as 'the man who predicted it two days before it happened'. Several invitations for radio interviews came in and, finally, one for television.

The TV invitation was from Independent Television News (ITN) and it was to appear on the late night current affairs programme *Dateline*. The subject was not Gagarin's flight but Britain's modest space programme. I can remember nothing about it except that I was very nervous and felt I had been a disaster.

But it was followed not long afterwards by an invitation to appear on BBC *Panorama* on the same subject. All that I remember was the opening, where I was standing on one side of that massive globe while Richard Dimbleby introduced the programme from the other. Most of what followed is a haze in my memory.

But in the hospitality suite afterwards, Grace Wyndham Goldie, the distinguished BBC producer, came up to me and said, 'Peter, it was very nice of you to agree to appear on our programme. We've always used Tom Margerison in the past but we've had a few viewers complain that they are sick of his face.'

Dr Tom Margerison, for several years the Science Correspondent of the *Sunday Times*, was an old friend of mine and I made a mental note – 'Never appear on TV often enough for viewers to get sick of your face'.

Tom was often popping up on different programmes, which gave me an opportunity to study his TV 'face'. He sometimes appeared to be sneering and I worked out that it was probably because he rarely blinked. As a result, tension made his lip curl. So I made another mental note that, if I ever went on TV again, I should make sure I blinked a lot, especially before speaking my first sentence. I also learned from Patrick Moore, the astronomer who had made the BBC's *The Sky at Night* compulsive viewing, the wisdom of being enthusiastic about what you say.

The Shannon file

It was ten months before America matched the Soviet Union in orbiting a man and, by then, the Russians had done it again. Gherman Titov went up in Vostok 2 on August 6, 1961, and the event commanded only slightly less coverage by the world's media than Gagarin's pioneering effort. Or was Gagarin's the pioneering effort?

Some months prior to Gagarin's orbit, there had been hints in Soviet publications that Russia's first spaceman would be one Colonel Ilyushin, son of the famous Soviet aircraft designer. That made sense – it fitted the Soviet love of heroic 'names' and the ambassadorial role which the first cosmonaut would undoubtedly have to play after the Kremlin had finishing parading him around the Soviet Union.

Space buffs watched for a launch. Nothing appeared to happen. Then it was announced that a Colonel Ilyushin, who seemed definitely to be one of the cosmonaut corps, had been seriously injured in a 'plane crash'. Subsequently he is believed to have died.

Rumours came out of Russia that Ilyushin had been hurt not in a 'plane crash' but after being launched to become Russia's first spaceman. But if that were true, why had Western monitoring stations not been able to pick up the launch?

I have always believed, from piecing bits of intelligence and published information together, that Ilyushin was to have been the first but that his launch booster blew up, as many Soviet rockets subsequently did, either on the pad or before it reached a height of 30 miles – the lowest point at which Western radar in Turkey and other points close to the Soviet border could have detected him.

In the same way, since Gagarin's death in a 'test flight of a military jet' was announced in 1968, I have pieced together evidence to suggest that he and his co-pilot – a Col. Seryogin – were actually testing the prototype for a Soviet Space Shuttle and not a military jet.

The Shuttle has since been put on display but never used in space.

But to return to Titov. Like Gagarin, he was given a hero's parade in Red Square and ITN decided to cover it 'live'. It was a Saturday morning and I was invited to make observations on the pictures from Moscow alongside Brian Connell, the veteran ITV current affairs commentator. It was a relaxed session, much easier than an interview – and I watched Connell using an aid which was to prove of enormous help to me in TV appearances in future years.

It was called a Shannon file and comprised a 15-inch tall steel cover, which opened like a book, with 84 flip-up metal holders inside for correspondence cards. On the cards, you wrote your own background notes about the events, people or objects which would be likely to appear on screen during your commentary. All you had to do was flip up the appropriate card heading and there, in front of you, were all the facts. When, subsequently, I covered eight Apollo moon missions 'live' for ITN – and many other special events as well, including the maiden flight of Concorde – I faithfully prepared my cards and loaded them into the file.

They gave me tremendous reassurance, but I never opened the file once during a transmission. Making up the cards had imprinted the facts on my short-term memory.

The first Americans go up

America soon hit back in the propaganda stakes. The launch of her first spaceman, Alan Shepard, was broadcast 'live', in full view of the world. So was the launch of Virgil Grissom.

Although each flight was a simple up-and-down 'hop' on top of a Redstone rocket – with only five minutes spent actually in space – showing them 'live' was a gamble which paid off. Each flight attracted almost as much world publicity as Gagarin's single – and Titov's 17 – orbits of the world.

It was gripping television, not least as we watched 'Gus' Grissom's capsule, the *Liberty Bell*, start to sink and the astronaut flounder in the water. What the cameras didn't show was something which I discovered later from the head of the Astronaut Office – that part of Grissom's difficulty was due to the left leg of his spacesuit being filled with U.S. dimes, which he hoped to sell or give away as 'souvenirs of space'!

The *Standard* thought it best that I should cover both stories from London, which I did from in front of a TV set, dictating my story into a telephone for a copy-typist to take down and rush to the print-room, so that it caught the last edition. But something which Lord Beaverbrook once said – 'All controversy is good – good for circulation' – made me take a dismissive attitude to Grissom's whole spaceflight.

On the day before it happened, Associated Press in London syndicated the *Standard*'s story to US newspapers. *The Oregonian* – under the headline 'Paper Pans Space Try' printed the following:

> The *Evening Standard* pooh-poohed Capt. Virgil Grissom's projected arc into space as a waste of time and effort. The paper's science reporter wrote that if there were a Society for the Prevention of Cruelty to Astronauts it would seem to have some grounds for protest.
>
> Compared with Yuri Gagarin's 108-minute orbit of the world, it is another flea hop. It can tell scientists very little that they do not already know. It will take America no nearer her avowed goal of the Moon.
>
> Yet, once again, political prestige and a national technological reputation and the life of an astronaut are being risked.

It took only a few hours after arriving at Cape Canaveral to cover the next American spaceflight – John Glenn's – to realise what bunkum I had written about Grissom. The ingenuity and sheer complexity of Project Mercury, as it was called, showed the human race at its greatest and I vowed never to play paper word-games again.

Murder at Cocoa Beach

The Cape, in those days, was feverish with activity – nearly every firing pad busy, Meccano-like gantries cloaking both military and 'civilian' satellites in anonymity, floodlights picking out any imminent launch and tannoys intoning the countdown – 'T minus eight hours and counting' until, hopefully, 'We have lift-off'.

Bars stayed open night and day, cabarets were packed at night. For John Glenn's launch, there was not one motel vacancy in nearby Cocoa Beach and the only way I could stay in the thick of it all was to sleep in a cabana beside the pool.

The motels had garish signs and space-age names – 'Polaris', 'Satellite', 'Gemini', 'Starlite' and so forth. I squeezed into the Starlite, which was where NASA had its Press Information room.

John Glenn took almost six weeks to get off the ground. Twice we trekked in the dark to the spectator stands, only to return in anti-climax as technical or weather problems postponed the launch. We didn't mind – there were plenty of minor stories to be dug out and phoned. On one occasion, an American reporter in the Press stand next to me, Martin Caidin, passed the time by speculating what might happen if the retro-rockets on Glenn's Friendship 7 failed to fire and he was marooned in space. It was hair-raising stuff but little did I know that it would one day be turned into a suspense movie called *Marooned*, scripted by Caidin.

A week before leaving London, Tom Margerison had asked me if I would be interested in taking over his job on the *Sunday Times* (he had just been appointed technical adviser to Lord Thomson, the proprietor). I said, 'No,' but unfortunately described it as 'a retro-grade step'. What I meant was that one issue a week was pretty tame stuff compared to eight editions a day. But it upset Tom.

However, I decided to tell Ronnie Hyde of the approach but say that I had already decided to turn it down and not use it as a lever to get a raise. One sunny afternoon at Cocoa Beach, I was sitting reading some NASA Press releases by the pool when a bellboy came round calling, 'Mr Fairley'. I opened the cable.

It read: 'Glad to recognise your loyalty by increase of fiver a week. Regards. Charles Wintour.'

The days began to drag a little. We started to develop con-sciences as we ran out of news to report. Then, in the fifth week, came some excitement.

Being the only London evening newspaperman at the Cape, I was the first up – in case London called. I went to breakfast in the Starlite's restaurant, which doubled as the 'Paladium Night Club' *(sic)* between 10 p.m. and 3 a.m. The previous evening I had watched a striptease artiste fix a fluorescent tassel to each of her nipples and somehow revolve them in opposite directions to music.

But on this particular morning, I found a group of motel staff watching the Dade County Sheriff measuring the distance be-tween the bar and a white chalk outline of a human body on the dance floor. It marked, the Bell Captain told me, 'the last of Liz'.

Liz was the motel's Bunny Girl – a voluptuous blonde whom most of the British contingent of reporters had made passes at, on one night or another, during the long Glenn vigil. Her jealous husband had apparently arrived around 2 a.m. and shot her.

Which, if any, of us prompted this murder I never found out, but the Sheriff told me that a full-scale manhunt was in progress, using a helicopter and armed patrolmen, across the swamp separating Cocoa Beach from Indian River. There were alligators in that swamp.

It was 2 p.m. London time and I dictated the story to the *Standard*, which ran it in the West End Final edition. The national dailies followed next day and we all felt better. Soon afterwards, John Glenn made it into space. The jealous husband shot himself before the 'gators got him.

First trans-Atlantic TV

On the way home from the Cape, I visited NASA headquarters for a series of briefings. One was about Telstar. Telstar was due to be the first satellite to relay TV pictures across the Atlantic and I had the good fortune to be given exclusive details of it and its mission, together with an excellent picture. The *Standard* led the paper with the story for most of a day.

When the black-and-white 'golf-ball' went into orbit on July 10 – four months later – its first pictures came in too late for British viewers. Just as well: the sound kept crackling with static and the first picture – the face of a NASA official – kept wobbling and breaking up. But I remember Ian Trethowan – who had been sent to Goonhilly Downs to report from the Post Office's satellite ground station commenting triumphantly, 'We have a picture. . . . a man in picture.'

ITN recorded the pictures and used them next day under the caption 'First pictures from space'. Then, at 11.45 p.m., Telstar came round in orbit again and ITN mounted a special programme, fronted by Andrew Gardner.

With Philip Purser, then TV critic of *The Daily Telegraph*, I was asked to comment on the pictures 'live' from the studio. They showed, first, President Kennedy giving a news conference, then a baseball game from Chicago and finally contestants for the Miss Florida title parading in the sunshine.

The quality was only slightly better and, having championed Telstar for weeks, I was very disappointed. I remember remarking, 'If this is the best that TV via space can do, I'd rather wait for film to arrive next day.'

It was harsh comment because what we were witnessing was a new era in communication and I should have had a greater sense of history. But no viewers rang to complain and, after Telstar, invitations to appear on ITN somehow became more frequent . . .

A call on the Hot Line

While in Washington on NASA business, I also requested a high-level briefing in the Pentagon on the situation in Vietnam. At that time, the US had 33,000 servicemen in Vietnam and its bombing raids on North Vietnam were creeping closer and closer to Hanoi: 349 Americans had been killed and 3,020 wounded. More significantly, a nuclear task force was on its way to the Pacific and three Polaris submarines were cruising off the coast of China.

The Army and Air Force generals and the admiral whom I interviewed were in grim mood and they pointed out, additionally, that the US Marine contingent at Da Nang had just been equipped with 8-inch howitzers which could 'fire either nuclear or conventional shells'.

As a result of the 90-minute briefing, I cabled what I still believe to be an accurate report. It read:

> America is prepared to use nuclear weapons if necessary in defence of South Vietnam. The issue means that much to her. But a whole host of conventional steps could and would be taken before any such 'go' nuclear orders would be given.

It went on:

> The Far Eastern situation has definitely moved up the first rung of the ladder of 'escalation'. None of the Pentagon officials to whom I spoke was prepared to say how many more rungs the ladder has and nobody was willing to define the precise circumstances in which use of nuclear weapons might be sanctioned. But I was left in no doubt that, if the situation demanded it, America would not flinch from pushing the button.
>
> We do have a tactical and strategic nuclear capability for Vietnam as for elsewhere in the world, I was told, 'but there is certainly no question of using it in the present situation'.

Next day, the *Standard* made it its lead story under the heading 'AMERICA AND THE ESCALATING WAR!'.

I flew back to Heathrow four days later as a political furore erupted. Tass News Agency had rung the Pentagon to ask for comments on my story and the call had been taken by a duty Press Officer who took a tough, 'So what?' line.

Tass quoted him verbatim. This then led to Nikita Kruschev calling up Lyndon Johnson on the 'hot line' to ask for reassurances that America was not preparing to use 'nukes' in Vietnam.

Obviously, I was not privy to what was said but afterwards Pentagon officials started to back-pedal on the story, pointing out that it was routine to have nuclear as well as conventional weapons in any theatre of war – it was all part of the Great Deterrent – but that that did not mean they would be used.

I said nothing.

'Where were you when they shot Jack Kennedy?'

Lord Beaverbrook disapproved of television. He was convinced that it would damage the newspaper industry because fewer people would buy newspapers. But Charles Wintour felt differently. He believed that, if an *Evening Standard* specialist was interviewed on TV – and clearly identified as from the *Evening Standard* – it would reflect well on the paper.

At first, I had to clear every appearance with Charles, then Robert Carvell (the *Standard*'s political editor) and I received a memo saying that clearance was no longer needed.

The very next day Geoffrey Cox phoned to ask if I had been invited to join a Ministry of Defence Press trip to Australia to report the launch of a British Blue Streak missile from Woomera. I had.

'Could you cover for ITN?' he asked. 'If you can, it means we can send our own TV crew.' I could. What I did not realise was that, because of weight problems on the aircraft, the BBC's representative would have to share the ITN crew.

A party of 14 reporters and a two-man TV crew set off in an RAF transport plane for Adelaide, re-fuelling in Libya and on the Indian Ocean island of Gan – one of the Maldives. Our plane. bless it, developed a technical fault in Gan, enabling us to go skin-diving and see the most amazing shoals of tropical fish, using gear lent to us by the RAF. I broke off a large piece of coral as a souvenir and also purchased a sword-stick and a 2 ft. high, fully-rigged model of a buggallo (native schooner), which then travelled with me around Australia – their sharp ends making me rather unpopular.

I had realised that the trip offered a big opportunity. Apart from news bulletins, ITN also transmitted a 20-minute feature programme, called *Roving Report,* in those days. It offered not only extra screen-time but a chance to be more imaginative. So I had read a book on Woomera, viewed nearly two hours of film about the rocket range before setting out from Britain and made an arrangement with the *Roving Report* editor to prepare a whole programme.

The BBC's reporter, Air Correspondent Reg Turnill, was not pleased. He insisted on having equal use of the crew. But he soon mellowed and before long we became friends. However, since we only had a day in Woomera, his initial stand on a principle meant the ITN crew – Len Dudley, Eric Vincent and me – almost running, in the heat of the Australian desert, to get enough material for *Roving Report* as well as a news item about the launch.

A different problem occurred when we reached the Snowy Mountains. The MoD had made arrangements for us to visit key points in the massive hydro-electric project and I had worked out that, by phoning ahead from the UK to arrange interviews and filming facilities, it should be possible to produce a second, 20-minute *Roving Report* in the time available.

But Len Dudley taught me an important lesson.

The hydro-electric project involved diverting the Snowy River (formed from snow melting off the Snowy Mountains) into a reservoir – then pumping the water up so that it could fall through turbines and produce a large amount of electric power. It was a story of Man meddling with Nature in a big way.

To open the story, I needed a location where I could speak to camera with the snow-capped mountains and the fast-flowing river behind me. Everywhere we went, Len kept holding up his fingers in the shape of a TV screen and saying 'Sorry, Peter, but that's all the viewer will see.' This went on for two whole days.

Finally, after negotiating many zigzag roads up and down mountains, we found the perfect location – a Bailey bridge across the Snowy River. But the only way to get all the story elements into the one picture was for me to stand on one parapet and Len to perch on the camera box strapped to the outside of the other, with the camera in front of him on the parapet itself.

Eric Vincent held on to Len's legs. But no sooner had I finished speaking to the camera than I overbalanced and toppled into the ice-cold water (fortunately, it was only waist-deep). To our chagrin, Len had already switched off – otherwise we might have made it onto the *It'll Be Alright on the Night* programme.

Back in London, we edited both *Roving Reports*. It was decided to transmit the Snowy Mountains programme first – at 6.20 p.m. on November 22 1963. It was a memorable programme – but for the wrong reasons.

An hour previously, President John F. Kennedy had been assassinated. The news stunned the world, not least me – for, despite subsequent revelations about his private life, he was (along with Winston Churchill) the man I most admired. The ITV programme controllers held a tele-conference to decide what to do. In the end, they not only extended news bulletins but cancelled all scheduled programmes for the rest of the evening except those of a serious nature. The Snowy *Roving Report* was considered 'serious'.

So I ended up intensely frustrated, sitting on a sofa with my family, watching my first real TV production being transmitted but yelling at the screen 'Get it off' and 'Tell us more about Kennedy'. I am sure millions of viewers felt likewise and switched to the BBC.

Insomnia and blindness

Between August 1962 and August 1965, six more cosmonauts and four more astronauts rode into space, each enjoying a few days of glory in the world's media. The ones who made the biggest impact were the first woman (Valentina Tereshkova), the first 'space-walker' (Alexei Leonov) and the two American Mercury astronauts, Scott Carpenter and Gordon Cooper – the last two for the wrong reasons.

Scott Carpenter – along with Pete Conrad, the most daredevil of the astronaut corps – blotted his copybook by taking a sandwich into space to supplement his official rations (bite-sized cubes of plasticised meat and semi-liquid concoctions in 'squeeze-tubes'). In those pioneering days, everything swallowed by the astronaut had to be approved, weighed, calorie-checked and analysed in the excreta. Sandwiches were definitely not on the menu.

Scott smuggled his contraband inside his Astronaut's Personal Preference Bag – otherwise known as the 'diddy bag' – a small bag in which the spaceman could load a few small personal belongings to create 'space mementoes' or souvenirs. It was the only item, until then, which was not checked by NASA officials or the ground crew.

Scott, unfortunately, took his sandwich out to eat when he was 100 miles above the Earth and it crumbled. Particles of bread and turkey floated everywhere in the weightless cabin. They so preoccupied him that he pushed the button to fire his retro-rockets (to 'kick' the spaceship out of orbit) three seconds late and overshot the landing area in the Pacific by some 700 miles – making his fellow sailors in the recovery force do an awful lot of extra steaming.

He was not court-martialled but he never flew in space again. Instead, he took his pioneering spirit and talents into inner space, becoming commander of one of the US Navy's Sealabs – capsules, fixed to the sea-bed, where divers could come and go, experimenting with techniques and equipment for living and working for long periods underwater. The inner-space programme, too, eventually became a subject area for me to cover and I met Scott the Aquanaut many times.

Major Gordon Cooper USAF went up in the last Mercury spaceship – Faith 7 – a year after Scott. He completed 22 orbits of the world and took a sleep over in Honolulu. To Earth doctors' amazement, he slept so soundly that he had an erotic dream – returning some interesting samples to Earth for analysis later.

The whole direction of America's space programme moved on from exploring the medical effects of space on Man to testing his ability to perform useful tasks, while travelling 'weightless' at more than 17,000 m.p.h. The Gemini programme took this a step further.

Gemini spacecraft were two-seaters and used the more powerful Atlas and Titan boosters, as opposed to the Redstones. The first, really ambitious flight took place in December 1965, when Gemini 6 and 7 linked up for the first 'rendezvous' in space. I persuaded the *Standard* to send me to Cape Canaveral to cover the event, but the Board of Directors had to approve the trip because the paper was in the middle of one of its periodic cost-cutting exercises. I left feeling that I had to deliver – or else . . .

Whether it was this worry or due to time-zone changes, I do not know but I began to suffer acute insomnia. While we were at Cape Canaveral, seeing Frank Borman and James Lovell off the pad and then waiting 10 days for conditions to be right to launch Wally Schirra and Tom Stafford, I slept four or five hours a night: in any case, there were all-night clubs available for shift workers and insomniacs like me. But when we transferred to Houston to report Mission Control's efforts to manoeuvre the two spaceships together, my sleep centre went haywire.

I was already very tired. But extra time-zone differences meant that I had to stay awake all night, to report the story and get it into the evening paper in London. I also worked hard to produce two 1,000-word features, with thoughts of that Board meeting adding pressure.

Suddenly it was all over. The astronauts landed safely and I could head back through New York to London. It was just four days before Christmas and I remember shopping in the snow in a fairy-lit New York, with Santa Claus stationed every few yards down Fifth Avenue, ringing his bell. Unfortunately, I could think of little else but the sharp pains which were developing in my eyes.

As soon as I got off the plane at Heathrow, I headed for the *Standard* and reported to the office doctor. He examined my eyes, said he could see nothing amiss, diagnosed 'stress' and told me to go home and rest.

Next day, the pains were worse. But it was Christmas Eve and a lot more shopping had to be done. At about 11.30 a.m., I paused for a coffee and rubbed one eye – which promptly blacked out. It stayed 'out' for about five minutes.

My family were great Christmas-lovers and played the game, that Christmas Eve, by going to bed without nagging, leaving us to discuss the trip and the strange eye problems alone. Then we filled the stockings, crept into the children's bedrooms to hang them up and retired to bed ourselves. By then, the pain was excruciating every time I moved an eyeball left, right, up or down. I remember going to sleep looking straight up at the ceiling.

Next morning, we were woken by the kids running in to show us the contents of their stockings. When I heard their excited cries, my first thought was, 'Oh great, the pain has gone.' My second was, 'Oh Christ, I can't see.'

I was totally blind.

CHAPTER TEN

Vision and Video

What do you do when you wake up blind on Christmas Day? Well, the first thing I did was blink – then think.

Blinking did no good. It was a total black-out, the only compensation being that the agonising pain had disappeared. I could even roll my eyes in comfort.

Thinking didn't do much good either. My first priority was not to alarm the children, my second not to alarm my wife. But we were expecting 16 people around the lunch table that day and there was no way that I could pretend that everything was normal.

I managed to act normally until the kids had returned to their bedrooms to play with (or eat) the stocking fillers. Then, as my wife operated the Teasmaid beside the bed, I said quietly: 'Look, I don't want you to worry but I'm afraid I can't see anything.'

Tea helped to relieve the shock. We agreed to tell the children over breakfast. While she bathed, I lay there quietly trying to work out the cause of my blindness. Having covered medical topics for a few years, the only causes I could think of were nasty – tumour on the brain being top on the list.

The children were wonderful. They laid the places carefully at the table, including the best glasses, telling me calmly to sit down because I kept bumping into things. So I did as I was told, sat on the sofa and made my bargains with God. 'Oh God, if you will only save me, I promise to get my teeth attended to, get spectacles so that I can read the telephone directory, go to bed at a reasonable hour, be a nicer person,' and so on.

I decided to look on every day thereafter as a bonus day (and I still do).

Then our GP arrived. He peered into my unseeing eyes with an opthalmoscope, took my blood pressure and asked a string of questions, starting with 'Have you been drinking wood alcohol?'

Irritated, I snapped back, 'Christ, Alan, what sort of a question is that? I'm not a bloody tramp – yet.' Then I remembered my new resolutions and apologised.

Eventually, he said: 'I can tell you what is wrong but I can't tell you why. We'll have to get you to a specialist.'

Apparently, the trouble lay not in the eyes themselves but in the optic nerves behind the eyes. He explained that these were like two cauliflowers on stalks and carried picture images from the eyes to the brain. Mine were 'grossly inflamed' – so no images were getting through. But what was causing the inflammation?

Specialists do not exactly hang around waiting for work at Christmas and it was three days before I could be seen by one. During that time I began to feel intensely sorry for myself. 'Why me, oh God, why me?'

In the end, it was worth the wait because I was able to see Kevin Zilkha, then a young but brilliant neurologist, working at both Kings College Hospital and the National Hospital, Queen Square. He put me at ease immediately when he said, 'I see a few cases of this a year and most of them get better.'

He explained that my condition was known as bilateral retrobulbar neuritis (inflammation of both the optic nerves) but that it had no obvious origin: tests were needed, including a lumbar puncture.

The houseman had a difficult job sticking a needle into my spine because of all the muscles from playing rugby and swimming, but the test at least showed that I was not suffering from multiple sclerosis. I was released to go home, keep taking steroids and rest.

The world became kindness itself, starting with my family and friends and continuing with all my office colleagues, including Max Aitken. Charles Wintour drove down to visit me. I could hear from his voice that he was deeply troubled by what had happened. He said he had not appreciated until then what a strain it must impose on a reporter to come to work each day with no idea what might befall him.

Days were no problem – I had plenty of telephone conversations to occupy the mind. But nights were difficult and I kept waking around 2 a.m. and groping my way downstairs to avoid disturbing my wife.

From the depths of the sofa, I kept wondering what I had done to deserve blindness and bursting into tears of self pity. The only thing which helped was an LP of Winston Churchill's great wartime speeches which I played over and over again.

Life settled into a pattern and started to become almost enjoyable. My fellow reporters managed to persuade the Royal National Institute for the Blind to loan me one of the first 'talking book' machines – a wooden cube with a mechanism which accepted a large audio cassette of recorded stories. I was not strictly entitled to one because I had not been confirmed as permanently blind, but it made a huge difference to my morale.

The first tape which I borrowed was *The Lonely Sea and The Sky* – Francis Chichester's autobiography, read by a melodious BBC actor – and the philosophy underlying it made me feel that my problems were nothing compared to those which blocked the path of the round-the-world-yachtsman-cum-aviator on several occasions during his lifetime. Every time, Chichester simply picked himself up, dusted himself down and started all over again. I stopped feeling sorry for myself.

A couple of days later, at 9 p.m., I had a call from Reg Lascelles, an old friend who had been put in charge of publicity at the Jodrell Bank radio-telescope. He rang to convey sympathy but went on to say that Professor Bernard Lovell's team had been tracking the Soviet spacecraft, Luna 9, which had landed 'softly' on the Moon's surface the previous day. They were 'listening in' at that very moment.

'It seems to be transmitting picture signals,' said Reg, ' but we haven't any equipment to record picture signals.'

I had an idea. Newspaper 'wire machines', as they are known, receive signals from all over the world and convert them into pictures. It would be another 10 hours before the *Evening Standard* opened but the *Daily Express* was in full swing.

I rang Derek Marks, then Editor, told him of my hunch and asked if there was anything the Manchester office of the *Express* could do by getting a wire machine out to Jodrell Bank. 'Leave it with me,' said Derek.

There then began a race against time. First, an attempt was made to convert a tape-recording of one batch of Luna 9's signals by playing them over a telephone line into the Manchester office and hooking up the wire machine to the phone. It failed. Professor John Davies, Lovell's No.2, realised that the equipment would have to be connected at Jodrell Bank if it was to work.

Spencer Carrington, deputy head of the *Express*'s wire department in London, picks up the story: 'We had the right piece of equipment – a portable, transistorised Muirhead FM/AM machine – and I decided to fly it to Manchester because the boys in our office there were ready to tear their six-foot version out of the wall and carry it on foot to Jodrell Bank, if necessary!'

The machine arrived at Jodrell at 7.a.m – eight hours ahead of the next appearance of the Moon above the horizon.

Bernard Nash, another *Express* transmission engineer, told me later how the machine was connected up and two trial runs carried out using the tape-recorded signals. Both produced only a blur.

'We were on tenterhooks by this time,' Bernard went on, 'but we decided to wait for a direct transmission from the Moon. At 3 p.m. we picked up the first signals. They lasted for six or seven minutes but the result was terrible – quite unrecognisable. Then three pictures were transmitted without a break. The first proved to be of exceptionally good quality and the second was just as good. We realised that the early failure had been due to the Moon being too low and picking up a lot of interference.'

The room at Jodrell Bank was crowded with excited scientists and tense technicians, all watching the revolving drum of which the pictures were built up, line by line, as a pattern of dots in different shades of black, white and grey. But I knew nothing of this.

Apparently, there was one moment, during the recording of the third picture, when the recording drum was full and had to be changed. Bernard said: 'The operator managed it very fast – we lost only a sixteenth of an inch of the picture at most.'

He added: 'We processed the pictures in a nearby lavatory and 10×8 blow-ups were printed. These were rushed to Manchester for re-transmission to London.'

The pictures – the first-ever close-ups – showed clearly that the Moon had an undulating surface, pock-marked with craters measuring from one to several feet across and pitted with thousands of smaller cavities. There were also hummocks in view.

The surface was virtually free of dust (which was a relief, since one eminent U.S. scientist had postulated that there could be as much as 20 feet of dust, which would play havoc with a manned landing). Under Luna 9 at least, the ground seemed fairly solid, with a structure like pumice stone.

That night, the *Express* had a world scoop. The Russians had not even admitted that Luna 9 was sending pictures, much less released any. But Derek Marks decided that the pictures were of such historic importance that the *Express* should share them with the world. They were shown on British TV that evening and virtually every daily newspaper in the world carried them next morning.

The *UK Press Gazette* devoted four pages to report 'the inside story of an outsize scoop' and the *Daily Express* took a double-page ad. in the *WPN* and *Advertisers' Review.*

It was just the fillip I needed – being made to feel useful and, despite blindness, that I could still contribute.

Spycatcher in the bedroom

About a week after the blindness struck, my wife took a telephone call from a man who called himself Brown and who said he was from 'the Security services'. Could he come and see me?

Vivienne told him of my predicament but he persisted, saying that it was important and he wouldn't need more than a few minutes.

My favourite relaxation had been reading spy novels and this call out of the blue intrigued me. What could I have done? Could it be something to do with Viva and Vanya in Bulgaria? Or the East German factory worker who had sought my assistance in arranging her escape to the West? Or the 'bugs' in the walls of the hotel in Warsaw? Or the olive stones which I had planted in cracks in the columns of the Acropolis in Athens when I could not find a rubbish bin? Had I been spotted?

Or did he want me to do things for the Security Service on trips abroad, under the guise of being a journalist?

He came next morning, when I was resting in bed, and drew up a chair. He introduced himself as 'John Brown from British Intelligence', which I took to mean MI5 – concerned not with foreign but with home affairs.

'Do you remember being by a swimming pool in Athens and talking about Professor Hermann Bondi?' he asked.

I did indeed. It had been during the previous year's International Astronautical Federation Congress, held in the Athens Hilton. That Hilton is built as a square around a 35 yard swimming pool and the meetings of the scientists and rocket engineers had taken place in different conference rooms around the pool. The shortest route from one meeting to another was via the pool. Seduced by the glorious sunshine, I had decided to combine getting a sun-tan with getting interviews by setting up my papers, typewriter and plug-in phone by the pool bar – the key US and Soviet delegates who were my targets for interview, would be bound to pass at some time during the week. And so they did.

But by the third day, the rest of the British Press corps had decided to do the same and it was after a pool-side snack that the subject of Professor Bondi came up. He had just been appointed chairman of the Ministry of Defence's space committee in London.

I remember sipping a glass of cold white wine and remarking 'Funny that a man who is a Communist gets that job'.

Nobody queried it and we had a short discussion about how his student days at Cambridge University must have coincided with those of Burgess and Maclean – and moved on to another topic.

'What made you say he was a Communist?' asked Brown from MI5. 'Because I had been told that he was,' I replied. 'Who told you?' came next.

I remembered quite well who told me but I was not about to lose my very best contact in the science world by revealing his name. 'I can't remember,' I lied, 'but I'm sure I wouldn't have said it if I hadn't been confident that the source was reliable – I don't deal in rumour.'

'Try and think,' he said. I waited then said, 'No, I'm sorry, I really can't remember. And I'm not likely to while I can't see – I can't concentrate on other things.' He went soon afterwards, leaving a number to ring 'if your memory improves'.

I never did get an approach to work for MI5 or MI6, although recently my old colleague Jon Snow, the Channel 4 newscaster, revealed that he was once offered £3,600 to work for them – but had said 'No thank you'. I am sure I would have done the same although, obviously, one of my colleagues out in Athens had connections with them.

Hermann Bondi, I am relieved to say, went on to survive his 'positive vetting' and become Sir Hermann, Chief Scientist to the MoD and, from 1983 until his death, Master of Churchill College, Cambridge.

I remain ashamed of my scandal-mongering. But an even bigger regret is that throughout my one and only encounter with a real-life spycatcher, I could not see his face.

Call from a blind man

After about three weeks of horrible darkness, I started to see light again, just a chink and only around the edges of the eyes – but definitely light.

I was allowed to wash and dry the dishes. At first, it was therapeutic. Then I began to resent the duty, wanting to get back to my sofa and the talking book machine. Finally, I snapped. To my eternal shame, I hurled the tea-towel at my long-suffering wife and shouted, 'God, I'm sick of this. I must do something more useful. I think I'll go down to Bromley Hospital and offer to talk to blind patients about space and the astronauts.'

Barely a minute later, the phone rang. A man's voice explained that he was 'Norman' and he produced radio broadcasts for a Hertfordshire hospital radio station. He wondered if he could come to see me and record a long interview about space, the astronauts and 'stuff like that'. He would edit the interview and then transmit it in between playing records of music.

'Did you know that I'm virtually blind – hopefully, its only temporary?' I asked. 'No,' said Norman. 'As a matter of fact, I'm blind myself.'

Norman came with his guide dog Pat a week later and we met them at Bromley North station and brought them home for lunch. By now, I was seeing quite a lot out of the corners of my eyes and I felt a bit of a charlatan for having said I was blind. We got on very well and recorded nearly three hours of interview, before he returned to Hertfordshire on the train, Pat faithfully leading the way.

I felt ashamed to think that my sight was returning, whereas Norman's never would. But I also felt amazement that my wish to do something to help the blind had been answered so rapidly. Could it possibly have been telepathy that made Norman ring at just that moment? I have always wondered. But it triggered that interest in psychic phenomena which was to result in those remarkable events before I left the *Standard*.

No such man as Superman

I began to see enough to read the headlines in the morning paper and to be allowed out for a walk on my own, up and down our road. I remember muffling up and walking for about 10 minutes. Then everything went dark again and I came home cursing.

I sat in a chair quietly and had a nap. When I re-opened my eyes, I sensed that my sight had improved to a degree better than ever. Next day, I took another walk and the same thing happened: vision was definitely improved. I rang Kevin Zilkha who asked me to come to the National Hospital next day.

When I got there, he had a lecture theatre full of medical students waiting.

He introduced me and asked me to read an eye test-card. I could only manage the top three lines of letters. 'OK,' he said. 'Now take some exercise – go up and down the lecture room steps.'

While I pounded 20 times up and down between the rows of students, he described my clinical picture to them. 'Now come and sit down – take as long as you want,' he told me.

After about 10 minutes of sitting quietly, I did another test. This time I was able to read five lines on the card – proving the point: exercise definitely helped. Kevin said he had never found evidence before but would like me to ring him weekly to report if the improvement continued.

I embarked on a punishing exercise regime, walking, jogging, swimming, even 'bicycling' upside down, with my legs pedalling the air, in the belief that it might be a gravity phenomenon. More and more vision returned. I found that gravity had nothing to do with it – any vigorous exercise helped.

By mid-March, I could see well enough to return to the office. The editorial floor looked as though it was full of a pale green gas and there was a hair's thickness of vision still blanked out in each eye. But I could read and type although, for a month, I went home early – without the usual briefcase full of work. I did not want to make capital out of anything that had happened to me, in deference to those less fortunate. But Charles Wintour said that there were lessons for others in my experience – particularly for people who continue to work when overtired or over-stressed – and insisted that I wrote a feature which the subs titled *The Day I Lost My Sight*.

It described the sudden onset and course of the illness, the lack of data about its cause and made a suggestion – that there should be a National Medical Data Centre, fully computerised, into which every scrap of information about unusual diseases could be fed, in the hope that electronic 'brains' might be able to spot clues which humans had missed. We are still waiting.

The feature ended:

> Perhaps the most pungent realisation after 93 days of darkness and half-light is that there is no such creature as Superman. He is a myth.
>
> I realise now that no man, no matter how easily he can shrug off minor infections, run for a bus, outsmart his rivals or achieve his personal targets, can assume he is indestructible.
>
> Whatever the cause of my temporary blindness, it has served as a salutary warning. Hence my new spectacles, the mended teeth, the less-frenzied approach to life. With other mouths to feed, I cannot afford again to take chances.
>
> And nor, I suspect, can you.

Rendezvous at the Ritz

Among my other bargains with God were never to use my eyes to read after 7 p.m. and never to agree to do anything that I really did not want to do – that, I believed, would produce noradrenaline, which in turn caused stress (as opposed to adrenaline which supplied energy) and that was a far more culpable killer than hard work. To this day, the bargain holds, with few exceptions.

In trying to work out the cause of the blindness, I had concluded that – in any case – I had been spending far too much time reading magazines and technical journals. These, when they did produce a story, produced only a minor one. What I had to do was to put it round the other way – keep asking, 'What is it that all of us do all the time?' and then try to find stories about those activities.

The logic went something like this: 'The first moment of life involves the heart. Yet do we know why the heart starts beating? Let's look at the latest knowledge of the heart.'

Next: 'All of us breathe 15 or 16 times a minute. The human lung and the bronchial tubes, if rolled out flat, would cover a tennis court. So let's look at the air that comes into contact with that "tennis court" – what is in it these days?'

Then . . . 'Most of us eat two or three meals a day. One fifth of the population is dangerously obese and one third is overweight. Yet there is only one Professor of Nutrition (John Yudkin) in Britain. Let's ask why we care so little about sensible eating.'

All *Standard* feature series had to run in fives – one for each day of the week. So the Thursday's topic became sex. There was no field of research moving faster than fertility and contraception, at that time. The intra-uterine device (IUD) and The Pill were going into widespread use (although not without their side effects); contraception by injection was about to be tried on volunteers: research was even starting into a 'morning after Pill'. On the infertility side, multiple births were resulting from treatment and test-tube babies were more than just fanciful talk. 'So let's sum up the latest state of knowledge,' I reasoned.

Finally, death: 'We are all dying all the time. The average lifespan in Britain is still "three score years and ten". Does it have to be? Can't we live longer? Do we want to live longer?' etc., etc.

The *Standard* published the series under the banner *The Stuff of Life*. My personal postbag, which until then had averaged 20–30 letters a week from readers, suddenly swelled to 200 in the week after the series and then 2000 the week after that. Clearly, the series had hit the button of interest. One letter was from the Editor. It read: 'Glad to see you are back in fine form. Just one little point . . . in the article referring to sleep, I think that the word "bonkers" is, although graphic, slightly unscientific. "Emotionally disturbed" might have been better!'

I kept asking myself 'What interests all of us?' thereafter. The stories seemed to get fewer but bigger. The *Standard* gave tremendous support, leading the front page with such unlikely topics as Aromatic Fluorocarbons (used to make new, tough, non-stick surfaces for utensils) and the Ruston-Hornsby AO Diesel Engine (offering much-improved performances and economics in shipping) as well as the increasingly ambitious activities in space.

Leaks of official reports come two-a-penny these days. In the '60s, they were still comparatively rare.

On Monday, October 10, 1967, the phone on my desk rang and a friend, an official of the Royal Society, said: 'Meet me for tea in the Ritz – I've got something which might interest you.'

Earl Grey, scones, strawberry jam and cream were served before he pushed a plastic bag towards me. It contained photocopies of proofs of a report, from a committee set up by the Government, to investigate why scientists and engineers were emigrating from Britain. It was dynamite.

'You can keep those,' my friend said, 'but don't say where they came from.' I paid for tea.

Next day, the Standard chose 72 point bold type to thunder from its final edition 'BRAIN DRAIN – STAGGERING FACTS'. It told how 6,200 scientists, engineers and technologists were leaving Britain every year for better-paid jobs abroad – double the number leaving five years previously. Two out of every five young engineers were quitting. It explained that the graduates – many of them PhDs – cost from £6,000 to £16,000 to train but were worth about £78,000 each on arrival in the US, where they were able to earn at least three times more in than in Britain. The story ended: 'The report concludes that Britain will have to pay them more – as a deliberate national policy if the Drain is to be stopped. Unless it is, the future well-being of Britain will be in danger.'

Radio and TV news bulletins led with the story that evening, attributing the story to the *Standard* because there was no confirmation from official sources. Next day, every national daily gave it prominence.

The *Standard* gave more details next day and we managed to interview a recruitment scout, prompting Jak to draw a wonderful cartoon showing schoolboys in a chemistry lab and a man in a Homburg hat and a big, fat cigar under the benches saying, 'Psst! I'm from the Massachusetts Institute of Technology . . .' I have it still. I also have a copy of Antony Sampson's book *The Anatomy of Britain* in which he gives me credit for creating the catchy phrase 'Brain Drain' and drawing attention to a national scandal.

It is my one and only contribution to history.

Face to face with the spacemen (and woman)

The early cosmonauts and astronauts were all required to be roving ambassadors and go on world tours after their missions, if only to reassure the general public that they were flesh and bone.

On their visits to Britain I met Gagarin, Valery Bykovsky, who spent five days in space inside Vostok 5, Valentina Tereshkova, the first woman in space and John Glenn, the first American to

orbit the Earth. Later I interviewed Neil Armstrong, the first man
on the Moon.

Glenn was charming and frank and I interviewed him for 20
minutes, at the end of which his NASA escort said, 'Geez, I've
never heard an interview like that.' I took it as a compliment and
said truthfully, 'It's easy to have a good interview if you are given
enough time. The longer you have, the easier it gets.'

That was true for the Armstrong interview, which lasted half
an hour. He was a shy, thoughtful interviewee, who gave the impression he would rather be on the Moon than at ITN. But the
highlight, as far as I was concerned, came when I asked him: 'When
you look up at the Moon now, at night, what goes through your
mind?'

He thought hard for a second or two, then answered quietly, 'I
remember places.'

The Russians were memorable for their vague or diplomatic
answers to questions and for their short stature. They arrived for
interviews inside long, black Zim limousines, squeezed between
KGB men and 'minders' from the Soviet Embassy in Kensington each of whom must have weighed, without exception, at least
16 stones.

Valentina's arrival at ITN's studios in Kingsway gave us a good
laugh.

Dressed in Women's Voluntary Service green and a pale cream
blouse, she came in through the swing doors of Television House
accompanied not by two 'minders', or even four, but by an entourage of 13 (two chauffeurs included). A small ITN reception
committee greeted her and then Valentina, the ITN men and all
the burly 'minders' went to get into the lift to go to the 7th floor
newsroom.

It would not budge.

Somebody pointed to the manufacturer's plaque stating 'Maximum Capacity 8 persons'. After some quick jabbering in Russian, the 'minders' insisted on staying with Valentina and so the
ITN party got out and walked upstairs, pushing button No.7 to
set the lift on its way.

Geoffrey Cox, as Editor, was waiting at the 7th floor to meet
her, along with several others including me. We waited. No lift.
We waited. Still no lift. Eventually the Russian party arrived,
puffing and panting, on foot.

It transpired that Otis Lifts really did mean it when they said

'Maximum 8 persons'. Nine 'heavies' and a rather chubby cosmonaut were too much. The lift had stuck between floors 4 and 5 and the entire party had to be pulled out by hand.

While Reggie Bosanquet interviewed Tereshkova in the studio, we had some difficulty explaining to the KGB men that the lift failure was really their fault and not a dastardly capitalist plot.

The newspapers loved it next day, with stories about Tereshkova getting into space and back without difficulty but not achieving lift-off inside Television House.

Tales of the unexpected

Space continued to excite the British public, and attending the meetings of the International Astronautical Federation (whose platform the Russians had chosen to announce the launch of the very first Sputnik in October 1957) became obligatory for anyone hunting for news or trying to get early warning of forthcoming events.

The cocktail party on the first evening was an opportunity both to have tête-à-têtes with men who had actually flown in space and to set up interviews for later in the week with the leading scientists and engineers who had sent them up, or who were planning future missions.

It was at the cocktail party before an IAF meeting in Paris that I found myself almost the last to leave, along with Bob Chapman (Science Editor of *The Evening News*) and Dr Randolph Lovelace, Director of the Lovelace Foundation Clinic at Albuquerque, New Mexico.

'Randy', as he was known, had been one of the team of medical experts who had devised the fitness tests for selecting U.S. astronauts. He was also a millionaire. That night he was 'on the town'.

'C'm on,' he drawled. 'Let's go somewhere nice and eat. I know a little place – went there last night and enjoyed myself.' We thanked him and followed him to a cab. I was a bit taken aback when he said to the driver, in an appalling French accent. 'The Sheherazade, *s'il vous plais*.' I knew the Sheherazade to be one of the most expensive restaurants in Paris. 'Good job he's a millionaire,' I thought.

The restaurant was nearly empty, despite the fact that it was almost 11 p.m. A four-piece group sounding like the Hot Club de France (including a guitarist who sounded like Jango Reinhart)

was playing and Randy commented, 'This is nice,' as we scanned
the menu. He ordered a bottle of vintage Moet et Chandon.

We all chose asparagus and lobster mayonnaise and talked space
medicine through the first bottle of champagne. The lighting was
low but Randy spotted two women sitting together at a table opposite. He ordered another bottle of Moet and asked the waiter to
invite the ladies to join us.

They were obviously escort girls but of the up-market variety,
fashionably dressed and with curves in all the right places. One
sat between Randy and Bob, the other between Bob and me.

Unfortunately, they spoke only French, Bob spoke none and
Randy virtually not much more than the '*s'il vous plais*' he had
used on the taxi driver. I was voted interpreter.

If there is one thing guaranteed to kill a flirtation stone dead, it
is having to concentrate on finding the right words to help foreigners, who have just met for the first time, understand each
other. Sure, the conversation flowed and there was quite a lot of
laughter – especially after Randy had ordered a third and then a
fourth bottle of bubbly – but, emotionally, I was soon drained
dry. The only plus point was when I saw Randy covertly pay the
expensive bill (which I later covertly pocketed in case it might
help me justify my office expenses for that week!).

At about 2 a.m., Randy left the table to go to the 'loo'. Ten
minutes later, Bob followed him. The girls and I waited and waited,
but they never returned. They didn't say goodbye – they just went.
It was all very embarrassing and the girls did not help, muttering
about Americans supposed to be 'polite' and the English 'gentlemen'.

Stupidly, I felt obliged to make up for my friends' lack of man-
ners by ordering another bottle of champagne. This, coupled with
an hour of hot jazz from the group, restored international relations, if not amorous feelings.

At 3 a.m., I said I must go. But the girls pleaded, saying that
they wanted to buy me a bottle of champagne for restoring their
'faith in ze English'. I finally left at 4 a.m. – but not without a
problem.

The problem was the bill, which was even higher than the total
on Randy's bill. Yet he had paid for four bottles of champagne
and three dinners, whereas I had only ordered one bottle of champagne. I realised that I was being ripped off and demanded to see
the manager.

The girls somehow vanished. They did not want to know. The manager arrived and explained that I had had two bottles of champagne and there had been 'ze music charge'. I grew very angry. 'Only one champagne,' I insisted. 'Non, two,' he insisted. 'But the ladies bought the second bottle,' I said. 'Non, m'sieur, you did.'

By now, a pair of obvious bouncers were homing in on my table. I decided to run for it, brushing them aside and managing to reach the cobbled street in one piece. To my relief, I saw one of those 'Break glass in emergency' boxes, mounted on a pole on the street corner. If ever there was an emergency, this was it.

I wrapped my hand in a handkerchief and smashed the little glass panel. To my amazement, a gruff voice suddenly came out of the interior. 'Oui?', it queried. I explained that I had been cheated over my bill at the Sheherazade. 'Wait there,' the gruff voice ordered. By now, I could see a hot discussion taking place by the restaurant door. Presumably, the bouncers wanted my entrails but the manager was holding them back. But it obviously could not go on for much longer.

I was impressed by the speed with which help arrived. But I shall never forget the scene as a tall, thin gendarme – a spitting image of Jacques Tati, the French comedian – swept round the corner on a bicycle, cape flowing. Dawn was breaking and damp cobblestones reflected the yellow of the street-lamps. Somehow, the pin-man profile of the gendarme, the angle of the bicycle and the swirl of his cape will live in my memory for ever.

I showed him my bill and produced Randy's as evidence of having been grossly overcharged. Then, in police language, we 'effected re-entry' and confronted the manager, who suddenly became charm itself, saying that 'There must've been a mistake'. He cut the total to a third and, when I had paid, offered to drive me back to my hotel. It was 5 a.m. and the IAF meeting would be starting in four hours' time.

En route for the Hotel Montalambert in his little green Citroen, I pompously brought out my pen and told the manager: 'Never forget that an English journalist always stays sober enough to count his drinks and know how much they cost.'

'I will give you a leetle advice in return, mon ami,' said the manager.

'When a lady in a nightclub offers to buy you champagne, it is you who are paying.'

'How's your grandmother, Reggie?'

Because of one exciting development in space after another, I began to appear quite often on ITN – usually as an interviewee on the late-night current affairs programme *Dateline*. The programme's presenter, more often than not, was Reginald Bosanquet.

I was always terribly nervous – indeed I later wore a Medical Research Council heartbeat monitor for a week and found that, when the cameras went 'live', my heart rate (which was normally 80) shot up to around 137. But Reggie knew how to calm my nerves – a drink or two – and, on one particular evening, we downed a gin or two and a bottle of burgundy.

I also used to hate any kind of rehearsal. We had developed a little ritual whereby the programme music, Reggie's introduction and his first question to me were rehearsed properly (for timing) but my answer (to check voice level) was always the same 'That's a very interesting question, Reggie, how's your grandmother? Have you taught her to suck eggs yet?'

On the night that America's lunar spacecraft, the unmanned Surveyor 1, made a 'soft' landing on the Moon, a second 'expert' – a real one – had been invited to appear on *Dateline*. He was Dr Gilbert Fielder, Head of Lunar Studies at Edinburgh University, who had never appeared on The Box before.

Because I knew that he, too, would be nervous, I decided to play the rehearsal straight, by answering Reggie's first question sensibly, and his second. But his third was about the cost of the mission.

The figure was in my briefcase but not in my head. So I said, 'Sorry – I can't give you the figure. I'll give you it later – blah, blah, blah,' and waved a hand casually. Reggie then interviewed Gilbert, said goodnight to the camera and the end-of-programme music came up.

The studio went 'dead'. Reggie turned and said, 'You were very relaxed tonight, Peter.'

'Relaxed?' I said. 'Huh, wait till we go 'live' – it'll be different then!'

There was a moment's silence, then Reggie said, 'Live? We were "live".'

I still wake in the night thinking how life would have changed if I had said the usual, 'How's your grandmother, Reggie?'

An award on the road to Apollo

The only professional prize that I have ever coveted was the Glaxo Travelling Fellowship, more popularly known as the Science Writer of the Year Award. Partly to keep my brain occupied while I was blind, I asked my wife to help me organise an entry and 'had a go'.

I have always kept cuttings of published stories and the ones which we selected illustrate the diversity of a science reporter's work in those days. They were:

1. A comparison between living and working in space and living and working under the sea (astronauts and aquanauts).
2. First results of tests to pre-select the sex of offspring in cattle, with their implications for human couples.
3. The first authoritative account of China's A- and H-bomb capability.
4. The Charing Cross Hospital dirty operating theatre scandal (described in Ch.6) and a solution (developed elsewhere) to the whole problem of cross-infection in operating theatres.
5. The first revelation that workers in the rubber and cable-making industries were at risk from toxic chemicals and were dying of bladder cancer.
6. An exclusive account of a dinner party given for four fortune-tellers and two psychiatrists, during which a code of ethics was drawn up to protect the public from charlatans.

In addition, some *World of Science* columns were attached, together with samples of radio scripts written for the BBC and Central Office of Information, and supporting letters from the Editors of the *Standard*, ITN, the COI's North America and Australasian programmes and the BBC's new *Tomorrow's World* programme, to which I had contributed ideas.

To my great surprise, I won. Apart from giving another fillip to recovery, it also gave me £500, which I spent touring America, investigating progress on the Apollo Moon programme.

It took me first to Cape Canaveral, where NASA officials showed me the new Saturn rocket launch pads; the half-constructed Launch Control Centre where myriad computers would monitor all the working parts of the boosters and the spaceships riding on top of them; the Vehicle Assembly Building (VAB) in

which the rocket stages would be mounted vertically one on top
of the other, like a child's building bricks, and The Crawler – the
world's largest moving vehicle – whose task would be to carry the
rockets, gantries and spaceships three miles from the VAB to the
launch pad.

There were not enough hyperboles even in *Roget's Thesaurus*
to convey adequately the scale of Project Apollo and the 'hardware' involved. Kennedy himself had described it as 'the biggest,
most complex scientific, engineering and technical challenge ever
faced by any nation'. But the enormity of it was hard for the layman to grasp, so I was constantly searching for comparisons.

In one feature sent from Moonport USA (as the John F.
Kennedy Space Centre was nicknamed), I tried some:

> Getting a man to the Moon means developing a spaceship larger
> than a railway locomotive – constructing a rocket heavier than a
> naval destroyer; creating a launch base the size of Woking; train-
> ing a new generation of fliers – the astronauts – and acquiring
> miles and miles of data about human behaviour under hostile con-
> ditions; completing the most thorough survey ever (of the Moon's
> surface); perfecting new techniques of navigation and guidance;
> developing strong but light new materials and mustering the skills
> of 400,000 people, the know-how of 20,000 firms and the brains
> of 150 universities and research groups. All in eight years.

The search for understandable terms was aided soon afterwards
by North American Rockwell, builders of the Apollo Moonship,
who gave each space reporter an Apollo reference book containing, among thousands of facts, several pages of 'gee whiz data' –
comparisons to make you gasp – such as 'The thrust of the engines in the first stage of the Saturn 5 rocket is equal to the com-
bined thrust of 54 jet fighters' and 'The VAB is so tall that, if it
were not air-conditioned, clouds would form in the top and rust
the rockets'. Subsequently, I developed a comparison of my own,
to give an idea of scale of spaceships and other objects in orbit
around the earth: how they measured against a single or a double-
decker bus. After using this a few times on ITN, members of the
public started to come up to me and say: 'Ah – the double-decker
bus man!'

British reporters also had a mass of space jargon to contend
with – phrases like 'launch window' (time available for a launch),
'eyeballs in' and 'eyeballs out' (astronaut terms for effects of

gravity during launch or re-entry into the Earth's atmosphere), BT (burn time for a rocket engine) and of, course, the now familiar CSM (Command and Service Module) and LM (Lunar Module). These never seemed to worry American newspaper readers but they were pitfalls in the path of us British and I developed a personal discipline of checking every report before it was set in type, to make sure that, if jargon had to be used, an explanation was given alongside.

While at the Cape, I bumped into a young English engineer, John Tribe, who had previously worked on Britain's Black Knight rocket project in Cowes, IoW, before emigrating to America. He had been part of the Atlas rocket launch team which sent the Gemini astronauts into space but had just been promoted to take charge of the Apollo spaceship's main engine once it reached Firing Pad 34 prior to a launch.

Over drinks, John told me how he arrived penniless at the Cape and needed a loan to buy a car but then, over the next six years, was able to buy two cars, two colour TV sets and his own 4-bedroomed detached house. 'Anything we want is never out of reach,' he added.

Before I left, he gave me his office telephone number at the firing pad. This was to prove invaluable when, five years later, news came that astronauts Virgil Grissom, Ed White and Roger Chaffee had been killed in a 'flash fire' inside the Apollo I spaceship, during training on the ground. NASA immediately imposed a news black-out but I was able to get through to John by direct dialling and, although we never revealed our source, the *Standard* was able to lead with a detailed, eyewitness account of the tragedy within an hour of it happening.

Von Braun and his monster rockets

From the Cape, my £500 took me to Huntsville, Alabama, where Dr. Wernher von Braun was only too keen to show a British journalist his 'baby'. Saturn 1 was arguably (for we did not know how far the Russians had progressed) the world's largest rocket. That night I wrote in my notebook, 'Saturn is not just a rocket – it is a staggering experience. It makes squibs out of all previous rockets. When you stand in its shadow, somehow you know America's might.'

Von Braun led me to a hangar, as clean as a housewife's pantry, where four of the giant boosters lay on their sides. They were 188 feet long and we needed to climb 32 steps to reach a platform on top of the side of one. Fully fuelled, each would weigh 520 tons.

The boosters I saw would be used to launch large satellites and to test a prototype, or 'boilerplate model', of the Apollo spaceship. But then the former German V–2 rocket designer took me into a drawing office and showed me blueprints for the awesome Saturn 5, the one which would be 'heavier than a naval destroyer'.

I remember his parting words: 'Saturn 5 will be the first rocket to be ruled by a democracy. It will have three computers in its first stage. Only when at least two vote "go" will we push the launch button.'

It did not always 'go' at the first attempt. But once it was airborne, it worked faultlessly every time.

Hospitality at Houston

Next stop was Houston, Texas – or rather Clear Lake City, some 20 miles away. There the main buildings of the Manned Spacecraft Centre were nearly complete, including Mission Control (from which each Apollo flight would be directed, from the moment the spaceship was clear of the firing pad to the moment of splashdown in the Pacific). When I saw it, it contained the biggest tangle of wires I had ever seen and the mind boggled at the cleverness of the engineers who would have to sort it all out.

Clear Lake City itself had only just been built as a multi-billion dollar speculative venture and it stood as a 'ghost town', buildings all ready to lease. I became the first overseas visitor to stay at the King's Inn Motel and was taken by the manager on a tour of the empty supermarket, shops, community centre and luxury homes, which were to become the hub of the astronaut community for two decades. It was eerie hearing everywhere the echoes of our footsteps.

When we got back to the Inn, the manager made me a member of the King's Inn Club – allowing me to drink in Texas on a Sunday – and introduced me to the Club's bunny girl. I was just getting on famously over two Brandy Alexanders – there were no other customers – when the phone rang. 'It's for you, Dixie,' said the bartender. 'It's him again.' I heard snatches of the conversation, during which the sum of $100 was mentioned.

When she came back from the phone, she had slipped a coat on and had her purse in her hand. The bartender told me that this often happened on a Sunday afternoon, when a particular Texan millionaire was lonely. I returned to my room to write. Somebody must have told the manager of the incident because, at around 8 p.m., there was a knock on my door. The Bell Captain stood outside with a tray bearing the ingredients of a Brandy Alexander – but not just one. There was a whole bottle of brandy, another of Creme de Cacao and a half-pint carton of cream. Beside these, a candy-striped box contained a table lighter in the form of the King's Inn logo (a knight's helmet with plumes) and a souvenir ashtray. He then said: 'Is there anything else you would like, sir – anything at all – I mean black, white, slim, well-built, blonde, brunette, red-head? You just tell me, sir.' I said, 'Thanks, but I have a lot of work to do.' When I stayed at the Inn a year later, I learned that both he and the Bunny Girl were in jail for vice offences.

The Lunar 'Bug'

Next to New York, to see a prototype of the first Lunar Module being built by the Grumman Aircraft Corp. at their factory in Ithaca. The module was often referred to as the 'Lunar Bug' and it looked remarkably like some monstrous insect, with four legs resting on footpads, a black-painted hatch in the 'nose' and windows resembling eyes on either side. One of the engineers who showed me around remarked: 'There's a kind of wartime stench to this thing – it reminds me of being in a tank.'

The LM was designed to land gently on the Moon, using a single engine and small manoeuvring rockets to guide it down to within a few inches of the surface. Shock-absorbing legs would then cushion the final impact. The inside of each leg contained a stack of rods of crushable, aluminium honeycomb and my guide insisted on giving me an off-cut, measuring 2 ft. 6 ins. long, as a souvenir of the visit.

It joins the coral, the three-masted buggalo and the shooting stick as classic items NOT to take with you on an aircraft. But it distracted the booking clerks from my other excess baggage and it proved a useful visual aid on ITN when men finally went to the Moon.

Breakfast cooked by a General

Finally to Washington, for a series of briefings on the medical aspects of manned spaceflight and the topography of the Moon.

In front of a huge map of the Moon, Dr Robert Jastrow explained how the Pioneers (which smacked their cameras full tilt into the Moon) and the Surveyor 'soft' landers would be followed by a series of reconnaissance missions to take detailed pictures, using spacecraft laden with cameras and transmitters, placed in orbit around the Moon. These would be used to select safe sites for the men to land. I was given a model of the so-called Lunar Orbiter.

It was quite remarkable how generous NASA officials and their science advisers were with information, photographs, maps, charts and models, once they realised the amount of coverage their space programme was getting in Britain. The nearest I came to a closed door was when I sought briefings on the medical problems of spaceflight and the fitness of the astronauts.

The man responsible for setting the fitness standards for astronauts was a consultant physician in the US Air Force, Brig. Gen. Don Flickinger. I asked for an interview with him but was told he was 'too busy'. I pleaded with the USAF Public Affairs Department but to no avail. So I looked up 'Flickinger' in the Washington phone book and found him.

'No, I didn't know you had asked to see me,' he said over the phone, 'but it's true that I am very busy'. In fact, he was about to depart for Albuquerque, New Mexico, to join his fellow NASA consultant, Dr Randolph Lovelace Jr, to conduct a further set of astronaut selection tests.

I must have sounded very disappointed because, to my amazement, he said, 'Look, I'm just about to cook breakfast. Why don't you take a taxi on over and we'll talk while we eat?'

When I arrived at his 10-storey apartment block near the Pentagon, he was in shirt and slacks, wearing an apron, wielding a slice in one hand and a frying pan in the other. 'One egg or two?' he asked. 'Sunny side up – or easy over lightly?' And so began a friendship which began with an excellent breakfast and briefing and stayed fruitful over many years.

It also led, by a curious set of coincidences, to my being invited to the Ministry of Defence Press Office in London years later and shown a newspaper clipping under the heading 'Hush Puppies'. It read, 'Met a guy from London this week, name of Pete Fairley. He had some interesting views on American women. "American women are the most seductive in the world," said Fairley. "The trouble is they never seduce you".'

More of that later. It's not one for the grandchildren. But if they do question me about the past, I can truthfully say that, when I wasn't busy being a general in the air force, I was busy having my breakfast cooked by one.

The rocket that rattled the ribs

November 9, 1967 – possibly the most exciting day of my working life. I was back at Cape Kennedy, this time wearing two official hats – one for the *Standard*, the other for ITN.

Along with some 300 other TV men and journalists, I was there to report the maiden flight of Saturn 5, the Western world's largest rocket, with an empty Apollo moonship on top. Nothing on the scale of this combination, the key to astronauts getting to the Moon, had ever been seen, much less felt, before. And feel it we did.

My first sight of it was when it was standing upright, held against a red gantry, on Launch Complex 39a. It was 364 ft. high – almost as tall as Nelson's Column – and weighed 2,700 tons. My first thought was, 'How do we communicate to the British TV viewer the true size of this monster?'

David Haylock, ITN's No.1 US cameraman, fitted a 20A zoom lens to his camera and a radio microphone on me. I stood about 50 feet in front of the firing pad with Haylock and the camera a quarter of a mile away in front of me. I had written a script which began: 'They are calling this the Big Shot – "big" because it involves the world's biggest rocket and "shot" because it will fire an object shaped like a bullet into space.'

Haylock started with a tight close-up of my face. On hearing the word 'big' in his earphones, he zoomed rapidly out to reveal the whole rocket and gantry, reducing me to the scale of an ant in the picture. It said it all in one.

Three days later, we were positioned on the Press stand, 3.5 miles from the launch pad, as Saturn 5 blasted off. Wernher von Braun, who had created the colossus, told us that, if we went any closer, our eardrums would burst. He wasn't exaggerating. If the whole thing had exploded, it would have done so with a force equal to a million tons of TNT.

There was a great belch of orange flame and smoke from under the rocket, which shot hundreds of yards to either side. Even as it gathered power on the firing pad for six seconds after ignition, I felt my whole rib cage rattling and an overwhelming roar in my ears. The vibration actually broke up a glass-sided commentary box at the side of our stand, dropping the veteran CBS TV presenter Walter Cronkite five feet to the ground.

It was so much more than we had expected, well-prepared as we were with 'gee whiz data' such as 'each of the 11 engines drinks three tons of fuel a second' or 'the rocket contains two million working parts' and, finally, 'Saturn 5 took six years to develop: it will take 16 minutes to perform'.

The booster functioned perfectly, each stage igniting on time and propelling the empty 40-ton spaceship (designated Apollo 4) into a single orbit of the Earth. The cone-shaped command capsule splashed down safely in the Pacific Ocean exactly 8 hours 37 minutes and 8 seconds after launch, only six miles from the ship waiting to recover it.

America was nearly ready to go to the Moon and I was nearly ready to go into television full-time.

CHAPTER ELEVEN
Into Camera

July 1968 saw a new era open for ITV. The second round of franchises went to 15 companies, including four new ones, serving 14 areas of Britain, and a new national TV magazine was created with the title *TV Times*. ITN continued to provide 'the network', as it was known, with news.

In the Spring of that year, Peter Jackson – with a reputation already for launching new magazines – was appointed Editor of the national *TV Times*, soon to occupy spanking new offices in Tottenham Court Road.

Peter wanted to launch the new programme journal symbolically, with a Saturn rocket blasting-off on the front cover and the theme 'Lift off into the future with the new *TV Times*' throughout the first issue. He rang me at the *Standard* and invited me to lunch to explore the idea.

The lunch began at 12.45 p.m. We were still sitting at the table at 5.45 p.m. By then, I had virtually agreed to quit the *Standard* and join *TV Times*.

Peter is a man-of-ideas who inspires others to have ideas and the conversation certainly sparked that afternoon. Neither of us sat down with the idea of my joining the new magazine but we found our professional minds so much in harmony that it seemed the logical thing to do. There was only one obstacle – my Beaverbrook salary was considerably higher than *TV Times* would wish to take over, much less increase.

'Leave it with me,' said Peter as we parted.

A few days later, we met for a drink and he told me that he had persuaded Nigel Ryan – who had succeeded Geoffrey Cox as Editor of ITN – and the Board of Independent Television Publications (owners of *TV Times*) to employ me jointly as Science Editor – in print and on the screen. I gave in my notice to Charles Wintour.

Apart from the first heart transplant stories – South African then British – there were few notable stories to cover while my notice was expiring and so I was able to devote a considerable amount of time to helping to plan the new magazine and writing copy for the first issue.

It was decided to link the magazine to the forthcoming launch of Apollo 7 and to include an interview with my friend at Cape Kennedy – John Tribe – and a photograph of his seven-year-old son, Stephen, in a spacesuit and helmet with a Saturn rocket blasting off behind him.

The first issue of the new *TV Times* appeared on September 21 and the launch was a great success. Apollo 7 blasted off on October 11 and was equally successful, a fact celebrated by its commander, Wally Schirra, with the immortal cry 'Yabadabadoo – that was a helluva kick up the fanny' as he fired his spaceship's main engine. The Media celebrated in a bar at Cocoa Beach with cocktails called 'Moonshot' – a gin sling containing no less than a pint of gin.

There was a mood of euphoria at the new *TV Times*. We all believed we were creating not just a TV guide but Britain's largest family magazine. There were major series in the pipeline, including one particularly ambitious one called *The Home of the Future*.

But the optimism soon changed to frustration as our ideas were put on hold or even 'binned' – because our owners and masters (the TV companies) insisted on limiting the number of feature pages, so maximising profits to bolster up their own incomes, which were falling below expectations. Audience figures and advertising revenue reflected the fact that viewers were simply not enjoying the new menus of programmes they had created.

When life became frustrating, I was lucky enough to have an escape route to the offices of ITN in Television House, Kingsway – and soon there was plenty to occupy me there.

By November, it was looking likely that NASA would be able to launch Apollo 8 – the first mission intended to orbit the Moon and return – on time. The planned date was December 21, with a six day flight spanning Christmas. But there were suspicions that the Russians might try to get there first – they had already sent two Zond spaceships to the Moon and back to map radiation levels, test communications and monitor the behaviour of small 'living organisms' – turtles, worms, fruit flies and the like.

There were very few people at ITN who believed men would go to the Moon that Christmas and it was quite difficult to persuade programme editors to allocate resources. However, on December 1, I was joined by Sue Tinson, then a young scriptwriter, and together we quietly got on with preparing film and other visual material, with a deadline only three weeks away.

With the help of Malcolm Beatson, ITN's highly-creative Head of Graphics and a space enthusiast, we designed a studio 'set' comprising a semicircle of panels covered with black felt, to represent outer space. Onto this we glued a large cut-out Earth and a smaller photo of the Moon. The idea was that we would indicate to viewers, at each news bulletin, roughly how far the Moonship had travelled, by pressing in large, yellow drawing pins.

We also borrowed a display dummy from a tailor's shop, which Jenny Groombridge, one of Malcolm's graphics artists, clothed in a life-like 'spacesuit' with a goldfish bowl for a helmet. Finally, we paid to have built a six-foot tall model of the Saturn 5 rocket to stand beside the newscaster's desk.

What the viewer never saw were the huge blown-up photographs of the Soviet Zond and Soyuz spaceships which we also prepared, together with a few reels of edited Soviet space footage and the letters CCCP (to stick on our dummy's 'helmet', to transform him from an astronaut to a cosmonaut) – we were that uncertain about who would go to the Moon first. But still few in Television House took us seriously until about a week before lift-off, when Sir Bernard Lovell, the Director of Jodrell Bank, gave a warning which set the adrenaline of every newsman pumping.

He called the mission 'Moon madness'. There was danger in the lift-off, he said, danger from radiation, danger of being marooned in orbit around the Moon, danger of crashing into the lunar surface, danger of re-entering the Earth's atmosphere too steeply and being fried alive, danger of missing the Earth altogether.

Suddenly, there was a degree of panic at ITN. Everyone wanted to view what we had prepared, look at our 'set', look at our transparencies and other visual material (especially our profiles of the astronauts) look at the mission plan, work out how key points on the flight might fit into planned news bulletins and what extra air-time should be asked for from 'the network' and so on. The commercial 'network' agreed to interrupt programmes for 'newsflashes' and to make room for more extended reports throughout the mission.

All too soon, it was December 21 – launch day.

If Frank Borman, Jim Lovell and Bill Anders felt anxious in their capsule, it was nothing to the way I felt in front of the camera. It was agreed that, whenever appropriate, the official ITN newscaster would start each newsflash and then hand over to me for an update. I would have been listening out, most of the time, to NASA Public Affairs officials giving minute-by-minute information from Mission Control in Houston over the international satellite link.

I was to speak directly to camera, wearing two earpieces – one feeding NASA sound into one ear, the other bringing instructions from the programme director in the ITN control room into the other. I found it totally deranging but said nothing because this seemed a real chance to establish a reputation as a TV Science Editor.

The mission went smoothly and to plan. The trail of yellow pins moved inexorably closer to the Moon and viewers began ringing to say that they enjoyed the 'set' and the clarity of the information given. 'Live' telecasts from the crew inside the Moonship were the highlights and I enjoyed these particularly because it meant that I did not have to speak to camera for more than a few seconds.

Exactly 25 hours after launch – and 119,000 miles out in space – Bill Anders reminded us all that Christmas was almost upon us by sending a message to his six-year old son, Greg. 'We saw Santa Claus earlier this morning,' he said, 'and he was heading your way.'

Christmas is a festive time but nowhere more so than at ITN, where about a third of the production and editorial staff have to remain on duty. There is a tradition that each member of Eurovision offers an hour of specially prepared programme to the international network for the enjoyment of those on duty throughout Europe and for their eyes only (as a result, some of the funniest as well as most nearly-pornographic material gets secretly transmitted).

At ITN, Christmas is also a time for celebration lunches and internal office parties and the fact that men were going around the Moon was not allowed to interrupt the fun – in fact, quite the reverse. Apollo 8 seemed only to add spice to the celebrations.

I remember it as a time of continuous temptation. I yearned to drink with the rest – in fact, the alcohol might have helped to calm my nerves – but I dared not. There is no worse 'crime' on television than to appear on screen in your cups.

Christmas Eve found the lunarnauts (as we began to refer to them) going round the back of the Moon, out of radio contact for the first time. It was a tense 36 minutes and we broadcast the renewed contact 'live'. 'We've got it, we've got it,' announced Houston, 'Apollo 8 is in lunar orbit.'

Each crew member gave his own first impression of the Moon. The one I remember best was Frank Borman's, 'It's a vast, lonely, forbidding type of existence – a great expanse of nothing that looks rather like clouds and clouds of pumice stone,' he said. 'It certainly would not appear to be a very inviting place to live or work.' It gave the NASA PR men the shudders and certainly killed any desire I might have had to go to the Moon.

Pictures followed, bearing this out. And then it was Christmas Day. It started, not unexpectedly, with a prayer from Frank Borman to the congregation of St. Christopher's Church in Houston, where he was a lay reader. Borman was a devout Christian and a strict disciplinarian, who believed in 'playing it by the book'. When Lovell and Anders produced three miniature bottles of brandy which they had hidden in their 'diddy bags' to celebrate Christmas, as Captain of Apollo 8 he confiscated them. 'No alcohol is permitted on duty or on Government property,' he reminded them. 'Here we are on both.'

None of this came out during the mission. Had it done so, it would certainly have prompted an extra toast, out of sympathy, from the crew on duty at ITN, where the merriment continued.

By the end of Boxing Day, we were all a bit jaded but there was still one party to go – 'Reggie's Hamper Party'. It was held in Bosanquet's office. We all chipped in with bottles of wine and Reggie provided a Fortnum & Mason hamper, including a huge pie. The party seemed to go on and on.

Because I was having to appear on screen, it was as important as ever to stay sober. But the two newsflashes which came during Reggie's party were a fiasco.

Although the news I heard in my right ear was good news (NASA merely describing manoeuvres which had been successfully carried out by the Moonship on its way back to Earth), it was the words I heard in my left ear which threw me and made me fluff my own words.

The programme director that evening was the legendary Diana

Edwards-Jones, a truly remarkable Welsh lady with a vocabulary of swearwords outstripping any man's and a reputation for quick action. While I was standing facing the camera in the studio, she was seated at the console in the Control Room, flanked by a p.a., a vision mixer and an engineer. To communicate with me, her microphone was linked to the earpiece in my left ear and she was supposed to press a switch when she wished to tell me something.

Unfortunately, the switch was left 'open' throughout the entire transmission both times. This page would be a mass of asterisks it I attempted to repeat, verbatim, her asides and snatches of conversation with others in the control room. I was not used to her language and, although no prude, I found it disconcerting.

'Listen Fairbags,' she said, after the second poor performance, 'if really is time you became more professional and learned to listen to selective talk-back.'

I snapped. 'I'd be more than willing to listen to selective talk-back if it was selective. But when I'm trying to hear what NASA is saying and speak to camera at the same time and I hear "assholes for breakfast, chaps" and "take the bugger tighter" in the other ear, I try to shut it out.'

Di realised then that she had left the switch open. We have been friends ever since.

'News at Ten' – a new concept

When ITN transmitted its first news on Sept. 22 1955, the staff numbered only 16 and the total airtime for its three bulletins – at 1 p.m., 5.50 p.m. and 9 p.m. – was just 30 minutes.

This was, however, in accord with the TV Act of 1955, which had laid down 'an irreducible minimum' of daily airtime for news on ITV, which had to be 'adequately funded'. During the 20 years of my association with ITN, each Editor (first Geoffrey Cox, then Nigel Ryan and finally David Nicholas) fought a continuous battle with the ITV regional companies (who ran 'The Network' and who funded our budget) to get more airtime and more cash. Far too many Chairmen, Managing Directors and Programme Controllers in those days regarded news as what Geoffrey, in his book *See It Happen*, described as 'an irritating extra which had to be fitted in somewhere'.

The first studio was located on the 8th floor of Television House in Kingsway, with the Newsroom on the floor below) but it was not custom-built and suffered from a lack of space and, especially, a low ceiling. The latter frequently made it insufferably hot, so that the newscasters frequently sat with buckets of 'dry ice' nearby to help them stay reasonably cool.

With the exception of a tin of Pancake, a dab-on pad and some talcum powder for the newscasters to apply themselves, there was no professional make-up. It had been decided that, on a news programme, interviewees and reporters would be hurrying into the studio at the last minute – even while the programme was being transmitted – without time to pause for make-up: better that all faces should glisten, it was reasoned, rather than *some* glisten and some not. Unfortunately, having been born in Malaya, my sweat pores opened at the slightest excuse and appearances 'on air' at Kingsway were always tinged with anxiety: would the camera be on me when the drop of sweat was still trickling down the nose, or would it have dripped off?

Television House became what Geoffrey Cox called 'the barrack square for a new generation of TV journalists'.

The pioneer newscasters Christopher Chataway and Robin Day, who did so much to win sizeable audiences for ITN from the start, moved on to higher things and were replaced by the no less appealing Ludovic Kennedy, Ian Trethowan, Antony Brown, Huw Thomas, Andrew Gardner and Tim Brinton – professionals in a new medium almost overnight.

'Unknowns' quickly became familiar faces on the ITN news – Reggie Bosanquet, Sandy Gall and Ivor Mills (all of whom started as reporters before turning to newscasting several years later), Michael Nicholson, Gerald Seymour, Alan Hart, Peter Sissons – who quickly gained reputations abroad – Tom St John Barry, the crime specialist and Julian Haviland, who made politics and Parliament his 'killing field', Peter Snow, the ubiquitous Richard Lindley and the two talented ladies, fashion expert Barbara Mandell and Lynne Reid-Banks.

Lynne actually wrote her first novel, *The L-shaped Room*, while she was at ITN. It was made into a film in the '60s, starring Leslie Caron and Tom Bell. The book has been described as 'a sensitive and moving story of a girl, pregnant and unmarried, taking a room in shabby lodgings while she worked out her predicament' and was rumoured to have been based on 'somebody at ITN'. We have all been trying to work out who ever since.

I was never on the staff of ITN but those who were quickly offered friendship and made me feel part of a team – a team which was lucky enough to be dealing with some of the most exciting news this century. There was virtually no training – certainly no format courses – we were all thrown in at the deep end and left to 'work it out' for ourselves. True, some were keener to appear in front of the camera than others.

But there were no prima donnas. The pressures of telling stories briefly but accurately – and at speed – left little room for vanity. We reporters were Indians not chiefs, orbiting planets rather than stars. Our reward was to get the story on.

It was the need to keep his talented staff and stop them defecting to rival TV organisations that was the chief motivation for Geoffrey Cox to intensify his battle with The Network to get the length of the main news bulletin increased to 30 minutes and its timing shifted to later in the evening. It took two years to win it.

Another factor helped – the introduction of satellite transmissions which allowed 'live' reports not only from America but from the Middle East to be brought onto British viewers' screens.

Three pilot 30-minute programmes were made with varying degrees of success but they were never broadcast. The individual programme companies remained largely hostile and over-protective of their own interests, especially as far as timings were concerned. Then, in 1967, the Independent Television Authority (ITA) proposed a new networking schedule which included a 'slot' for the late evening bulletin at 10 p.m. instead of nine.

News at Ten was born. For the first time since the birth of ITV, the news was accepted – at least by the ITA – as the 'central pillar' of evening viewing, instead of as an interruption. The only criteria laid down were that it should be 'markedly different' from other bulletins and 'built around a central personality'.

Previous experience had shown the problems of having one 'personality' handling a long and complex programme and Geoffrey, in his wisdom, insisted on two – Alastair Burnet, aided by Andrew Gardner on Mondays, Tuesdays and Fridays and Andrew with Reginald Bosanquet on Wednesdays and Thursdays. The combination proved a winner.

Geoffrey also believed in what he called 'integrated news packages', which quickly helped to make *News at Ten* 'different'. These involved the reporter researching and writing his own script, speaking the introduction, links and finale to camera and voicing over the commentary himself. This could either be done 'in the field' or recorded back at ITN in the studio, after the film or video tape had been edited. In other words, the reporter became his own producer in the field, he acted as director as well, although it would be a fool who did not consult and take advice from the camera crew.

As a result, a variety of different styles began to develop on screen – all adding to the interest of *News at Ten* – and many friendships were forged between camera crews and reporters, who formed sub-teams. Next day came the inquests.

Although more air-time meant that longer news reports were possible, time remained a tight constraint. If ITN were to over-run its allotted 'slot', programme companies would have to can-cel advertisements, which in turn would mean a loss of revenue. So before going 'on air', every item – whether visual or verbal – was timed with a stop-watch at least once. The items and their timings were then listed on a sheet of paper, known as the output running order, which was circulated to senior production and editorial staff.

A production assistant sitting beside the bulletin Director in the Control Room, armed with a stop-watch and a calculator, kept a continuous check on progress. If the bulletin was under-running its schedule, extra stories (usually two- or three-line items, known as 'shorts') were included: if it was over-running, these stories were cut. Another option was to leave out the 'And fi-nally. . .' item which usually ended the news and provided an op-portunity for a little light humour.

The same p.a. was also responsible for counting out aloud the last 5 or10 seconds of the story being transmitted, to give the newscaster his next cue: she then 'counted in' the first 5 or 10 of the next report, so that it could be switched onto the viewer's screen precisely on time.

Geoffrey Cox had gladly accepted 'The Network's' insistence on a commercial break in the middle of *News at Ten* because it allowed two minutes for the mathematical juggling to take place in the Control Room (and fresh advice to be given to the newscasters through their earpieces) before Part Two of the pro-gramme went ahead.

Everybody at ITN was aware that there were just 12 seconds of leeway. If *News at Ten* over-ran by more, a commercial would be lost and all hell would break loose. It is a testimony to the fine work done by the much under-rated p.a.s that it almost never did.

Teleprompter – the vital tool

An essential aid in news bulletins was the Teleprompter (Autocue in the BBC). It was a system which gave the viewer the impression that the person speaking to camera had memorised the words, whereas he was actually reading them.

Words to be spoken were first typed onto a four inch-wide roll of paper which was moved under a TV camera by an operator turning a handle. The words were magnified and projected by mirrors onto a small TV screen in front of the newscaster or reporter in the studio.

It took much of the strain out of speaking to camera. Many viewers did not realise that a crib was in use, although early Teleprompters were detectable because the projection screen had to be positioned above, below or at one side of the camera and the newscaster's eyes were noticeably angled. It was only when engineers developed a 'wrap around' version, to fit in front of the camera lens itself, that it became true 'magic' (virtually the only way to detect its use today is if the user is wearing contact lenses and the slight movement of the eyeballs scanning the words picks up reflections of the studio lights: the eyes appear to be, literally, 'twinkling'.)

Although the Teleprompter helped many to achieve professionalism, its prime purpose was as an aid to precise timing. When the words were typed, they were counted. Although it varied slightly from person to person, broadly speaking we worked to the formula ' three words equal one second' or '180 to the minute'. So when the total of words was known, the time needed for the item 'on air' could be worked out accurately.

Unfortunately, even the best systems can break down. For this eventuality, the p.a. who typed the story onto the roll of paper also typed it onto foolscap pages. These were known as 'greys'. One copy was given to the newscaster or reporter and a second to the programme Director.

Most newscasters developed the technique of glancing down briefly at the 'greys' before carrying on reading off the Teleprompter, finally shuffling the pages together (and sometimes putting a pen away) in vision at the end of the news. But I remember vividly the night when Teleprompter broke down and I had no 'greys'.

It was a night when news had come in, just before *News at Ten* went on air, that the American space station called Skylab had developed a major problem. One of its 'wings' (huge panels of solar cells, on which it depended for power) had failed to unfurl properly. The craft had also developed a slight wobble.

I barely had time to confirm the news with NASA in Houston and scribble my story for the p.a. to type for the Teleprompter before it was time to race downstairs into the studio. I reached it, along with the p.a., just in time to hear Reggie announce the 'bongs' (headlines in between strikes of Big Ben). The first was 'The American space station Skylab is in trouble – we'll have a report from our Science Editor, Peter Fairley, in a moment. . . .'

The 'props' manager had arranged for a 3-foot-tall model of the space station to be placed on the studio floor and I took up position, standing by it. The Teleprompter operator was busy with scissors and glue inserting my Skylab report into her roll of stories as Reggie reached the end of the 'bongs' and started his lead-in to the Skylab news.

Each news item on the roll always has a catchword above it, indicating where to start reading. My catchword should have been SKYLAB. The red light came on above my camera, indicating that it had gone 'live' but, instead of SKYLAB, the catchword 'LONRHO' appeared, along with the first two lines of the Lonrho story. The operator had stuck the Skylab story in the wrong place.

What does one do?

It is a psychological side-effect of using an electronic crib that, when the words are committed to a roll of paper moving in front of your eyes, your brain places total reliance on the screen on which they are appearing. It has to be all Teleprompter or all 'greys' – there is no halfway mode. Unfortunately, because I was standing by the Skylab model, my 'greys' were on a table 10 feet away.

I asked to see a playback of the news afterwards. I found that I had coughed twice and then cleared my throat before 'ad libbing' about the Skylab problem. The two coughs had bought sufficient time to allow my brain to take back the facts from the machine and give me the confidence to ad lib.

It was my second *momentus horribilis* in television and I can
never hear the word 'Lonrho' without reliving it.

The key colour

Appearance is obviously important on television. Performers never
fail to let the taxman know how much they spend on their clothing, their hair etc., although some of the ITN newscasters, in
those days, often wore smart jackets but casual trousers because
the camera never showed them below the belt.

Reporters were different. They might be revealed standing, or
having to walk across the studio to some visual aid. So although I
had never been sartorially minded, being appointed ITN's Science Editor made me do something about my wardrobe.

The *Daily Mirror* had once described me as 'portly' – and *World
Medicine* as 'portly-built but with ferocious energy'. Nigel Ryan
had threatened to include a clause in my freelance contract stipu-
lating 'must stay in reasonable shape'. So I was determined, for a
start, to buy clothing which was slightly too large in the hope of
appearing slimmer than I actually was. I also went on a diet for
three months (the reward for which was to lose nearly two stone
but to discover that I had diabetes).

Just before joining ITN, I had been invited by the BBC to take
part in some experimental colour TV programmes, the longest of
which was a documentary about fire. During these, I observed
that, although reds and oranges and greens stood out vividly on
the screen, the most faithfully reproduced colour was actually
blue.

So when the time came to select a 'TV wardrobe', I bought
seven blue shirts, seven pairs of blue socks, four subdued blue
ties and an expensive blue suit. But when ITN went into colour
in 1969, it was decided to use an electronic system for making
pictures appear, as if by magic, behind the newscasters as they
sat at their desks. It was called Chromakey – chroma coming from
the Greek kroma, meaning colour, and key being any one, chosen colour.

No pictures were actually visible in the studio – merely a hard-
board panel in the chosen colour, hung behind the newscasters
shoulder. The pictures were loaded into a machine elsewhere and
electronically mixed with the signal output of the camera facing

News at Ten with Alastair Burnet and Andrew Gardner.

ITN's front-line team for Apollo 15 mission: (standing, left to right) Valerie Morrison, Frank Miles, W/Cdr. Gordon Sharpe, Peter, David Nicholas, Diana Edwards-Jones, Christine Lomas, Carole de Caux, and (seated) Reginald Bosanquet and Jim Irwin.

The ITN Apollo team: (left to right) Frank Miles, Jane Burdett, David Nicholas, Diana Edwards-Jones, Paul Gawith, Nigel Warrack, Alastair Burnet, Christine Lomas and Steve Wright. In front is Fred Hickey and Peter.

The watch presented to Peter by Dick Gordon, who wore it on the Apollo 12 mission.

Dick Gordon (Command Module Pilot for Apollo 12), seen here with Diana Edwards-Jones and Peter, joined the ITN team for Apollo 16. He became such an anglo-phile that ITN bought him a rolled brolly, bowler and briefcase.

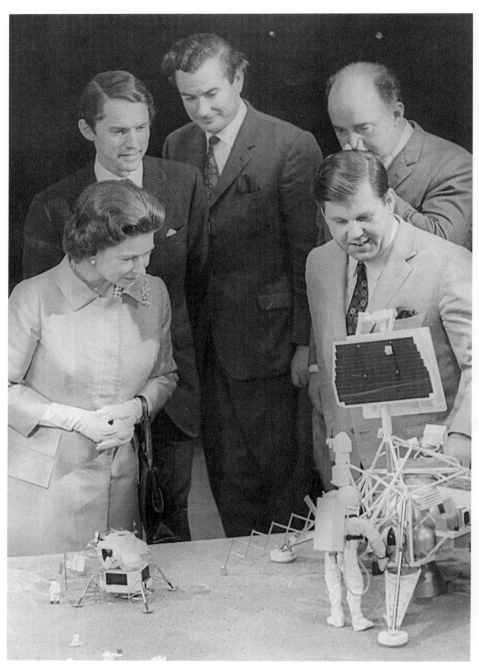

HM The Queen talks to Peter when visiting the News at Ten studios, with Nigel Ryan, Alastair Burnet and Paul Haney looking on.

Interviewing Neil Armstrong.

Peter and his sons in spacesuits.

Peter in ITN studios covering the Apollo 8 mission.

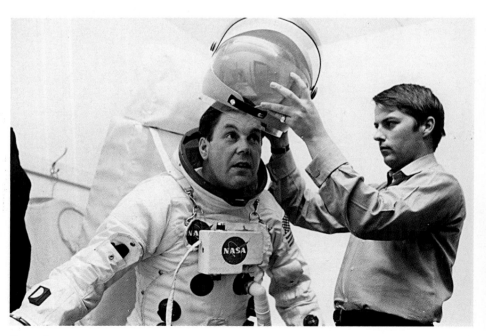

Peter the astronaut.

Peter describing the future of space exploration on viewing the model of the 'shuttle'.

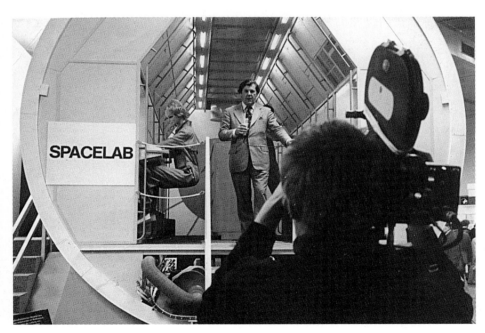

Visiting the Spacelab exhibit.

The 'father' of space medicine, Dr Hubertus Strughold, shows Peter a 'moon tank' in which problems of space flight are studied.

the newscaster. Whenever the camera saw the key colour, it over-printed the externally-fed picture.

To my disgust, ITN chose blue for Chromakey. It meant that all my new blue clothing was useless for television: if I wore it in front of the camera, the viewer would see Chairman Mao's hordes or the Vietnam war or a spaceship or whatever, marching all over me. So I had to go out and buy a fresh set – fawn, brown, bottle green – anything but blue.

A few years later, a different technical system was introduced and I was able to wear the blue items although, by then, not all of them fitted. But the principle of wearing over-large clothing paid off because there were many occasions when Nigel Ryan stopped me in the corridor saying 'Gosh, Peter, I believe you've lost some weight' – when I hadn't.

'Whoops – I've broken it'

NASA's efforts to meet Kennedy's aim of landing a man on the Moon before the end of this decade, continued on schedule. Apollo 8 was followed by Apollo 9, the first and only time I saw men actually ride a Saturn 5 rocket into space from Cape Kennedy. It was almost as gripping as the maiden launch of the giant rocket, with the added angst of seeing men risking their lives.

Jim McDivitt, Dave Scott and Rusty Schweickart tested the full Apollo spaceship in Earth orbit and checked rendezvous and 'docking' procedures between the CSM and the LM before re-turning to Earth. I spent some of their time in space flying to Houston and recording a number of short TV reports on the 'hardware' that would be used when man actually landed on the Moon.

I feel a bit sheepish, now, admitting that, to introduce many such items, I wore either a spacesuit or NASA coveralls (white overalls), in the belief that it would add interest and realism to the story. I cringe now when I look at some of the old footage. I seem like a child who cannot resist dressing up, although clambering in and out of spaceships can lead to clothing 'snagging' on projec-tions and at least the NASA suits saved my own from getting torn.

One report was recorded on the lawn in front of the Astronaut Office of the Manned Spacecraft Centre at Houston. It was a demonstration of the Moon 'tool-kit', an aluminium frame, like a clothes horse, onto which various specially developed tools for working on the lunar surface were clipped.

Bob Gordon, the NASA PR man assigned to look after TV crews, had managed to get us a prototype to handle and demonstrate to camera. All went well until I came to the 'lunar hammer'. I had brought along some lumps of rock to show how the hammer would produce smaller samples for return to Earth, and I picked up one piece of rock and tapped it.

The hammer broke. 'Geez,' cried Bob, wheeling around with his head in his hands. 'You shouldn't have done that. I signed for that. They'll kill me.'

Pointing out that it was as well to discover a defect on Earth rather than during a walk on the Moon did nothing to mollify him and we were never able to show the actual Moon tool-kit in our pre-launch reports.

Instead, ITN built a replica kit of its own. I still have the hammer from it.

A lesson from Hollywood

Another of these reports was filmed in Downey, a Los Angeles suburb, where North American Rockwell was constructing a line of Apollo Command Modules to carry three astronauts at a time to the Moon.

We were mid-way through recording a piece to camera from the cramped interior of one module, with me wearing a ridiculous, polystyrene 'snoopy hat' to demonstrate how astronauts would sleep without hurting their heads while 'weightless', when my opposite number from ABC Television, Jules Bergman, arrived saying he had to film in a hurry.

That in itself might have been all right, but he came with an entourage of 10, including a 'pushy' p.a. who told us to break off our 'shoot' while they did theirs. 'Like hell,' said David Haylock, my cameraman, and we carried on. But we needed several 'takes' to complete each passage to camera because the ABC crew refused to lower their voices. It was the only time I had trouble with one of the big American TV networks, most of whose broadcasting staff were only willing to be helpful to a lone Limey.

That week-end, before moving on to Washington, I joined a

public tour of Universal Studios. It proved invaluable. One part of the tour was a stop at Sound Stage 7, where the indoor sequences for many movies involving famous film stars had been shot. Our guide explained that, because these were highly-paid people, shooting was always planned so that they had to wait around as little as possible.

If they didn't actually need to kiss or hug, one star would be shot from one angle one week, talking his or her lines into thin air. The co-star would be shot from the reverse angle the next week. The performances would be spliced together in the editing suite.

I then realised that I could shoot my little packages for ITN in the same way. Because ITN was the poor brother of ITV, there was always pressure on reporters to get the maximum material from any foreign trip. I had plenty of ideas for two- or three-minute 'pre-launch packages' (the Apollo spacesuit, space food, the urine collection device, the backpack for moon walking, the rocket escape system, etc.) but little time to shoot them.

The answer, as Universal Studios showed me, was to shoot parts of several stories in one location, other parts in another location, others in a third – and so on – thereby minimising the time needed to pack up the TV equipment and move around. As long as full scripts and scene lists were sent back to London with the video tapes, an editor could piece them together like a jigsaw.

In one visit to Houston prior to Apollo 15 (the first time a roving vehicle was used on the Moon) I succeeded in shooting 11 such packages in two days.

High Society – and a slap in the face

Return to Washington coincided with an annual congress of the International Astronautical Federation. In my conference pigeon-hole, I found a gilt-edged formal invitation to cocktails with Brig. Gen. Don Flickinger, the general who had cooked me breakfast.

I accepted and turned up to find his flat full of Washington High Society, with a sprinkling of astronauts, other US generals and admirals, various space officials from different countries and a galaxy of elegant women.

The general, who was between marriages No.3 and No.4, was clearly on terms of affection with most of the women and, after we had exchanged greetings, he murmured, 'Stick around at the end – don't go.'

The party bubbled for two hours and I spent most of the time talking to Dr 'Randy' Lovelace, whom I had last seen in Paris when he walked out of the night club leaving me on my own with the two champagne-loving escorts (he was full of apologies and explained that he had begun to feel queasy and 'needed some medication back at the hotel').

The need to go suddenly became infectious at the Flickinger flat also and, within 15 minutes, the party had shrunk to five men and five women – including 'Randy' and me. 'If you're all game,' said General Don as he gathered us around, 'I've booked supper at The Bird's Nest.'

Game? I certainly was, for it was the club named after Charlie Byrd, the great jazz saxophonist, where another of my musical idols – George Shearing – was playing piano.

After introducing us to his fiancee, Marylin, and then to the others present, we all piled into cars for the drive to the Nest. The Shearing Quartet was playing as we sat down at a table set for 10.

I found myself opposite an ash-blonde in a figure-hugging black dress, called Susan. She told me she was a Pan Am air steward-ess. We both ate butterfly-tailed shrimp and lemon cheesecake and the evening became magic, with Shearing playing many of my favourite tunes and Susan recounting some of her foreign journeys, touching my hand with one of her black-gloved hands from time to time. Although Shearing was blind, he insisted on coming over to say 'hello' to the party. I had several minutes of conversation with him because he, too, was English and wanted to know what was happening in Britain.

Around 1 a.m. we all returned to the general's flat, where he invited us to the ballet the following evening. And so began an unforgettable week – hard work by day and society life by night.

I hired a dinner jacket for the ballet and then hung on to it for the rest of the week as further invitations followed – to the thea-tre, a dinner in the Mayflower Hotel, several more cocktail par-ties in fashionable parts of Georgetown and even a small reception in Congress. Jokingly, we referred to ourselves as 'Flickinger's Follies'.

Susan and I were drawing close. We asked to be excused the final evening's programme and went alone instead to dine and dance at the Sheraton, where Bill Snyder and his orchestra was playing. We danced close, too.

Before midnight, she invited me back to her flat for coffee. The doorman called a cab and I was a bit disconcerted to hear her give the driver an address on the outskirts of Washington.

I remember her perfume. I remember trying not to sneeze as her fur stole brushed my face when she rested her head on my shoulder throughout the 20-minute drive. I remember paying off the taxi and walking to her ground floor apartment, her arm tucked in mine.

But the thing I shall never forget is her stepping inside, turning round and without a word – slamming the door in my face.

To this day, I know not why – except that, quite early on in our relationship, I had told her that I was married. Perhaps it was her way of telling me to remember my wife.

Silence is golden

The last step in the Apollo programme to land men on the Moon was to test all the 'hardware' and the complex manoeuvres needed as close to the lunar surface as possible. Apollo 10, with astronauts Tom Stafford, Gene Cernan and John Young aboard, went up on May 18 and were away from the Earth for 192 hours.

When the Lunar Module had detached itself and descended to within nine miles of the surface, there was a 'live' telecast from the Command Module showing the fragile, black-white-and-gold LM looking like an insect against the grey backdrop of mountains and craters. This telecast coincided with Thames Television's *This Week* programme and a number of 'experts' were invited into the Aldwych studio to comment on the pictures as they came in from the Moon.

The programme was a shambles. Each 'expert' felt he had to have a say and kept butting in, usually just as one of the astronauts started to speak, so that the poor viewer barely heard a word from Gene Cernan or Tom Stafford who were inside the LM.

Among the watching millions that night was a man who instantly took this lesson to heart – David (now Sir David) Nicholas, then Deputy Editor of ITN and the executive in charge of all our news coverage of the Moon landings. 'We must never trample over "astronaut sound" again,' he told me sternly.

This instruction was reinforced a month later when ITN's Apollo team, David, Sue Tinson, Di Edwards-Jones, Frank Miles (a senior news writer) and me – booked the 'office' of the Boot and Flogger pub in Southwark for lunch, in order to plan our coverage of the 'really big one' – the Apollo 11 mission in which two men would walk on the Moon. The 'office' was a glassed-off inner room close to the bar and it became the venue for ITN's ops. planning for all the early Moon missions.

We had obtained a copy of the official NASA flight plan, a document nearly two inches thick, in which every single event and action by the astronauts was listed in sequence. We went through this with a fine toothcomb for nearly three hours, helped by plates of meat and cheese and some excellent vintage wines. It was decided that Alastair Burnet should front all the 'special' programmes and inserts into news bulletins, assisted by Paul Haney (the ex-NASA official who, until then, had been the 'Voice of Apollo' and knew the Moon programme in detail) and me.

It was a great relief to have Alastair 'fronting' the show because it meant that I could get useful visual aids ready off-camera, as they became relevant, and 'chip-in' with comments without feeling the strain of having to speak to camera.

It was also decided to create a more elaborate studio 'set' with a more authentic 'astronaut', although still with a goldfish bowl for a helmet! Frank Miles offered to summarise and anglicise the flight plan and distribute it to all the key people – including production staff – taking part in ITN's coverage.

A week later, I was sitting on a radiator chatting to the Editor's secretary, when the Board Room door opened and Lew Grade came out, cigar in hand, to go to the 'loo'. 'Peter, my boy,' he beamed. 'It's OK. You're going to get what you want.' I did not know what he meant but apparently David had made out an excellent case for a special programme budget.

Later we learned that, for the actual landing, ITN would be linked with an extended *Frost* programme in the hope of attracting a majority audience. It worked. The majority was 6–1 – the first time more viewers had watched ITN coverage of a major news event rather than BBC News.

It was something the 'Beeb' never forgot.

Man walks on the Moon – we sweat

To a journalist who had specialised in space coverage for 12 years, what happened on July 21, 1969, should have been the greatest story of all. I remember it for different reasons.

Firstly there was 'JOS' – Jackets Off Situation, as we termed it – when the three of us in the studio (Alastair, Paul Haney and myself) were allowed to appear in shirtsleeves for the first time, in recognition of the hottest night of the year. The temperature actually reached 92 F and we went into our 'live' coverage of the Moon landing with fans blowing the vapour from a semi-circle of blocks of 'dry ice' (solid carbon dioxide) at us, along the studio floor.

Then, on David's orders, we had to keep totally silent for five minutes before and five minutes after the actual touchdown on the Moon, to allow the astronauts' voices to be heard clearly by the viewer. I sat there watching a TV monitor with my hand clamped over my mouth.

To our great delight, James Burke and the other BBC pundits seemed not to have learned that lesson and viewers told us afterwards that it spoiled their show. Not only did some of them speak at crucial moments but they showed four different countdown clocks flickering away over the corners of the 'live' pictures from the surface of the Moon.

We told our story, during the self-imposed 10 minutes of silence, with the aid of one-line captions. These were programmed by Frank Miles and faded up onto the screen by Di Edwards-Jones – but only for as long as it took for the eye to read each one. Otherwise, the pictures from the Moon were left 'clean'.

My next memory was a feeling of anti-climax which persisted until Neil Armstrong and Buzz Aldrin decided to take their Moon walk earlier than scheduled. I had expected to feel elated during the historic occasion. Instead, it all seemed terribly routine. This was probably because we had all 'mugged up' the flight plan so thoroughly that we knew what was going to happen next – and it did. The only thing the flight plan couldn't tell us was what the first words from the Moon's surface would be.

They turned out to be, 'One small step for Man – one giant leap for Mankind'. Subsequently, I found out that the line had been written by Jan Armstrong, Neil's wife, and that he had fluffed it. What he should have said was 'One small step for a man – one giant leap for Mankind', which actually makes sense. (Jim Irwin, who drove the first Moon car, told me later 'He got it in the neck when he got home').

By the time NASA announced that, instead of having a sleep after all the post-landing checks on the LM had been completed, Armstrong and Aldrin would take their Moonwalk early, David Frost had finally handed the programme over to ITN and millions of viewers had gone to bed, intending to get up again around 5.30 a.m. to watch the men emerge.

We kept going.

The ghostly figures of the spacesuited men, hopping around in one-sixth gravity conditions and using their lunar tool-kit to good effect (without anything breaking) will never fade in my memory. It was riveting television.

When it was all over and the astronauts were back in the 'Bug', ITV took a commercial break. David Nicholas came into the studio with a 'Well done, chaps,' and then told us that one of us would have to remain in the studio to introduce a video tape recording (VTR) of the Moon walk, not once but again and again – until 6 a.m., our official transmission restart time. They all turned and looked at me.

I remember sitting in the studio throughout the night, feet up on the desk (when the camera was not focused on me) sipping champagne out of the upturned astronaut's ' helmet', until it was time to introduce the next VTR.

The *Guinness Book of Records* stated in its next issue that I had set 'a national record for continuous on-air appearance' – 17 hours 22 minutes and 16 seconds – but I would have preferred a different record. Before the Eagle landed, Alastair had been handed a news agency report about a viewer in Cheshire having won £10,000 for a £1 bet on man walking on the Moon 'before the end of this decade'. He had placed the bet three years earlier.

Seven years earlier, when von Braun was showing me his Saturns, I would have bet on that – and the odds would have been even longer. But it never occurred to me in those days that you could bet on such things.

From studio to pen and book

To do the Apollo 11 story full justice, I decided to write a book, called simply *Man on the Moon*. The publishing house of Arthur Barker agreed to produce it in hardback and Mayflower Books in paperback form.

I knew that I had rivals and that speed onto the booksellers' shelves would be crucial to sales success. The others were free to concentrate on their writing, whereas I had to help cover the story on TV as well.

It was agreed that the printers – Wilmer Brothers of Birkenhead for the hardback and Cox & Wyman of London and Reading for the paperback – would pre-set 11 chapters, leaving me to write Chapters One and Two (covering the landing and Moonwalk) as they were happening.

I booked into the Waldorf Hotel (just around the corner from ITN's studio) and set up my typewriter in a first-floor bedroom. Every moment that I was not needed in the studio was spent tapping out the story with one finger (nobody has ever taught me to use more).

I finished the two chapters – 10,000 words – just 20 minutes after President Nixon finished greeting the returned astronauts on the deck of the carrier USS *Hornet* in the Pacific. A taxi rushed it round to Arthur Barker's offices in Winsley Street. There then began a most frustrating month.

I discovered that, in the agreement struck between Arthur Barker and Mayflower Books, there was a clause barring the paperback from appearing on sale earlier than three weeks before the hardback was ready.

The paperback was printed in a week – the hardback not for seven. During the interval, tens of thousands of copies of *Man on the Moon* sat locked away in a warehouse somewhere in the Home Counties, waiting for the Birkenhead printers to complete their more expensive version.

To make it worse, I walked into the Kingsway branch of W. H. Smith a fortnight after splashdown to find a major promotion taking place for one of my rivals' books, *Invasion of the Moon, 1969*. It had a clear run of the market for a fortnight.

Even more galling was to discover that the author was none other than Peter Ryan, the brother of Nigel – my editor at ITN!

CHAPTER TWELVE

Action Man to the Rescue

A pollo 12 was the mission where the men walking on the Moon burned out their TV camera, hit it with a hammer for good measure and left ITN facing hours of booked broadcasting time and no pictures.

Pete Conrad and Alan Bean were due to recover pieces of an old Surveyor robot which had been sitting on the Moon for four years: scientists wanted to see how the materials had stood up to the hostile environment of the Moon. Among our visual aids, for coverage of that mission, we had obtained a beautifully-engineered one-fifth scale model of Surveyor from Hughes Aircraft Corp. ITN Graphics had built a table 'moonscape', out of papier mâché and grey sand, on which to stand it.

With no pictures (other than one unchanging view of Mission Control in Texas), we were all worried about how we were going to illustrate the 'live' broadcasts from the lunar surface. Then, over breakfast, someone remembered that the toy 'Action Man' was to the same scale as the model of the Surveyor spacecraft on our sand-table.

At 9 a.m, Malcolm Beatson raced to Hamleys in Regent Street and bought the astronaut version of 'Action Man'. Our broadcast was due to start at 10.30 a.m. In that time, his graphics team succeeded in painting, dressing and equipping the model to look like Pete Conrad, who had the task of cutting bits off the old Surveyor.

We positioned the little man next to the three-legged spacecraft, just as the programme title-music, *Footprints on the Moon,* was starting.

'Astronaut sound' came through clearly over the satellite link and I spent the next two hours crawling, out of sight of camera, to adjust the position of Action Man (vis-à-vis Surveyor) to match the 'live' commentary. The scene was so realistic that Di had to keep putting the caption 'Simulation' over it. Several times, over 'selective talk-back', I heard a Welsh voice saying, 'Thank Christ for that bloody model'. It gave us pictures to sub-title which were relevant to the mission: the BBC had only 'talking heads'.

A question from the Queen

Shortly before Apollo 12, ITN had moved its entire operations into a brand-new studio-cum-office complex at 48 Wells Street.

The official opening by the Queen happened to coincide with that mission and it was arranged that she would formally open the new building by pulling a cord to reveal a plaque, temporarily mounted on the wall of Studio 1, before going upstairs to the Newsroom. She was then to press a button in the Control Room to start the 5.50 p.m. news bulletin.

Studio 1 was where we had our Moon 'set', including the sand table. It was agreed that she would meet the Board of ITN in the studio, walk to the plaque and pull the chord, then be introduced to David Nicholas, Alastair Burnet, Paul Haney and myself before going upstairs.

Paul Gawith (the studio floor manager) wearing headphones, was to let us know when the Royal party had arrived and this he did with the cry, 'Her Majesty has arrived at the front door'.

At this, several of the 13 Board members – dressed in their Sunday best shot to attention. They remained so, looking increasingly sheepish and I heard Alastair murmur, 'I'd like to see the door open, a whole load of OBEs thrown in and a voice say "they're up for grabs".' At that moment, the studio door did indeed open and the Queen walked in, accompanied by Nigel Ryan, then Editor.

We had obtained a handsome, 1/50th scale model of the Lunar Module from Grumman Aircraft Corp. and David Nicholas presented this to the Queen after she had opened the curtains hiding the plaque. 'That'll go very nicely on the nursery mantelpiece,' she replied. I then showed her the sand table, explained Action Man – and off she sped to meet the Newsroom staff.

We were all very tired. Most of us had had little sleep and the tension of the 'live' Moon walk was over. My blindness had taught me to cat-nap whenever possible and so I put my feet up on the sand table and asked Paul Gowarth to 'wake me on lift-off'. He did so, just before the bulletin started. But it seemed an unusually long time before the ITN logo disappeared off our monitor screens and the face of Andrew Gardner, one of the newscasters that evening, appeared.

After the bulletin had finished, the Queen agreed to meet the staff more informally in the upstairs Club and we piled into lifts to be there ahead of her. Carpets had been specially laid. I happened to be standing with a group of three other ITN reporters, near the entrance, when the swing doors opened.

The Queen came straight to me. 'Mr Fairley,' she said. 'How do you do it?' I thought, 'What a question from a Queen!' And asked her what she meant.

'How do you manage to go to sleep just before all that exciting news goes out?', she replied.

'I didn't realise you saw that, ma'am.'

'Saw it?' She said, with a twinkle in her eye, 'I saw it on a dozen television sets.' I realised then that the picture from the camera focused on the sand table area must have been switched by the vision mixer to every 'spare' monitor in the control room. 'What is more,' she went on, 'you were actually snoring.'

Her mood was so light-hearted that I felt emboldened to say something back. 'Can I ask you a question, ma'am?' She nodded. 'How come you are the only person who's been allowed to start the news five seconds late?'

'That's a very good question.' she answered. 'Was it only five seconds? You would have thought, with all the button-pushing that I've done in my life, that they would have trusted me on my own. But there were so many fingers trying to do it for me that it took me time to reach it.'

Everyone at ITN that night has their favourite Queen story. Andrew Gardner's is of what happened when the Queen reached the Newsroom.

He and Reggie Bosanquet used to sit opposite each other at a desk equipped with old-fashioned typewriters. On these, they would compose the 'bongs' – headlines for *News at Ten*. They were working on these when the Queen and her entourage approached.

Andrew recalls:

Suddenly, with the Queen no more than six feet away, Reggie leaped from his seat, elbowed me out of the way and typed in a new top story headline. He then stood respectfully aside as Nigel Ryan, David Nicholas and Her Majesty reached my desk. I glanced down with growing horror at what Reggie had just typed and quickly spooled it out of sight.

After the usual niceties, David – who had spotted the sheet of paper in my typewriter – said: 'Andrew, I'm sure Her Majesty would be interested to see how you are getting on with this evening's headlines.'

I could feel the sweat dripping down my neck. I fixed David with a lethal glare and said : 'I don't think so David – they're not ready yet.' To cover my embarrassment, I grabbed the circulated list of available stories and began a garbled explanation to the Queen as to which would make 'bongs'.

When the Royal party had moved off, I ripped the sheet of headlines from the typewriter and tore it into pieces.

In capital letters, at the top, Reggie had typed: 'ONE OLD QUEEN MEETS ANOTHER'.

Secrets of sound

Working at the new ITN House – next to the Middlesex Hospital and close to Wells Street Magistrates Court – was like exchanging the cramped conditions of a submarine for the spaciousness, if not of a battleship, at least of a cruiser.

Six floors instead of two; a penthouse restaurant and bar, two studios instead of one, with 70 adjustable lights in the ceiling and a huge, curved backcloth (known as a cyclorama or 'cyc') in the larger studio; a scenery or 'props' store between both; four cameras, instead of two, on the floor of the larger studio and three in the smaller; and a host of film editing machines, video tape recorders, preview and commentary rooms located within easy reach of the Newsroom – even a make-up room. We were no longer the poor brother of the TV world, 'making do' with obsolete equipment in cramped conditions, but a state-of-the-art television station proud of its assets.

With prior warning, we began to show wives, partners, families and friends around the new empire, usually ending up in reserved seats at the back of the Control Room to watch a news bulletin go out. I never knew a guest who departed without being amazed by the tension and precision of it all.

The highlights of my personal, conducted tours were always Teleprompter and 'grams'. 'Grams' was short for 'gramophone records' but it also included cassettes and tapes containing recordings of hundreds of different sound effects. This was the empire of Alfie Wilson, a short, shy man who was a genius at finding the right music or sound effect to 'underlay' a particular scene or programme – or at creating his own. For example, Alfie formed the volunteer ITN Choir, one of whose tasks was to record World War Two songs for use over shots of the D-Day beaches, or whistle World War One tunes for shots of the trenches.

One of Alfie's team was Josie, a motherly figure with an amazing memory, who could pull a 'gram' from its storage rack almost without looking. She used to put on a party piece to impress on guests the importance of sound to TV news. First, she would play a recording of a reporter's commentary without any sound underlay – just total silence. 'Boring, isn't it?' She would ask. 'Sounds as though there's something wrong.'

Next she would play the same recording but mix in a little 'atmos' natural background sound, recorded on record or tape. It might only be the sound of an empty room, or a quiet garden. 'Makes all the difference – sounds real,' she would point out. 'Want to hear the Queen going up the Thames in *Britannia*?'

Josie would pull seven or eight records or cassettes from her library and mix in one after another. First, we would hear the thrum of *Britannia*'s engines and the turning of her screws: then she would add in the cries of seagulls, then the 'whoop-whoops' from Thames tugboats, followed by a gun salute from the Royal Horse Artillery at the Tower of London and finally the cheers of crowds lining the Embankment.

Her *coup de grâce* was to tell my parties of visitors that virtually every rifle shot or burst of machine-gun fire heard in film reports of the Vietnam war was not recorded in Vietnam but supplied by 'grams' and laid over the pictures at ITN by herself or one of her colleagues. 'I like to think that we helped to save lives,' she would say. 'The system avoided the need for a sound recordist to go onto the battlefield – only a cameraman.'

Danger in the letter 'S'

Shortly after Apollo 12 returned safely to Earth, I was asked by Thames Television to appear again on their children's programme *Magpie*. By then, I had become *Magpie*'s unofficial science reporter, commenting on a variety of topics but mostly on events in space.

Compared to the pressure of ITN, the fairly relaxed atmosphere of the *Magpie* studio at Teddington was welcome and I was always made to feel at home by the youthful presenters – Tony Bastable, Susan Stranks, Pete Brady and, latterly, Douglas Rae.

On this particular day, Pete was giving a party after the 'live' transmission and he invited me to drive back with him to his Chelsea mews flat, wash off the make-up and become the first guest. As more guests arrived, I found no difficulty in downing several champagne cocktails until, suddenly, Pete appeared saying 'ITN's on the phone'.

How they tracked me down I never found out. But Frank Miles broke the news that the first pictures of the Apollo 12 Moonwalk, taken by the astronauts, were on their way to London Airport. ITN would be mounting a 'special' at 11.30 p.m. I was to front the programme.

I took a taxi back and went straight to the saloon bar of the 'Green Man', just beside our studios. 'A baguette of French bread, some cheese and a jug of lime juice, please,' I said. As soon as they were finished, I ordered a second round.

As mentioned earlier, there is no greater 'crime' in television than to appear drunk on air. It is a cruel medium, not only reproducing the sound of words being slurred but showing up, on camera, tiny blood vessels in the nose and cheeks which the human eye cannot see.

Fortunately, I had only to speak a couple of sentences to camera – to introduce the Moon pictures which were taken by cameras on the astronauts' chests, after the TV camera had been broken. But I also had to speak about 20 minutes of commentary off-camera. I prayed hard that the 'blotting paper' would work.

I went into the studio with a sickening feeling that this could be my last appearance on TV. However, I had worked out two opening sentences to speak to camera, neither of which contained the letter 'S'. I had also decided to speak as little as possible over the pictures.

The studio camera went 'live' and I forced myself to look alert and speak the two sentences without slurring. Then I settled back, out of vision, and spent the time finding words of commentary which had as few 'Ss' as possible. They came out at an average rate of one sentence a minute: the 'blotting paper' was only partially working.

Totally drained, I left the studio and passed the ITN switchboard where Jo Redding, the senior operator, was trying to cope with a deluge of calls. I feared the worst. But to my amazement, Frank told me next day that most of them carried the same message: 'That's one of the best programmes ITN has done.'

As David Nicholas had realised six months earlier, when the pictures are good silence is golden – silence without an 's', that is.

Apollo 13

By the time the next Apollo spaceship – Apollo 13 – was ready to leave Earth, the BBC had decided it was more than time that they won back their audience for space news. I have never been able to find out the total of their budget for covering that ill-fated mission but it was reputed to be £250,000.

With the money, they built a huge studio 'set', including life-size replicas of the Command and Service modules and the Lunar 'Bug', together with mock-ups of many of the items of equipment which were due to be used during the mission.

By co-incidence, I happened to be sitting outside the Board-room – again talking to the Editor's secretary – when Lew Grade came out . This time he barely glanced at me but snarled out of the side of his mouth, 'Space is dead' – and walked on.

We learned that there would be no special budget and that the ITV companies would allow no extra airtime to be given to that mission. Almost as if to rub it in, the BBC started to trail their coverage of Apollo 13 earlier than usual, showing their new 'set' again and again, to attract viewers.

The excellent film *Apollo 13*, screened 25 years after the event, gives a pretty accurate representation of what happened two days after Jim Lovell, Fred Haise and Jack Swigert set off from Earth on what most of America (and certainly Lew Grade) believed would be a routine – and therefore boring – mission.

At precisely 5.11 p.m.- half an hour before our early evening news bulletin instruments at Mission Control in Houston regis-tered a major malfunction aboard the spacecraft. A few minutes later, the voice of Jim Lovell came through.

It is at this point that the film is in error (not that it matters much). It depicts Lovell as saying 'Houston, we have a problem.'

In fact, he said, 'Houston, we've *had* a problem.' Because, by then, the crew had been able to work out roughly what the problem was. A short-circuit had ignited insulation close to one of the oxygen tanks linked to the No. 2 fuel cell, causing it to explode and rip off a complete side-panel from the Service Module. It also caused a total loss of electrical power.

Suddenly, everybody became alive to the drama. Unfortunately, because of the budget cut-back, ITN had no special visual aids when the explosion occurred. But we did have Airfix models of the different spaceships and I remember going to the 'loo' with a pair of scissors and cutting a jagged hole in the side of the Service Module to indicate where the explosion had occurred. We made it in time for the news bulletin but it remained virtually our only visual aid for the next four days: we watched life-sized demonstrations going on in the BBC studio with frank envy.

The world held its breath as engineers at Houston worked out a course of action, using the Lunar Module as a 'lifeboat'. In this, the crew could conserve their resources and just about survive. The astronauts steeled themselves against the intense cold and the build-up of expired carbon dioxide.

The plan also involved the crew firing their main engine to send themselves around the back of the Moon before heading for home. ITV agreed that we should put on a 'special' to cover this crucial manoeuvre – the slightest error and they would be lost in space and die from lack of oxygen.

In any event, it would be a night of tension, which might end up as a marathon programme and the deaths of three brave men.

An unusual panel of pundits assembled in the ITN studio for the open-ended programme – not only 'experts' on space and space medicine but people who had faced near-impossible odds during their lives and overcome them. Among these was another of my personal heroes – Douglas Bader, the legless wartime fighter ace – and I remember David Nicholas having a problem helping him to his seat on the 'set', which had originally been designed for that day's coverage of The Budget.

Hastily added to that 'set', but out of sight, was an item which had been built originally into the Apollo 12 'set' – a small refrigerator, to fit under my desk. For Apollo 12, it had been filled with white wine, a bottle of gin and some tonics.

Remembering how 'horses necks' had stimulated the *Evening Standard*'s reporting team during the grim night of the Lewisham train disaster many years previously, I stocked the fridge. this time with brandy and bottles of dry ginger ale.

As midnight passed, the story became a series of peaks and troughs – peaks of excitement, as crucial manoeuvres were carried out, and troughs of waiting to see the results. There were unusually long periods of silence from the spaceship because of the need to conserve the astronauts' energy and power supply.

These gaps provided plenty of opportunity for our pundits to make their contributions and for me to swallow some Dutch courage.

The final moments of the engine 'burn' were almost unbearable. The silence went on much longer than expected and it began to look as though the worst had happened. Suddenly, we heard Jim Lovell's voice.

I am not sure why the studio camera turned to me at this point but I remember making some emotional comments, with a tear or two trickling down my cheeks, before Alastair closed down the programme. It was nearly 3.30 a.m. As the guests left the studio, I noticed that the brandy bottle was half empty.

Next morning, Nigel Ryan called me into his office. As programme's go, it had been a success. But he said simply: 'Don't ever do that again – don't ever let your emotions show on air.'

I no longer believe it was the brandy. When I saw the film 25 years later in a Leicester Square cinema, I blubbed again – at the same point and just as much. Tension and relief are powerful emotions and Hollywood had managed to capture them perfectly.

The watch that went to the Moon

It is ironic that it took a near-disaster to re-kindle the fickle public's interest in Moon missions but we never encountered a problem in getting extra air-time to cover Moon missions again.

Paul Haney was dropped from the team (on the grounds that his expert knowledge of the Apollo project was becoming outdated) but he was replaced on each programme by an actual astronaut who had flown to the Moon – first Dick Gordon (Command Pilot aboard Apollo 12) and then Jim Irwin (who drove the first Moon car during Apollo 15). As personalities, they made an interesting contrast.

Dick was met at London Airport by Frank Miles and said,

almost straight away: 'Frank – I'll be frank. I'm only here really for two things – booze and birds.' Jim arrived six months later with a question: 'Is there anywhere where I can get a game of tennis?'

We managed to supply all their needs and there is little doubt that the astronauts found ITN's informality and friendliness to their liking. After one particular night on the town, Dick Gordon took his watch off his wrist and pressed it into my hand, saying, 'Pete, I'd like you to have this as a memento of my visit.'

The U.S. astronauts were supplied with Omega watches with certain extra features – a built-in stopwatch and the equivalent of a tachograph around the rim. This one had the added attraction of having been, apparently, to the Moon.

I waited until next morning before producing it again. 'You may not remember giving me this last night.' I said. 'I can't possibly accept it.'

'I remember perfectly well – and I want you to have it.' Dick said, murmuring something about having 'sold my soul to the digital guys' and needing to be seen wearing digital watches.

The stopwatch on the Omega proved really useful for timing scripts and editing recordings and I wore it constantly: but I wondered for a long time whether it really had been on Dick's wrist as he circled the Moon. Then it started to lose time (due to a speck of dust) and I was obliged to take it into Omega's service bureau in London for repairs. Omega keep a record of the serial numbers of 'VIP watches' and, when I told them that this one had once belonged to Dick Gordon, they checked.

It had indeed been used during the Apollo 12 flight.

Curiously, the watch went in for repair just prior to the first Apollo–Soyuz mission – a mission to link an Apollo spaceship with a USSR Soyuz spaceship 140 miles above the Earth and transfer two of the U.S. crew into the Soviet cabin. The actual transfer coincided with *News at Ten* and I had to comment on the 'live' pictures. For five minutes, there was plenty of action. Then nothing much happened until, suddenly, the left wrist of cosmonaut Alexei Leonov appeared to float up towards the on-board camera and we saw, plainly – an Omega watch.

'That's interesting. ' I said into the microphone. 'That's the space watch which the Americans used on their Moon missions. The Apollo crew made a gift of three of those to the Soyuz crew when they were training together for this flight.'

Hardly had I made the comment when the mid-news commercial break started. When this happens, the ITN studio goes 'dead' and everybody bustles about, getting ready for Part 2 of the News. Those in the studio have no idea what ads are being shown during the break (ITN has no involvement in commercials they are sold, produced and transmitted from elsewhere in ITV).

As soon as the news ended, I was summoned to Nigel Ryan's office. 'I've had a complaint from a member of staff that you deliberately 'plugged' the Omega space watch,' he said. 'In fact, it's suggested that you are in the pay of Omega. Are you?'

I did not understand. I had not mentioned the name Omega when I drew attention to the watch during the 'live' telecast. Who was putting the boot in?

Nigel explained that the commercial break had begun with an ad for the space watch, naming Omega as the manufacturer.

'I was totally unaware of that,' I explained, 'and I'm certainly not getting any back-handers from Omega – or anyone else, for that matter.'

'I was sure that was the case.' said Nigel. But he refused to name his informant.

It was the only unpleasant experience I had during 18 years of working for ITN. But next morning I rang the watch repairer. 'Just in case you might have been thinking of repairing that VIP watch free of charge,' I said, 'please don't. I shall pay when I pick it up – and I'd like a receipt.'

'Freebies' and the ethical code

Although ITN is part of commercial television, it has always fought to remain untainted by commercial pressures. Reporters are not allowed to appear in advertisements, nor to accept money or gifts from manufacturers, nor to accept 'free' flights.

I had to refuse several lucrative offers and the only 'freebie' I ever took was a lunch at Au Savarin restaurant in Charlotte Street. I went there with Jim Irwin, who had come hotfoot from London Airport with a lump of Moon rock which he had collected during his 'drive' in the strange-looking Moon 'car' on Apollo 15.

The piece of Moon, weighing about a quarter of a pound, was on a velvet cushion locked inside a steel box. Jim refused to hand it in at the cloakroom, insisting on keeping it under his chair while we ate. Afterwards, he hurried back to ITN alone, while I finished my coffee and settled up. 'Were there diamonds inside your friend's case?' Queried the *Maitre d'*, conversationally, as he presented the bill on a saucer. 'He seemed very anxious about it.'

'Not diamonds,' I said. 'Something more valuable.' I explained that my guest was Colonel James Irwin, U.S.A.F., who had been to the Moon on Apollo 15 and who, during his drive in the first Moon 'car', had collected samples of rock, one of which NASA had allowed him to bring to London.

'You mean it was Moon rock under that chair – under one of our restaurant chairs? Exclaimed the *Maître d'*. 'Hey, Mario, hey Luigi come here.' Two other waiters in tails came over and all three spent a while chattering in Italian and pointing at the patch of carpet where the steel box had lain, as if it had started to glow with fluorescence.

'*Signor*, it is a privilege,' he added. 'Your meal is complimentary.'

I gave up arguing.

'Slots' galore

The final four Apollo missions went like clockwork.

Apollo 14 – with a landing in the hilly Fra Mauro region of the Moon by Alan Shepard and Stuart Roosa, leaving Ed Mitchell circling in the Command Module above – stands out in the memory for two particular reasons.

One was that, in the cause of science, Shepard had smuggled a golf club and some balls into his tool-kit in order to test the effects of one-sixth gravity on a golfer's drive. Unfortunately, NASA took a stuffy attitude and the camera was never allowed to show it.

The second was because Nigel and David negotiated enough airtime from 'the network' for us to hold a phone-in with viewers posing questions 'live' to Alastair and then Alastair turning either to our resident astronaut (Dick Gordon) or to me for answers.

Di, with her lightning reactions, was in the Control Room, ready to 'pull the plug' on any viewer who tried to swear or be obscene, but none did, although I believe that a four-second delay was put into the line to ensure that she had time to act.

As a yardstick of the revival of public interest in the Moon, we were allowed to broadcast no fewer than nine special programmes – one of them three hours long – to tell the story of Apollo 14. Space was most certainly not 'dead'.

For Apollo 15, we had a lot of fun – or rather others did – with a life-size model of the Lunar Roving Vehicle, or 'Moon Car'. Each time the studio was opened up, it had either travelled to some new position or was loaded with a bizarre cargo. But the TV pictures of the real Moon Car, driven by Dave Scott and Jim Irwin around a feature known as Hadley Rille, were so fascinating that we hardly used our studio dummy.

The astronauts spent more than 19 hours on the lunar surface and went either for a walk or a drive three times. We covered each excursion. One interesting feature was that the car (which they nicknamed 'the bucking bronco') bounced around so much in one-sixth gravity that they had to wear seat-belts, even though the maximum speed was only 8 m.p.h.

Getting Jim for our studio team for the last two Apollo missions was something of a coup and his expertise and quiet comments somehow had a calming effect on all of us. He was one of three astronauts who had felt an overpowering closeness with God on the Moon – indeed, by the final Apollo landing he had founded an evangelical mission in Colorado Springs called 'High Flight' with the object of using his extra-terrestrial experiences to help recruit 'believers' from all around the world. But apart from giving each of us an autographed copy of his book, *High Flight*, he never thrust religion down our throats or even voluntarily raised the subject when he was with us.

It is always inexplicable when such a man, a 'doer' rather than a talker, a keep-fit fanatic, abstemious in habits, a man with a true vision of the future, should be pole-axed by a heart attack and die before he was 60.

With Jim Irwin available and a well-organised team thoroughly familiar with the mechanics of Moon missions and their TV coverage, the last two Apollos posed no problems for ITN – except how to cope with the sense of anti-climax after they were over. The energy and sense of camaraderie which they engendered, not just within the Space Unit but within the whole of ITN, is something I shall always treasure.

But space apart, getting 'network' approval for anything smacking of feature (as opposed to news) material was still extremely difficult: sure enough, the documentary which I had in mind, drawing the whole Apollo story together using the voices of the scientists, engineers and astronauts who actually made it happen, was rejected as an ITN production.

So I hawked the idea around.

Anglia TV were the first to respond. They said they liked it and appointed John Phillips (ex-ITN) as Producer/Director, which suited me fine, and Brian Connell as Editor. After agreeing a script and a list of the Americans whom we should feature in the story, John and I set off for New York, where we picked up a TV crew, before going on to Washington, New Orleans, Cape Kennedy, Huntsville and finally the Johnson Space Centre near Houston and its surrounding astronaut community.

Everyone bent over backwards to give us what we needed. My previous visits to Houston paid off and we were not only handed, free-of-charge footage of the missions themselves which had never previously been seen, but allowed an even rarer opportunity – access to the wives of the lunarnauts.

They were pleased to be interviewed. Lurton Scott, wife of David Scott of Apollo 15, told me that when they looked up at the Moon at night, 'We don't look at it as the romantic thing some people sing about – we see it as an old friend which Dave has visited and where, some day, he may go again.'

She revealed that, when the Apollo 15 capsule splashed down safely into the ocean, she was watching the drama on TV when the doorbell rang. 'A man was standing there with a bouquet of roses.' She went on, 'Dave had ordered them to be delivered at the exact moment of splashdown.'

Sue Bean, wife of Alan Bean of Apollo 12, recalled how her husband had taken her into a flight simulator during training and shown her a group of craters on the Moon model called The Snowman. 'On the night he landed, I heard him say I have The Snowman in sight.' She went on,' It was his private way of telling me everything was all right.'

Dick Gordon of Apollo 12, who had given me the Omega watch, told the film crew I look up at the Moon now and say, 'Gee – I wish I could go back again.'

Dr Thomas Paine, who headed NASA during the whole of Apollo, was more sombre. He told me that when he looked at the Moon, he only saw 'missions where we might have lost astronauts.'

'Occasionally I see a ghostly Flying Dutchman of a spacecraft circling the Moon.' He went on, 'Then I see the future and think to myself that, before the end of this century, the first human child will be born on the Moon.'

Wishful thinking, Tom.

Tom Paine made a phone call and soon we found ourselves the first media men ever to be allowed to film inside the Astronaut Office at Houston – the 'holy of holies' where each spaceman had his own room, decorated with his own space souvenirs, family photographs, awards and trophies. We met most of the Gemini and Apollo astronauts, some on camera, some privately, but I discovered a fact of life which I would rather had been kept secret.

Cy Baker, the head of the office, took us into a small room flanked with pigeon holes containing portrait photographs of every astronaut. In the centre, a giant photocopier was churning out colour copies of the crew of Apollo XI – Neil Armstrong, 'Buzz' Aldrin and Michael Collins – wearing spacesuits and standing in front of a large-scale Apollo mission badge.

To my horror, I noticed that when the photographs came out of the photocopier they were overprinted with the men's signatures. 'To cope with public demand,' Cy explained, 'it was the only solution. Otherwise they'd have died by now from writer's cramp.'

After that, I made sure that any autograph which I collected also had some personal message beside the signature.

We were only in Houston for three nights but on one of them I called up Paul Haney, our friend from ITN Moon coverage days, who was then living in a beach house at Galveston, 20 miles south along the Texas highway. 'C'mon down for a barbie,' he insisted.

It was a warm summer's evening and we had finished all our filming, so we had no other commitments. We changed into casual clothes and I drove John to the beach house.

After just one glass of white wine (the smallest amount in an evening for years) a plateful of grilled 'links' (U.S. sausages) and many reminiscences, we set off up the highway around midnight. After about 18 miles, we came to lines of rapidly – flashing lights, indicating road repairs and guiding us down a kind of funnel. After exiting the funnel, there were several more wooden barriers and I became confused as to which of the two lanes to drive in.

Since there was no other traffic, I decided to stay in the middle.

After a minute or so, I vaguely noticed a flashing yellow light in the rear mirror. But there were so many flashing yellow lights, by then that I took no notice especially since it stayed roughly in the same position.

Suddenly, it moved and a siren wailed loudly. I pulled onto the hard shoulder as a Texas Highway Patrol car shot to a halt in front of me, blocking my path.

Two young patrolmen got out with guns already in their hands. 'Spread,' one said. 'Put your hands on the car, feet apart.' I had seen it done on the movies. What I was not expecting was the violence of their 'frisking', which included squeezing my private parts. 'OK, let's see your driver's licence,' said the more Spanish-looking of the two.

'I don't have it with me,' I said. 'We're from England and I left it in my room at the motel.'

I explained that we were filming a documentary about Project Apollo and had been visiting a friend at his beach house in Galveston; because it was such a warm evening, we had put on sleeveless shirts and slacks and come with nothing but a few dollars. Everything else was back in the Kings Inn at Clear Lake.

'I am arresting you, sir, for not carrying a driver's licence and for crossing the median line in the road. You must accompany me – Officer Delgado will drive your car with your friend,' he rapped out.

We drove in convoy for about 5 miles until we came to a low brick-built building with the sign 'Texas Highway Patrol – La Marque'. I was booked in, after another body search, and led through into a room with four iron-barred cells. John was left, sitting on a bench by the booking clerk. Each cell was occupied.

I was still in a state, if not of shock then of surprise, especially when two of the occupants, clearly drunk, mouthed obscenities at me. The patrolman told them to shut up and indicated that I should enter a fifth 'cell' – a rope cage, hanging from the middle of the police station ceiling.

It was swinging gently and resembled one of those rescue baskets lowered down from a helicopter to astronauts, after splash-down. But at 2.a.m in a Texas jail, the only appeal it had for me was as an additional barrier against the drunks.

By now I was getting annoyed. I demanded to be allowed to use a telephone to contact the British Consul in Houston. But that bit of bluster merely prompted the question, 'Sir, would you like us to breath-test you?'

Although I had drunk only one glass of wine at Paul's, I was not sure if Texas State law allowed a driver any alcohol in his veins. So I shut up and waited for the inevitable paperwork.

It was explained to me that I could leave only if I deposited 'bail bonds' of a sum set by a judge. It was by then 3 a.m. They said they could provide the judge, despite the hour, if I accepted the terms he set (two bonds, eventually, at $25 each.) I only had $20 with me but John stumped up the balance.

We were both furious and almost decided to drop the Moon video and substitute one about the Texas Highway Patrol. But after breakfast, I rang Paul, who said he knew a lawyer who would handle it and I should try to forget the incident.

Obviously, I never have. But Paul's lawyer friend was a World War Two bomber pilot, who said he had spent 'many happy days' with the Suffolk folk in the Bentwaters area and was upset to hear of my experience. He managed to get $25 rebate on the grounds that it would have been nearer to have driven to my motel to see the licence than to have locked me up at La Marque.

But I am still $25 worse off – for crossing a white line in Texas. However, I did receive a letter of apology from the Police Commissioner at La Marque, saying that his men had 'over-reacted'.

The one-man Olympics

In the absence of anyone professionally qualified, I was asked to cover medical – as well as science – news for ITN. One of the first assignments was to fly out to Mexico City to film a 'curtain-raiser' for the 1968 Olympic Games, which had been nicknamed 'the medical Olympics' because of the problems which the athletes would face performing in thin air, 5,000 feet above sea level.

Unfortunately, none of the athletes had arrived.

At school and in the Army, I had won cups for the 400 metres, which was the same distance as the track around the Olympic stadium. In order to demonstrate the effects of oxygen deprivation on runners at high altitude – without any runners there seemed little alternative to running the 400 metres myself and being filmed at the start and finish.

The local ITN 'stringer' – an American university lecturer

whose last camera commission had been in the Korean War 15 years previously – borrowed a pair of shorts, a T-shirt and some 'spikes' for me. It was arranged that I would run the complete circuit as fast as I could, to produce the maximum breathless effect, pick up the microphone lying on the grass by the finishing line and speak two memorised paragraphs of script to camera.

The American said he would switch off after the start and just film me in the final straight because he only had an old clockwork camera which would need to be re-wound after 20 seconds. So I would have to get the words right.

We started. I had barely completed 100 metres before the effects of high altitude began to make me pant hard. By 200 metres, I was straining for breath. As I entered the final straight, I was in distress and could see only a red mist. But somehow the finishing line passed below and I could just make out the shape of the microphone.

'They're calling these. . .' I gasped, with a huge gulp for air between phrases, '. . . the medical Olympics – "medical" because of the medical problems which the athletes will have to overcome next month due to the high altitude.' I forget the words of the second paragraph now but, whatever they were, I got them out without a 'fluff' and slumped to the ground, all energy gone.

'Geez,' said the cameraman, 'that was great. But I'll have to ask you to do it again because I lost you from frame for the last five metres and it'll look like it's faked.'

I was speechless, physically and metaphorically. And it was 20 minutes before I recovered sufficiently to run the last 50 metres again. This time he got it right – and the effect was just as dramatic. But in all the medals awarded at and after those Olympics, I made certain that there was not one for the cameraman

Was this the face of Jesus

I was about to go home early from ITN one afternoon, to go to a birthday party, when there was a call from Reception to say that a man, who would not give his name, was insisting on seeing me.

He turned out to be a young film director who had just completed a movie for an American Christian foundation about the Turin Shroud. 'We believe this shows the face of Christ conclusively,' he said, producing a can of film. 'If you haven't used it by tomorrow, I'll have to offer it to the BBC.'

I had never heard of the Turin Shroud but I was not going to admit it – the whiff of news was strong. We found a film editor who laced up the 16 mm film for us to watch. Fortunately, it began by explaining the background to the shroud.

The shroud itself was in Turin Cathedral, locked away behind glass. It was claimed to be the gravecloth in which Christ was wrapped after he was taken down from the Cross. Legend had it that it had been smuggled out of Jerusalem to Turkey, fell into the hands of the Crusaders in 1204 and finally reached Turin in 1578, after being partially damaged by fire.

For three centuries, the Turinos paid scant attention to it until, in 1898, a photograph was taken which caused a sensation. The faint ochre marks on the cloth suddenly came to life. With highlights and shadows reversed, a positive image appeared, in place of the negative: full-length back and front views of a naked, crucified man could be clearly seen.

But who was the man?

Two French scientists next presented a paper to the French Academy, stating that the marks were almost certainly a mixture of blood, sweat and embalming fluid – they had produced similar stains on cloth in their laboratory. 'The man of the shroud was Christ,' they concluded.

Then, in 1977, a team of American scientists were allowed to examine a small strip of the cloth and concluded that the marks were 'strongly suggestive of actual blood'. At the same time, all the photographic images taken of the shroud were sent to a U.S. Air Force space research laboratory for computer enhancement.

It was these last two pieces of detective work that the rest of the film was all about. I was fascinated. We watched as the computer turned a flat photograph into a 3-D image of a man with a long nose, straight lips, sunken eyes, long, tousled hair and a short, straggly beard.

Was this the face of Christ?

I thought, 'Either it is – in which case, I've been given the story of a lifetime or it isn't, in which case it's a fake. But it's a good story anyway.'

I thanked the director, promised to return his film next day, said goodbye and went in search of David Nicholas, then Editor. We replayed the whole film in a fourth-floor viewing theatre

'Christ,' he said, using both meanings of the word, 'let's get crack-ing.'

We had just two hours to transfer the film to video tape, write a script, edit the film and voice the commentary, before the recording had to be ready for *News at Ten*. We made it with two minutes to spare.

The fact that carbon-dating later put all the 'evidence' back into question and that the controversy over the shroud is still raging – is neither here nor there. That night, I had 'on air' my second-longest TV news report ever – 5 minutes and 45 seconds.

Pre-natal exercises in Yorkshire

When ITV was re-shuffled in 1967, the consortium of business-men and TV executives who were after the Yorkshire franchise invited Geoffrey Cox to prepare their case to put before the Independent Broadcasting Authority. Geoffrey, who had become Sir Geoffrey the previous year, was still Editor of ITN. So much had to be done undercover, which was not easy when you are surrounded by a closely-knit team of newshounds and rumours are rife.

My wife Helen (whom I married in 1987 some years after Vivienne, my first wife, died) was then Geoffrey's secretary. She recalls how hardly a day went by without some sleuth from the ITN newsroom trying a cunning approach to confirm the rumour. Fortunately, nobody suspected my involvement.

Geoffrey believed that Children's Programmes and Science should form important components of the consortium's plan and asked me to help write the Science part of the bid. I, too, was sworn to secrecy.

It was a great opportunity to put forward ideas which had been burning in the breast for several years and I thought hard for about a month before putting a plan for several documentaries – and whole series of science and technology programmes – on paper. It was an unwritten understanding that, if the bid succeeded, Geoffrey would take a senior management position and at least some of my ideas would become 'hard' projects.

The consortium won. Geoffrey chose to become Deputy Chair-man, a post with little influence over programme-making, but our ideas still seemed safe because Yorkshire's first Programme

Controller was to be none other than Aubrey Singer, Head of Science Features at the BBC, and a man with a reputation for making serious subjects interesting.

After the celebrations were over, a hectic period of studio construction, staff recruitment and programme planning started, mainly in Leeds. As so often happens when new ventures get under way, cliques gathered and power blocs quickly formed within Yorkshire, none of them including Geoffrey (who still had to spend most of his time at ITN to ensure a smooth take-over by the new Editor, Nigel Ryan) or Aubrey Singer (who still had to serve out a term of notice at the BBC).

Then came a shock. Aubrey decided to stay put at the BBC. It was announced that another BBC man – the live-wire Donald Baverstock, who had become a legend from his days with *Tonight* – would become Programme Controller instead of Aubrey.

'Don't worry,' Geoffrey assured me. 'When he's had time to settle in, I'll make sure he contacts you.'

Almost a year went by with no word from Baverstock. Then, one afternoon, he phoned me at *TV Times*. 'I'd like to see you next Wednesday evening – can you make it, boyo? I'll be having dinner in the Queens Hotel that evening, why don't you join me for coffee afterwards?'

Gee, thanks, Donald. Not 'would you like to join me for dinner?' but 'Why don't you join me for coffee afterwards?' However, I pocketed pride and accepted, got out the folder of ideas, arranged to stay the night in Leeds and, in due course, kept the date.

He hadn't suggested a time so I dined alone at a side table and, in due course, watched Baverstock, Ward Thomas (Yorkshire's Managing Director) and Tony Essex, another of the BBC 'old boys', have a well-lubricated, noisy dinner in the middle of the Queens' restaurant. Their coffee was served at 10 p.m. by which time I reckoned it was my turn.

He had clearly forgotten 'Who?' He queried as I introduced myself. 'Oh yes.' He then apologised to his fellow diners, who promptly took their leave, and started to speak volubly.

'Listen, boyo,' he started, 'you can forget about science programmes. All we're going to do is to make 13 programmes for youngsters about becoming an engineer.'

I was flabbergasted. Apart from his rudeness, it amounted to a complete rebuff for my carefully thought-through programme ideas, which were designed to dent the BBC's monopoly in the coverage of science.

He hardly let me get in a word and every time I went to open the folder, he held up a hand and said, 'I don't want to hear those.' Instead, we discussed the lives of great British engineers and current advances in technology At midnight, he got up, we shook hands and he left with the words 'So, boyo, if you want to earn a few bob, give me the names of 13 really good engineers and put them down on paper.'

It was the last time I saw Baverstock and the 13 part series *I Want to be an Engineer* came 'on air' within a year with no help from me. I am ashamed to say that I just could not swallow my pride. However, there was an interesting development two years later.

I learned that Baverstock received a phone call from the IBA in which he was asked, in no uncertain terms, what programmes Yorkshire TV had produced, or were in the process of producing, to keep the promises made in their franchise bid for substantial coverage of Science.

I was told that, as soon as he put the receiver down, he shouted from his office, 'Get me that bugger Fairley.'

Working on a lower floor at the Television Centre, Leeds, at that time, was a young producer called John Fairley. My informant told me that John was summoned immediately to Baverstock's office and told to prepare a series of Science programmes. He did so (and subsequently went on to become Programme Controller after Baverstock died).

But there was cause for further disappointment. With the entire world of scientific discoveries and advances to choose from for its new science series, Yorkshire decided to devote the whole of the first documentary – 50 minutes of airtime – to a surprising subject.

Rats!

CHAPTER THIRTEEN

Widening Horizons

ITN's coverage of the Apollo missions to the Moon led to many invitations to appear on other ITV programmes, some serious, some light-hearted.

One of the serious occasions was March 2 1969.

Wynford Vaughan-Thomas, the legendary BBC war correspondent but, at that time, Director of Programmes for Harlech TV, had invited me to cover the maiden flight of Concorde. The 'live' commentary would be fed by Harlech to the ITV Network.

Strictly speaking, it was a job for Richard Dixon, ITN's Air Correspondent, but he was also ITN's Industrial Correspondent and he was committed to attend a TUC conference on the date of the flight.

Wynford, with his lovely Welsh lilt and irrepressible sense of humour, was another of my heroes and I spent four days fact-finding at British Aerospace's Bristol factory to make sure that I had plenty of commentary material, in case the flight was delayed. I was keen to live up to Wynford's expectations.

The flight was due to last 30 minutes and take the airliner, at sub-sonic speed, from Filton aerodrome on the outskirts of Bristol to Fairford in Gloucestershire.

I assembled all the 'gee-whiz data' onto cards and loaded them into my Shannon file before reporting to one of Harlech's outside broadcast directors at the Filton control tower. There I also met Brian Epps, Concorde's flight engineer, who introduced me to his wife as well as to Mrs Cochrane (wife of the co-pilot) and Mrs Trubshaw (mother of the pilot).

We arranged for me to interview Mrs Epps in front of the control tower during the 'blank' 30 minutes while the airliner was in the sky, before it landed at Fairford. She would provide 'the human touch'.

A Harlech sound engineer then took me to the commentary point – an old telephone box, positioned on a mound overlooking both Concorde, as it waited to take off, and the control tower, where the relatives of the crew would be watching.

I felt a bit like Dr Who in the box, waiting to set off to meet the *Tardis*. It was so cramped that there was barely room for a 9-inch TV monitor and my chair. Using the tall, metal Shannon file was out of the question. So I unloaded the cards and stuck the most important ones around the bottoms of the windows, although I do not recall glancing at any of them: Concorde's history and statistics were firmly in the memory.

Take-off was perfect. My commentary felt comfortable – we showed a cutaway of the relatives smiling with relief immediately after the airliner's wheels had left the ground – and the interview with Mrs. Epps went well. Two hours later, I was on a train back to London.

At about 8 p.m., the telephone rang at my home. It was Wynford.

'Congratulations on today,' he started. 'Commentary at its best.' This from the maestro! 'I'm afraid, though, that we had to make an on-air apology this afternoon – I hope you don't mind.'

An on-air apology? For what?

Wynford explained that, after the networked 'live' broadcast, Harlech had received a phone call from a viewer in Yorkshire who said that she – not the woman described by me as 'Mrs Cochrane, the wife of the co-pilot' – was the real wife of James Cochrane. 'That woman is his common-law partner,' she had added, demanding a public apology.

'We took legal advice,' said Wynford, 'and apparently we would have been in the clear if you had left out the words "wife of" – merely referring to her as "Mrs Cochrane". "Wife of" made it actionable.'

'No sweat,' I said. 'I'm sure you appreciate that one can't go up to people whom you intend to mention on air and ask was she really married to that man. Anyway, you were jolly lucky that I held back what was on the tip of my tongue to add.'

'What was that?' asked Wynford.

'I was about to add – and very natty she looks today in a nice, new maternity outfit.'

A drop in the ocean

Harlech evidently forgave me because it was not long before they agreed to make a documentary – which I had submitted as a synopsis – about super-tankers.

It was the year after the *Torrey Canyon* disaster, in which that super-tanker had been driven onto rocks, splitting into pieces and discharging most of its oil.

This had resulted in a major pollution problem, leading to thousands of seabirds dying and marine life being affected for miles around.

During coverage of the accident, someone had told me that the average super-tanker needed 1.5 miles to come to a halt – a statistic which intrigued me and set me researching the whole super-tanker scene.

Harlech assigned one of their best young directors, Euryn Ogwen-Williams, to the programme – a Welsh speaker with a great sense of fun – and we arranged for British Petroleum to provide the 'star' – a super-tanker called *British Inventor*.

Super-tankers have to keep moving to be economical and we were told that under no circumstances should we delay the ship, which was sailing from Kuwait to Rotterdam. So we and the crew flew out to the Canary Islands and lived it up for a few days until the tanker drew level – then flew out by helicopter, to be lowered, one by one, onto the deck with the camera gear. The call came at 4 a.m. while it was still dark.

I remember three things about the trip. The first was that I was able to complete a year's overdue expenses for ITN, while not wanted 'on camera'.

The second was that, because of the risk of a tiny spark causing a fire, only a clockwork (not an electronic) camera could be used. This meant that all my speeches to camera had to be completed within 22 seconds – before the camera needed re-winding.

The third was the bicycle ride. *British Inventor* was nearly a quarter of a mile long and an old, sit-up-and-beg bike was provided to help any crew member who needed to check valves, or other equipment on deck, to get around.

We decided that filming a cycle ride, from the stern to the bow, would be the best way to illustrate the scale of things. So Euryn positioned the camera (and himself) on the bridge: I positioned myself on the saddle. At a wave from the director, I started pedalling towards the bow anchor.

I remember thinking that the Bay of Biscay was relatively calm that day. But the slight incline of the deck prevented me from seeing the actual swell.

Just as I reached the bow, the biggest wave I have ever known came up and over, drenching me and sluicing the bike along the deck until a projecting pipe finally brought us to a halt.

Euryn said it was the funniest thing he had ever seen in years of filming. And that one did make *It'll be Alright on the Night*.

Magpies and Beasties

Magpie appearances became even more frequent and, as 'one of the family' I was invited to take part in two Christmas shows in successive years.

For the first, each of us was asked to state our 'dearest wish'. I said mine was to 'fly' like Peter Pan and I remember Tony Bastable saying that his was to interview the Prime Minister.

Two days later, Thames TV's *Magpie* office rang to say that *Peter Pan* was not being performed in London that year. 'OK,' I said. 'What about *Mother Goose*? I've always wanted to play the goose.'

A researcher arranged an appointment with a theatrical costumier in Hammersmith, where I was kitted out with stockinged 'legs', webbed 'feet' and a one-piece, fibreglass body – like a yacht's hull – with feathered 'wings'. The 'neck' and a grotesque 'goose's head' were attached to the body separately.

I was told to pull on the leggings and climb into the outfit through a large hole in the underside of the fibreglass hull.

The following Tuesday, I reported to 'Wardrobe' at Thames' Teddington studios, to be helped again into the goose outfit. The presenters had spent the whole morning rehearsing, but they all attended one final dress rehearsal, which also involved me.

It was agreed that Sue Stranks, at the end of her 'dearest wish' item, would be startled by a goose waddling up to her. 'Hello, my dear, I'm Mother Goose,' I was to say, using a West Country accent.

She was then to reveal that the goose was actually Science Editor Fairley and explore the features of my costume – hidden toggles to make the huge eyelashes blink, separate 'legs' and a ledge within the fibreglass 'body', to allow an actor to store small 'props' (properties).

The props. I had chosen were a paperback novel, an alarm clock, a sandwich, a half-bottle of Drambuie and a liqueur glass. Having produced these, like gifts from Santa's sack, I was supposed to waddle off.

Rehearsal went well. So did 'live' transmission. But by the time it was over, the inside of the outfit had become insufferably hot and I decided to try to get out of it as quickly as possible, instead of waiting until the end of the show for Wardrobe's help.

As soon as I was 'off camera', I knelt down and tried to use the studio floor as a lever to push the fibreglass hull up over my shoulders. Unfortunately, I overbalanced and lay rolling about like a giant egg on the floor, helpless.

Possibly because it was Christmas, more probably because I had downed too much of the Drambuie during rehearsals, it all suddenly seemed terribly funny and I burst into a mad cackle, webbed feet kicking wildly. I knew that that should be safe because the next item – Tony Bastable's interview with Prime Minister Harold Wilson – had been pre-recorded and I had heard Tony explain his 'dearest wish' to the viewers and the studio go 'dead', as VTR rolled and the item started.

What I was unaware of, in the middle of my cackling, was that VTR had broken down and the studio had gone 'live' again, to allow Tony to apologise and give a summary of what the PM had said.

'Please don't ever do that again,' said a livid programme producer afterwards, 'the viewer must have wondered what the hell the 'noises off' were all about.'

I apologised. But I did feel it a pity that the studio director had not had the courage to swing a camera round to show the source of the cackling – a 'friend of *Magpie*' wishing, more than ever, that he could fly away like Peter Pan.

A dragon at Woburn

Despite the gaffe, I continued to be a 'friend of *Magpie*' and was invited to take part in the next Christmas 'special' – Christmas at Woburn Abbey.

Part of the objective was to use up the residue budget and no expense was spared to re-create a traditional, Victorian Christmas at a stately home, including paying the not-inconsiderable location and appearance fees of the 13th Duke of Bedford and his Duchess, the former French socialite, *Mme* Nicole Milinaire.

The Duke was charming, if a little absent-minded, but Nicole had a reputation for being 'difficult' – which she proceeded to live up to by delaying the 'shooting' of her scene (an interview with one of the presenters) for 90 minutes while she became finicky about her make-up.

I was to take part in two scenes – charades in the Great Drawing Room and a scene in the Duke's study where a miner would arrive, hot-foot from the laboratory of Sir Humphry Davy, with news of the invention of the miners' safety lamp.

For the latter, my face was blackened, I wore a dirty shirt, knee-breeches and helmet and carried a Davy lamp and a stuffed canary in a cage (miners used to test for methane gas by watching the antics of a live bird). For the charades, I was squeezed into the rubber costume of a gruesome-looking dragon, complete with 'spines' down the back and a flexible tail.

Because of the Duchess' arguments with her make-up lady, we were unable to 'shoot' either scene before lunch. The Thames OB unit numbered at least 12 (excluding actors) and 'Unit Catering', in a converted double-decker bus, had been laid on in the Abbey car park to cope with all the hungry mouths. We were given 30 minutes.

I wasn't hungry but I was thirsty. I didn't like the odours coming from the bus, so wrapping my dragon's tail into the driver's seat beside me, I drove off to Woburn village and found the 'Bedford Arms'.

The public bar had the usual lunch-time clientele – an elderly man and woman, three men playing dominoes, a couple of farm workers with pints of ale and a young man with oil-stained clothes – presumably a garage mechanic, waiting for a blowsy barmaid to finish pouring his lager.

The elderly couple carried on talking. The domino players never looked up. The farm workers looked up, then down again. The young man took his lager with hardly a glance and the barmaid kept a straight face as I said, through the dragon's teeth, 'A pint of bitter, please.'

I drank it, head pushed back and tail brushing the floor, and ordered another half before saying 'Goodbye' and leaving the pub. The 'Goodbye' responses sounded perfectly normal.

I am convinced that dragons must drink at the 'Bedford Arms' every day of the week . . .

What's on the other side?

Another programme idea which was accepted outside ITN – this one by Rediffusion – was for their religious *Last Programme*. It went on air just before the station shut down for the night.

With the development of new resuscitators, patient ventilators and life support machines, I had been interested for some time in seeking answers to such questions as 'When patients apparently die but are revived, are they conscious of 'crossing over'? Do they get a glimpse of what's on the other side'? Do they meet God?'

The idea was put up to Rediffusion as a week-long series and it was one of the last programmes they transmitted before the company lost its franchise to Thames Television.

I and the programme researchers located various men and women who had experienced clinical death, yet somehow revived. The interviews were interesting but disappointing, in that the nearest we got to evidence of 'crossing over' was a housewife who felt the sensation of travelling on a trolley down a long glass corridor into total blackness. She refused to acknowledge that what she had probably experienced was being taken, partly anaesthetised, on a trolley to a hospital operating theatre.

For the final Friday night programme, we had invited the Rector of Framlingham, Suffolk – Canon Martin Bulstrode – to comment on the descriptions given by the 'resurrected'. I had never met Martin before but, over wine in the Green Room, we formed an instant rapport. He had been a submarine commander and worked in the Oxford and Cambridge Mission in Southwark and had a rich, earthy laugh. He was also interested in space.

The time came to go into the studio for the interview. *The Last Programme* title music rolled. I summarised to camera what had emerged from the interviews earlier in the week and turned towards Martin. 'And with me tonight,' I began.

Suddenly my memory went. How did he pronounce his name? Was it Bulstrode or Bullstrode? I had heard it pronounced at least twice before but nervousness suddenly made me unsure.

'And with me tonight is the Rector of Framlingham, Canon Martin Bulstrode.' I knew in a split second that I had got it wrong but it became doubly apparent when the Canon's face reddened and he shouted . . . 'Bullstrode, man – like bullshit.'

Fortunately the programme was being recorded at 3.p.m. and not going out 'live'. We had a good laugh in the Green Room afterwards and my bullshitting Canon sent me a suitably irreverent Christmas card every year afterwards until, sadly, he died.

An acorn – but no oak tree

Phil Garner, then Assistant Head of Local News at Anglia TV was another who watched ITN's space coverage with enthusiasm. One afternoon, I had a phone call inviting me to Norwich to discuss 'something which might be of mutual interest'.

When shown into his office, I found Jim Wilson – Editor of the local news and current affairs programme *About Anglia* – there too. What they suggested did indeed interest me.

They asked if I would like to travel to Norwich every Monday and record five minutes of science or medical news for inclusion in that night's *About Anglia*. To distinguish it from the rest of the local news, they proposed calling it *Fairley's World*. They offered £75 a time, plus train fare.

Ever since taking part in the shaping of the first 13 *Tomorrow's Worlds* for the BBC, I had been trying to persuade executives in various ITV companies to mount a challenge to the BBC's highly popular programme – but to no avail. Might not *Fairley's World* be a little acorn from which a great oak could grow? In any event, five minutes was a lot of air-time compared to my normal average ration on ITN bulletins of 1–2 minutes. In word terms, it was the equivalent of a whole page newspaper feature as opposed to a single column.

I was introduced to *About Anglia's* director, Bill Perry, and in my enthusiasm offered to buy him lunch in the Royal Hotel opposite the old Corn Exchange (where Anglia had its studios) in order to talk through ideas. It was an unfortunate precedent. Bill was a friendly man but he turned out to have gourmet tendencies and he obviously thought I was being paid a 'star' fee, for he ordered nothing but the best every Monday for the next six months! He enjoyed our lunches so much that I hadn't the heart to say, 'It's your turn, Bill.'

We decided to give each *Fairley's World* a theme, rather than hop from one random item to another and the first theme was 'Labour-saving'. I had been collecting kitchen gadgets for years, so I packed them in a suitcase, along with a piece of film showing a robot lawnmower cutting a lawn while its master sat in a deckchair, and took the first train from Liverpool Street.

Rehearsals went fairly smoothly, Bill and I had lunch and then we recorded.

I remember donning an apron, standing at a kitchen table, then at a waterless sink, trying to stop my hands shaking. This was largely due to the floor manager mouthing 'Hurry up'. and gesticulating that, to avoid over-running, I would need to cut at least one demonstration. Fortunately, the film of the robot lawnmower ran without a hitch and earned the comment 'fascinating' in the *East Anglian Daily Times* next day, with no comment about the presenter.

Fairley's World days took on a pattern – early up the railway line, morning rehearsals, lunch in the Royal, record after lunch. For my fee, I was expected to generate the programme content, obtain any 'hardware' or demonstrators needed, pay for any entertainment (including Bill's lunch) and then cart the whole lot back to London again in the late afternoon all for £75. But there was another, less tangible reward – the 'slot' gradually lengthened. Viewers were writing favourable letters.

We covered 'spare part' and transplant surgery, satellite communications, technical improvements in TV, Post Office 'memory diallers' and anti-vandal systems for telephone kiosks, as well as more homely topics such as new fabrics and furniture materials.

Although the programmes were supposed to be about science and technology, I tried to introduce 'popular' ways of interesting the viewer. Three efforts stick in the memory in detail.

The first was the second *Fairley's World* we ever transmitted. The theme was 'Warmth at Home'. Manufacturers were persuaded to build different types of double-glazing in the studio, ordinary coal was burned in a revolutionary smokeless stove and, to demonstrate the effectiveness of a new kind of duvet, I arranged for a friend of mine called Carol who was a model, to appear from a deep-freeze, wrapped solely in the quilt.

'She can't wear nothing,' cried Bill, aghast. 'She must wear at least a night-dress.' So my friend was despatched to Wardrobe and returned for rehearsal in a rather old-fashioned gown which she clearly did not like.

The three of us talked about it over lunch, pointing out that a night-dress would reduce the impact of the item, because it would be introducing a second layer of insulation. But Bill was adamant. However, just before recording started, Carol – who was a striking brunette with a stunning figure – excused herself for a moment and went to the 'loo. When she returned, she climbed back into the deep-freeze with her back to the camera and snuggled down. Just before a studio hand closed the lid, she gave me a wink.

Sure enough, when I opened the lid after introducing the item, there was no sign of the night-dress. But, between us, we were able to indicate that she was nude underneath but perfectly warm, without her dropping the duvet.

'Cut,' said Bill, after I had finished explaining the principle of the new material. He came into the studio. 'OK, you win,' he said. 'I'll buy that.'

I reckoned lunch that day was value for money.

Less pleasure came from a programme a month later on 'Security'. We had arranged for various devices using an invisible beam, either to protect them or to activate them, to be positioned in a semi-circle in the studio. They included window catches which would ring an alarm if you tried to open the window, a floodlight which would illuminate if you stepped on a mat, a safe protected by an invisible beam which would trigger a shrill burglar alarm and a beautifully-crafted, tabletop model of a driveway, garage and car.

The 'sonic key' for opening up-and-over garage doors was still in the realms of Hollywood in those days but it was about to become available in Britain and I was keen to show the model in action.

The items took a long time to set up in the studio, rehearsals were slow and lunch was late, so there was no time for a final rehearsal before recording time was upon us – and no time for re-recording hiccups either.

The red light went on in the studio, I managed to explain the programme to camera without any 'fluffs' and walked to the showpiece window frames. I lifted the sash of the first: no bell rang. I turned the handle of the second: no bell rang. I stepped onto the mat to illuminate the floodlight: none of the several attempts worked. But we still had the safe and the model.

I was supposed to don a black-and-white striped T-shirt, put on gloves, a baggy, black cap and a mask in a rather puerile attempt to suggest I was a professional safe-cracker. I did so and moved stealthily towards the safe. My hand went through the protective beam, turned the handle and even removed the 'loot' without a single alarm sounding.

Bill tried a re-run but it still refused to function.

The car and garage were still worth a short *Fairley's World* on their own, so I memorised a fresh intro and prepared to activate.

The car activated – it leaped to maximum speed in 0.8 seconds Unfortunately, the garage door did not. It stayed shut. Worse, the impact of the 1:20th scale coupé buckled the up-and-over door so that it never would work without major repairs.

Fairley's World failed to go out in *About Anglia* that Monday evening. Was it sabotage – or gremlins? Whichever it was, it did nothing to boost my confidence for the following week's programme which had the theme 'Personal Security'.

For this, I had arranged with a firm of security glass manufacturers in Leeds to build a bullet-proof glass coffin, which would be stood on its end and into which I would climb. Once the lid had been closed from the back, three shots would be fired at me from a revolver. There had been a recent attempt to assassinate a Middle Eastern ruler in a motorcade, but his life had been saved by the bullet-proof glass in his limousine.

The Leeds firm, which had provided the glass for the car, asked, 'How bullet-proof do you want the glass to be?' I replied, 'The same as the Sultan's.'

The Ministry of Defence allowed us to use a disused airfield near Norwich for the recording, which included a demonstration of trying to break toughened shop-window glass (manufactured by a different firm) with a pickaxe.

After the catastrophes of the first programme on security, I was tempted to call off the coffin demonstration. Although I am a fatalist, believing that I shall only die when my 'number is up', there were others to consider. I was, after all, a married man with children and should act responsibly. So I tried hurriedly to organise some special life insurance. But no one would take me on for less than £150 – which equalled the fee for two whole programmes! Besides which, I wanted *Fairley's World* to be talked about (although preferably not because of my death).

I don't remember who the marksman was, except that he was someone whom Anglia found, and I had to sign a legal disclaimer for Anglia's lawyers – in case something went wrong.

It wasn't until I was standing in the coffin, waiting for the camera to roll and the first shot to be fired, that I finally realised what a daft act of bravado it was. The fact that the bullets caused nothing worse than some splintering of the outer layer of the glass was neither here nor there. We should have hired a stuntman.

This point was emphasised when the pickaxe penetrated the shop-window glass. It was supposed not to. But it did. So we had to devise different words to explain it away.

My misery was further deepened when I got home that night. My wife was in a strange mood, barely speaking a word. I guessed she had somehow found out about the coffin. 'What's wrong,' I asked.

'You know what's wrong,' she answered.

'No I don't,' I pleaded. 'C'm on – tell me.'

'You know perfectly well – stop making it worse. Just admit it.' She glared at me.

I remember feeling cold metal behind my back as I pressed against one of the steel-edged kitchen tops. 'Nothing happened – it was perfectly safe,' I said. 'It was just a bit of fun.'

'A bit of fun?' She exploded. 'You call adultery just a bit of fun?'

Adultery? I really did not know what she was talking about and she realised it from the look on my face. It transpired that, during the day, she had received a phone call from Barclaycard asking whether I had changed my home address. Which was correct – the one on their records or the 'Tiptree Cottage, Basingstoke' given by a 'Mr and Mrs Fairley' when they paid by Barclaycard for a double room at the Great Eastern Hotel, Liverpool Street, the previous night.

I told Vivienne that I had actually spent the night in a single room at the Royal in Norwich and had paid the bill (as with all hotel bills) by American Express. I made her ring the hotel, who confirmed it. She relaxed a little and I saw no reason to volunteer the glass coffin escapade – local Anglia programmes were never shown in Kent.

Next day, we got to the bottom of it all. I remembered that I had last used my Barclaycard (as usual with fares, to keep accounts simple) to pay the return rail fare to Norwich. I must have left it by the ticket window. Some young couple (the hotel receptionist described them as 'show-offs') must have found it, studied my signature and then forged it on the hotel cashier's Barclaycard slip. I suspect that the Basingstoke address was false too. The only truth was that they had had a free night on me.

I was furious. Barclaycard immediately cancelled the card, although by a miracle, it never surfaced again. I pretended to be angry with Vivienne too – for doubting me. But I couldn't keep it up for long. If fate were to hear even a whisper of hypocrisy, I might not be spared the bullet next time.

The E-type suit

Throughout the *Fairley's World* series, I wore one particular suit – for a good reason. It was made from a new polyester yarn developed by Dupont, knitted so tightly that it was hard to tell it from worsted. It was blue, smart, kept its shape well and was said to be stain and water-resistant. In fact, according to the manufacturers, 'if you fall into a swimming pool, you can get out, shake yourself like a duck – and go on to a wedding'. They called it 'the E-type suit'.

Dupont let me have one in advance of it being marketed and paid an East End bespoke tailor to make it fit me . I promised to wear it on all *Fairley's Worlds* and on all long journeys, especially by steam train, giving progress reports to viewers.

One Monday was a particularly lovely summer's day and I decided to drive to Norwich, instead of taking the train, breaking the journey at Dedham, Essex. An old school friend, Gerald Milsom owned a much-renowned hotel called Le Talbooth there. Before dinner, he joined me in the bar and we up-dated our news.

I said I was en route for Anglia's studios, where we would be recording a *Fairley's World* on new materials and the future of clothing. I said I was wearing a futuristic suit – the E-type suit – and repeated Dupont's publicity claim about waterproofing and the duck.

Quick as a flash, Gerry picked up a soda syphon from the bar, said 'Let's put that to the test,' and squirted me up and down for several seconds.

The suit was certainly waterproof. Unfortunately, we had forgotten that between the finely-knitted strands, there were tiny holes. The water ran off onto the bar carpet as it off a duck's back. But my shirt was soaked underneath and I had to eat in the kitchen, away from the other diners, while it was dried.

A few days later I was lying prone on the sofa at home, reading, when Vivienne suddenly said, 'What's that flash of white between your legs?' I looked down. To my horror, the entire crutch of the E-type trousers was missing. It had simply fallen out.

I reported to Dupont. 'Ah,' they said, 'that sometimes happens – it's the pillball effect.' I couldn't believe my ears.

Apparently, when the man-made fibres rubbed together, they generated heat and friction caused them to break and curl up into tiny balls. 'We're hoping to develop an F-type suit which won't have pillball problems,' the PR man added. 'Would you like one when it's ready?'

But I had had enough. To hell with the future. The crutch might have dropped out of those trousers on screen. From then on, it would be good old, traditional Marks and Sparks. And it was. . . .

Golf in bare feet

Dupont provided me with two other inventions for the Anglia programme 'The Putter of the Future' and a pair of Corfam golf shoes.

The putter was the idea of a Dupont scientist for correcting any inborn tendency which a golfer might have to putt repeatedly to the left or right of the hole. The head was semi-circular and adjustable, with a completely flat base. It was made of hard, black rubber, across the top of which two parallel white lines were painted. It came with a stand-up card marked in degrees.

The scientist had studied several hundred golfers and observed that very few could putt a ball straight. Some consistently putted one degree to the left but nearly 80 per cent naturally hit the ball one (or even two) degrees to the right. It was a function of eyesight, he believed, when the head was bent over the putter.

The way to find out was to stand over your putter, put down a ball and direct a fellow golfer to place two more balls, one four paces away, the other eight, in what you saw as a straight line. You would then lie down beyond the third ball and look back along the line. The position of the middle ball would indicate whether you were a natural 'left hooker' or a 'right hooker'.

This could be confirmed more accurately with the calibrated card, placed on the golf course or on a carpet. Its central line was your aiming point. If you putted 10 balls at it, marked the card where they struck and took the average, you could adjust the putter's head one or two degrees to left or right, to compensate for your eyesight. On the green, all you had to do then was to point the parallel white stripes, on the top of the club-head, at the hole and the ball *should* go in.

It worked. The card showed me to be a 'two degree-to-the-right' man and I adjusted the putter head accordingly. An Anglia TV crew recorded the whole procedure on the local golf course and I putted from 10 yards in one.

Every true golfer will know that it was a fluke – beginner's luck. When I took 'The Putter of the Future' to Sanderstead, Surrey, to play in a *TV Times* vs. Directors of W. H. Smith match, every hole required several putts. The ball went straight for the hole, sure, but it stopped short or overshot by anything up to five yards.

The reason was the huge, flat base of the club. Several square inches of rubber coming into contact not just with the ball but with the grass, caused either friction or the head to 'stab' at the ball.

There is a happy ending, however.

In 1974, I was invited as a 'celebrity' to take part in the *Exchange Telegraph* Golf Day, held at Moor Park. I knew Moor Park to be a splendid course with a famous history and I was flattered to be invited, so I didn't let on that I was known by my *TV Times* colleagues as 'the world's worst golfer'. I took along 'The Putter of the Future', by then a scientific curio, as a distraction.

It certainly proved to be that, unfortunately for the industrialists, members of the racing fraternity and PR men who were Extel's guests, it bucketed. By 9 a.m., greens and fairways were flooded and both courses had to be closed.

Bacon and egg breakfasts, coffees laced with cognac, billiards balls and playing cards were produced in turn but, by 11.30 a.m., there was a definite 'What shall we do next?' atmosphere and the Extel staff were scratching their heads.

'What about The Putter of the Future?' I suggested, explaining what it was and how it worked. 'We could set up a competition in the Long Bar.'

An empty tonic water bottle was set at one end of the 25 yard-long carpet, a 10p piece placed on top, a golf ball set down and 40 high-spirited men took turns to try to knock it off. None did. An Extel director replaced the coin with a £5 note. Again, everybody failed.

'C'mon Peter, you haven't had a go.' Somebody said, to a chorus of, 'Yeah, you try it.'

Without swerving a centimetre, the ball went straight for the bottle and the note fell off. It was the second time I had 'holed in one'. They nearly lynched me, but by then it didn't matter. Lunch was served.

A year later I was back at Moor Park for the same Extel Golf Day. It was very wet but the courses were playable. Over the obligatory coffee and cognac, the news was broken that I was to partner the Assistant Secretary of the Professional Golfers Association in a Stableford competition.

'But I'm no good at golf,' I spluttered. 'I haven't even got a handicap. I only play for fun.'

'Don't worry, old boy, I'm no good either.' said the AS of the PGA. 'I'm an administrator – we'll just go out and enjoy ourselves.' But his kit, in the locker room, looked suspiciously better than mine and I wasn't happy.

The first hole was not exactly a disaster but he won it easily. To my surprise, he indicated that I should tee off ahead of him at the second, although it was customary for the winner to go first. I thought he was being polite. I wished he wasn't, because I was a bundle of nerves.

As feared, my drive shot off at a tangent of 45 degrees and landed in the rough. He went down in three, my ball took seven. When we put the pin back in the hole and I got out my card, he said, 'Perhaps you'd like me to mark your card you're probably not familiar with the rules of a Stableford.'

'Bloody cheek,' I thought. 'First he wants me to tee off first, then he doesn't trust me to mark my own card.' I declined frostily, saying that I did know the Stableford rules.

My drive off the third was even worse than off the second and I got drenched hunting for the ball. But it wasn't the wet that worried me. Dupont had given me a pair of two-tone, imitation crocodile-skin golfing shoes made out of a new man-made material called Corfam. I had shown them and explained their virtues on the Anglia programme, and I thought they would make another ideal distraction for Moor Park. They were hideously flashy.

Unfortunately they were not properly 'broken in' and the unyielding Corfam material was beginning to cause blisters. I decided to take them off, tie them to the golf bag and play in socks. To my horror, I found the socks had holes in them so I played in bare feet.

I will never forget the look of total disgust on the AS of the PGA's face when this so-called 'celebrity' partner finally appeared from the rough, hair matted, shoes swinging by their laces, feet bare. Thereafter, he not only insisted on my teeing off first, he seemed deliberately to direct his own shots as far away from my ball as possible. He apparently could not bear to be seen in the same company.

We played hare and tortoise all the way to the 18th, with me not only needing extra time to hunt for balls (I lost four) but to make sure that my wet, numbed feet did not step on any sharp objects.

He had vanished inside the clubhouse by the time I reached the last green. So I never knew whether he witnessed the final act of desecration. I untied the flashy brown-and-white shoes from the golf bag, tied the laces together again and, in the manner of an Argentinean cowboy trying to capture a bull, twirled them three times round my head and hurled them into the middle of the ornate pond that is one of the architectural delights of Moor Park.

Alas, they are no longer there. An Extel man rescued them and had them mounted on a teak block to use as the booby prize in following years. My 'celebrity' role was over, at least at Moor Park.

From one medium to another

Anglia seemed to like my contributions – I certainly liked Anglia. Everybody I met seemed friendly, there was a relaxed atmosphere throughout the old Corn Exchange and the Royal Hotel, opposite, was the only place in the world where I ever found the seaweed delicacy known as samphire.

Although the fee never went up, the programme blossomed until it was actually longer than the rest of Monday night's local news. Then a situation developed which was common in many ITV companies – the NIH (Not Invented Here) factor.

When *Fairley's World* reached 23 minutes and made the content of the Monday night local news top-heavy with science, it was taken off for a break while its future was considered. One option (certainly my favourite) was to turn it into a 30-minute, self-contained science feature programme like the BBC's *Tomorrow's World*. But, although Anglia had a Documentaries, Natural History and a Farming Department, it had no Features Department. So it would have meant giving the programme a separate budget and its own production team.

That was where the NIH factor came in. I was an ITN man. I was also Jim Wilson's protégé. So among his well-established colleagues, there was no support for an 'outsider's' programme which might have taken away some of their own budget money. *Fairley's World* never went up the railway line again.

I had, however, acquired a quite different ally in Anglia by then – one of its film directors, Forbes Taylor. Forbes was a senior figure in the industry – a member of Council of BAFTA (The British Academy of Film and Television Arts) – but I remember him better as the director of one of the first Robin Hood series (the one starring Richard Green where every episode started with an arrow twanging into the trunk of a tree) and as the man who made me realise that film directors really do shout 'Action'.

The National Research Development Corporation had asked me to write a book for them about inventors, to celebrate their 21st birthday. Forbes had read it and thought it would make a good film.

He persuaded Anglia to put up a reasonable budget, we drew up a shooting schedule and I took a fortnight's holiday from ITN and *TV Times*. One of our first tasks was to re-create the laboratory at St Mary's Hospital, Paddington, where Alexander Fleming discovered penicillin – luckily, we found one of his medical technicians still living and he could remember its muddle down to the last notebook and pen.

I remember picking a dandelion that had gone to seed and a member of the crew dangling out of a window above the lab, and trying to blow its delicate white 'hairs' in through Fleming's window to simulate the penicillin spore accidentally landing on a Petrie dish containing gel. It took us five dead dandelions and about 20 'takes' before Forbes was satisfied and even then we had to wait until the next day to see the film 'rushes' to be sure the effect was as planned.

Another item in the film was about inventors designing 'robot housemaids'. We went to Queen Mary College, Whitechapel and filmed Professor Meredith Thring's version, which resembled a washing machine with an articulated arm. It cleared a breakfast table of dirty dishes for the benefit of the camera but couldn't find the sink to put them in. 'We're still working on developing an eye,' the Professor assured us – but his grant ran out before he did.

At Warwick University, the electronics research laboratory had progressed as far as developing 'an electronic dog' which could 'see' and 'feel' its way around the kitchen but could not pick up anything. While we were there, Forbes and I were invited to lunch in the Fellows' dining room. Before lunch, we had a drink in the upstairs bar and from its window I noticed four red-brick houses grouped around a neatly-trimmed lawn.

There were several unusual features about the houses. All four were hexagonal in shape, had flat roofs and were linked together by what seemed to be a long, brick-built corridor. They also had only one small upstairs window, where one presumed the bedroom would be.

'What are those houses?' we asked the Dean.

'Oh those are the "mathematicians' houses" – they're each occupied by higher mathematicians and their families,' he replied.

'Why do they have a corridor linking them?' asked Forbes. 'Are they a commune?'

'No,' he said, 'it's to give them room to work out their equations. There's a blackboard fixed to each of the living room walls and it continues down the corridor and into their neighbour's house. If they don't complete their calculations inside their own home, they simply carry on down the corridor.'

'And why is there just one tiny window upstairs?' I chipped in. 'It can't give much light in the bedrooms.'

The Dean laughed. 'We researched carefully before these houses were designed and built,' he replied. 'For some reason best known to themselves, mathematicians don't like much light in their bedrooms.'

The imagination boggles.

It was a race against time to fit into fortnight 'shoots ' at locations as widely spread as Warwick, Cambridge, Sizewell in

Suffolk, East and West London, Reading and Southampton, especially since Forbes worked to a ritual which never varied, despite the need for speed. Our mini-bus would draw up as close to the location as possible. Forbes and I would get out and look for the best spot for filming. He would then go back to the mini-bus to fetch the cameraman. The pair of them would 'hum' and 'hah' for a few minutes – then the cameraman would go back to summon the rest of the crew and get the equipment.

Once the camera and any lights were set up, nothing was allowed to happen until Forbes had said 'Action.' There were always several seconds of silence before the guru spoke and I found these disconcerting, especially if I was trying to quell the 'butterflies', remember my words and look straight into the camera lens.

After the first week, I spoke to the crew about it and we decided to play a joke on Forbes. Looking back now, it seems childish but at the time it seemed very funny – and it did solve the problem.

From a toyshop in Southampton, we bought cap-guns, toy grenades and a noisy child's machine gun. The crew equipped themselves with the guns and me with a grenade. The final scene in the last day's 'shoot' was set inside the Control Room of Fawley power station and I arranged with the crew to put it safely 'in the can' before we played around.

The sound recordist then pretended that he was not happy with the sound on the first 'take' and would like a second. We got back into our positions.

'All settled?' Queried Forbes. 'OK, then ACTION.'

We gave him action, The machine gun rattled, the cap pistols fired and I tossed the grenade, laden with even larger caps, at Forbes' feet where it went off with a loud bang.

His face was a picture – totally aghast at first, then wrinkling into a smile. But he had his revenge. In a later movie we made together, he never said 'Action' once, he simply said, sarcastically and in front of everybody: 'If you're sure you're ready, Peter, then perhaps we can start.'

At the end of the microphone

On October 17, 1973, Londoners heard a new sound – Capital Radio. Although primarily broadcasting music, it had a Talks

Department whose head, John McFarland, asked me if I would like to contribute to current affairs programmes on days when science, technology or medicine came into the news in a major way.

It was not my first taste of radio – I had been recording occasional 'one-off' interviews for the BBC for years and had even presented 13 *Science Now* programmes from Broadcasting House the previous year – but it was the first time a radio station had asked me to be their Science Editor.

John and I had our first meeting at 96 Piccadilly, which Capital had rented for six months until its studios and office complex were ready in Euston Tower. I had last known '96 Piccadilly' as an elegant night spot, featuring good food, a romantic atmosphere and the music of Stephan Grappelli who, apart from being a virtuoso on the violin, was godfather to a friend of mine, Donatien Bottard. Don and I and several of our fellow officer cadets, used to race up from Aldershot and dine and dance at 'the 96' until the small hours of many Sunday mornings in 1949.

Now it was the focal point for people's energy of a different kind.

Reggie Bosanquet used to describe ITN's newsroom as 'organised chaos'. To an outsider, Capital Radio's temporary headquarters was certainly chaotic but the organisation was less obvious, apart from the fact that the chiefs seemed to occupy a central bank of desks while the Indians rushed around them with thousands of pieces of paper.

I told John that I would be delighted to work for Capital, especially since Euston Tower was within walking distance of both ITN and *TV Times*. And so began a decade when I was lucky enough to be able to communicate simultaneously in three different media – print, vision and sound – on a daily basis.

Capital also set up a Children's Programmes section, to which Maggie Norden and David Briggs became the main contributors and which eventually came under the control of Bryan Wolfe, an imaginative producer with a strong stage pedigree.

The main output of the Children's section was a two-hour programme, on Sunday afternoons, called *Hullaballoo* and it was not long before I found myself contributing two tape-recorded packages to *Hullaballoo* each week. One was called *Wow* and contained facts, figures and topics which might make a young listener say 'Wow'. The other was called (yes, you've guessed it) *Fairley's World*.

After a while, we replaced *Fairley's World* with *Backstage*, a series which investigated what went on behind scenes in the theatre which the audience never saw (or should never see) – how Peter Pan 'flew', for example, how Jack's Beanstalk 'grew', the work of 'Props', 'Wardrobe' and so forth. I interviewed Anita Harris and Tommy Steele in the course of going backstage a dozen or more times and was pleased to find that they were just as interested in the Apollo moon missions as I was in their theatrical world.

The fees were, in Capital's own words, 'token' and it took me hours to cut and assemble the quarter-inch tapes, which formed the three items, in my study at home each week. To get enough material for *Fairley's World*, I lugged a 10 lb. Uher tape recorder and a Stenhauser microphone wherever I went in the world – an oil rig off Stavanger, the streets of Paris and Brussels, Cape Canaveral, Los Angeles and the 'deep sea fishing capital of the world' – Bimini Island in the Bahamas – were just some of the overseas locations.

Carrying radio equipment did not help the airline baggage allowance problem but I enjoyed the work as recorded radio is less stressful then TV as well as being cheaper, simpler to edit and easier to rearrange. It was also satisfying to have access to the right medium for stories which had strong sound elements in them, such as funfair hubbub, noises from circus animals, the cries of traders in markets, or the parades of musicians and cartoon characters up Main St in Disneyland.

One *Fairley's World* might have been better broadcast in the *Wow* slot – it certainly made the eyewitnesses gasp. It was about the world of gliding and Bryan Wolfe, who was crazy about flying and subsequently became the Flying Eye traffic spotter over London, had 'friends in gliding'.

We met after lunch one Sunday at a small airfield in Bedfordshire, where a biplane and glider had been prepared for take-off. I was to interview members of the gliding club and record a commentary from the rear cockpit of the biplane – the towing aircraft – as we took off. Bryan was to pilot the glider, under instruction, behind me and record a separate commentary as he (hopefully) picked up a 'thermal' (current of warm air) and soared skywards. We would then splice the recordings together.

We climbed into flying suits. The club members gathered around for interviews and helped us into our respective cockpits, passing the tape recorders in after the seat-belts had been fastened. I was facing the tail of the biplane, Bryan was in the front seat of the glider. Everybody waved at everybody, the engine roared and we trundled forward. I felt a tug as we took the strain of the tow-line and, after what seemed like a lifetime, the bumping over the grass stopped. We were airborne.

I had tested sound levels and adjusted my Uher to cope with the engine noise while I commented non-stop over it. I could see Bryan grinning. Then the moment came for the glider to release the tow – and the grin disappeared. Instead of riding a thermal into the heavens, he nose-dived. Fortunately, his instructor managed to get the nose up just before the glider hit the ground and only slight damage was done.

We all said 'Wow' and that particular *Fairley's World* ended up in the waste bin.

Bryan may have felt differently but it wasn't my worst moment in radio. For that I have to thank Frank Cousins.

Frank, a respected trade union leader, had just been appointed Britain's first Minister of Technology. It was an interesting appointment, especially since it was more in his nature to fight Governments than be part of one. I went to interview him in his brand-new office in Millbank Tower, taking with me a piece of advanced technology – my trusty Uher.

'I'll give you five minutes, lad,' he said tersely, 'and no more. I'm very busy.'

I opened the leather carrying case, took out the tape recorder and laced up a fresh 5-inch spool of tape, talking all the time about the questions I wanted him to answer. 'All right,' he said. 'Let's get on with it.'

The interview seemed to go well and I was preparing to take myself and the machine out of his sight, without even uncoupling the microphone, when he suddenly said, 'Now let's hear what I said.'

I re-wound the tape and began to play it back. Silence. I went 'Fast Forward' – then 'Play'. Still silence. There wasn't so much as a hiss on the tape, much less a word.

Frank was not pleased – and said so. We investigated and discovered that, by a one-in-a-million chance, the manufacturer had reversed the tape so that the backing passed through the recording head instead of the magnetic side. But it was something I should have checked – and would have checked, had I not felt under pressure to meet his five-minute deadline.

'Do you want to do it again?' he asked, as he saw a new spool being readied. 'Yes please,' I said, 'so long as you've got the time.'

The second interview, as so often is the case, was not as interesting as the first, despite the fact that the questions were the same. But I wasn't pushing for perfection and, when he seemed satisfied with the playback, I was happy to cut and run.

It goes into my book of nightmares – a Technology Editor, interviewing a Minister of Technology, who could not operate a tape recorder. Even worse, the interview was never used.

CHAPTER FOURTEEN

A Little Fame – but no Fortune

Six years at *TV Times* were a mixture of ups and downs – ups first, downs later. When the new magazine was launched, the management put me 'on parade' as part of a round-Britain roadshow, to which advertisers, news wholesalers and magazine distributors were invited. I was described as one of their assets – a staff man actually working in television news, appearing regularly on screen and covering a range of interesting subjects.

As part of the agreement to join the staff, I was promised my own office, furnished as I wished and carpeted wall-to-wall, with my own secretary and an assistant, if required. I declined the assistant, brought my secretary from the *Evening Standard* and went out and selected a curved executive desk in teak, teak filing cabinets, a teak coffee table and, most important, a teak wardrobe in which I could keep the E-type and other suits, clean shirts, ties, underpants and socks, for use if a call came to appear on ITN.

But right from the start there was a mean streak in the management of *TV Times* and when I actually moved in, after serving the statutory three months at the *Standard*, I found that the office had been cut to half the promised size and I had been issued with what I described, in a note of protest to the management as 'an exaggerated prayer mat'. I pointed out that, having spent £700 on some fine, new office furniture, it would be a shame to ruin it by installing it on a tilt, two legs of each unit on the carpet and two off.

'Only the Editor and Deputy Editor are allowed fitted carpets' a return note from the Company Secretary stated. 'It would need a Board meeting to change this ruling.'

'Have it.' I wrote back. But I clearly was not going to win and I did not want to cause problems at that stage, so I brought in my own carpet contractor, asked him to match the colour and batch number of the 'prayer mat', turn it around and stitch on a new piece so that it covered the whole floor.

I got my satisfaction from feeling drawers and doors open smoothly and from visualising, when the day came to leave *TV Times*, walking off with half a red carpet rolled up under my arm. But of course, when that day did finally come, I had better things to do . . .

It was a joy to work with an Editor who was always cheerful and full of bright ideas and who believed that science and medical topics would broaden the appeal of what he firmly believed would become 'Britain's biggest family magazine'. Peter Jackson and I soon became close friends. He asked me to be a godfather to his son, Nicky, and I, in turn, introduced him to a friend of mine, Marie Woodhouse, who was an excellent secretary currently looking for a job. She then not only worked for him for more than 10 years but became his second wife.

As Peter had planned, subjects covered by me 'on air' were linked, whenever possible, to features in *TV Times*. The Mexico Olympic stadium run, for example, triggered a research project to find out 'What makes an Olympic Champion?', with the results announced in a major spread in the magazine. Every Apollo space shot was accompanied by a relevant feature in the programme journal. News of a surgical advance became the excuse for an investigation into how close to 'Spare Part Man' medical science was coming.

In another series, we looked at the future of 'the Box' itself. This, although relevant, did not have a direct link to an 'on air' programme and eventually an edict was issued that, to save space (and so costs), only features relevant to actual TV programmes were to appear in *TV Times*.

Out went a major project we had in the pipeline called *The Perfect Home*. Instead, I tried to think of as many off-beat science ideas as possible which could be used in TV programmes and then written about in that week's issue of the magazine.

I had a lot of help from Dr Christopher Evans, a research psychologist at the National Physical Laboratory. He later wrote the best-seller *The Mighty Micro*, but sadly died soon afterwards.

Chris had a first-class brain, but he was an eccentric. I first met him over lunch at 'The Printer's Pie' in Fleet Street – quite a smart restaurant. But Chris arrived, constantly tossing back a mane of black hair, wearing a T-shirt, jeans and open-toed sandals and carrying a handbag.

'Oh God,' he said as we sat down, 'I should have worn socks.'

Although his research was officially into voice-pattern recognition (for possible use in controlling computers) he knew the value of publicity. Any money which it might attract would supplement his limited Government budget. So when I moved to *TV Times*, we devised two research projects which would involve Chris, make interesting 'live' TV and provide feature material for the programme journal.

One was to investigate whether images in commercials shown during evening TV would feature in the dreams of viewers that night. Peter Jackson was enthusiastic and so we booked two rooms at the Queen's Hotel, Manchester (one large and equipped with two TV sets), and travelled up by train to arrive with our tape recorders and notebooks by 6 p.m.

We then wined and dined in the large room, back to back. The waiter who served our dinner onto lap-top trays clearly thought we were nut-cases, one of us sitting there watching BBC, the other watching ITV. We didn't explain.

Each time we saw a striking image in an ad – such as a giant packet of washing powder, or a car roaring straight towards and over the camera, or a child swimming in a sea of Smarties – we would give a quick description into the tape recorder and note the programme position and time.

Next day, a team of six researchers, armed with questionnaires, made doorstep enquiries at 250 Granada-land homes to find out if the products in the commercials had 'come through'.

We found that, in the dreams of about 20 per cent of the viewers, they had. Granada gave a short report in its local evening news, Chris and I wrote it up in *TV Times* and we sent copies to the companies whose products had featured on screen. It was hardly earth-shattering news. But it was original and it made a good story.

Another of Chris' ideas was to measure the stress under which TV presenters and newscasters were under when the camera went 'live'. This broadened into research to measure the energy used by disco dancers appearing on *Top of the Pops*. We had a mutual friend in the Electronics Department of the Medical Research Council, Heinz Wolfe, who was anxious to try out an ingenious little heartbeat counter, developed for use by cardiac specialists, and he was happy to lend us a dozen for our experiment.

The counter, about the size of a pencil torch, worked by using the electrical signal from each beat of the heart to cause a chemical change in a strip of a special metal: the tiny, glass reaction chamber, inserted into a machine in the lab., turned the chemical signals back into electrical pulses, which were then counted. The number of pulses, divided by the number of minutes for which the device was worn, told the researcher the heart rate of the wearer. The higher their number, the greater the load imposed on the heart.

I wore one for a week of appearances on ITN. To my consternation, we found that my heart rate went up to an average of 137 beats per minute from a normal 80. Andrew Gardner's, Reggie Bosanquet's, Ivor Mills' and other newscasters whose heart-rates we tested, although increasing when the camera went 'live', were much lower overall.

We fitted 12 to assorted disco dancers in Granada's *Top of the Pops* studio and found, on playing the counters back afterwards, that their heart-rates ranged from about 120 to 140. But their levels were due to physical exercise, whereas mine were due to nervousness and stress.

I have always hoped that the Lord does not allot each of us, before birth, with a total of heartbeats. If he does, TV appearances have certainly shortened my life expectancy.

Those that got away

Most of our ideas for projects were greeted with enthusiasm by Peter Jackson – indeed some were his own – but two proved impossible, despite the effort put into them.

One was 'Smelly Telly', the other, 'the Bath Books'.

Among my contacts in those days was a chemist working on the development of synthetic fragrances for use in 'scratch n' sniff' patches. He approached me to see if *TV Times* might be interested in running some competition in which readers would scratch patches impregnated on a page of the magazine and identify the different fragrances or odours released .

Unfortunately, the 'only if it's on TV' rule was being strictly applied at the time and Peter had to turn the idea down. But we were not finished.

Some 50 different smells were available from the chemist's 'scratch n' sniff' bank – bacon, burnt toast, newly-mown grass, cedarwood, banana custard, oranges, soap and several ladies perfumes among them – and I worked out a synopsis for a TV murder plot in which the viewer, with *TV Times* on his lap, would have to scratch at clues in pictures similar to those on the screen to be able to work out who dunnit.

We hawked the synopsis for *The World's First Smelly Telly* around the drama departments of all the ITV companies. We needed a script writer, actors and actresses, a director, a producer and a budget to create something worthy of networking. But it was another case of NIH (Not Invented Here). 'Who is this chap?' I could hear them say. 'A science man from ITN? Does *TV Times* expect us to use up budget on this crackpot idea?'

So Smelly Telly went back into the 'TV Ideas' folder in the filing cabinet.

The Bath Books went a little further down the road to reality. Another of my contacts was involved in the development of plastic paper – sheets of various weights and dimensions with many of the characteristics of paper, made out of a special plastic which was waterproof and stain-proof.

Peter, Stan Glazer, the Art Director, and I thought hard about applications for *TV Times*, but beyond a stain-proof holder for the magazine or reproductions of past *TV Times* covers as mats for lap-top TV trays, we could see none. We suggested various applications to the book publishing arm of Independent TV Publications, which rejected it on grounds of the capital cost involved.

The idea of plastic books was novel in the early 70s and we were convinced of the potential, so we formed a private group (and nearly a company) to exploit it outside *TV Times*. One idea was plastic bath-books for mother and baby – a step-by-step, steam-proof and splash-proof illustrated guide for new mothers, faced with the nightly challenge of bathing and dressing baby, and a give-away submersible, colourful picture-book for the little darling to play with in the bath.

Katie Boyle was co-opted with a view to approaching manufacturers of talcum powder, skin cream and baby lotion for sponsorship.

We drew up plans and designs for underwater notebooks for divers, oil-proof car maintenance manuals, a plastic recipe book for cooks and even a *Lazy Gardener's Guide* which could not only be wiped clean of garden stains but contained a calendar of 'minimum tasks'.

But nothing 'gelled'. Everywhere we turned, we were either too revolutionary or too expensive and, because we had busy alternative careers to pursue, The Bath Books eventually joined 'Smelly Telly' back in the filing cabinet.

So too did 'Viewability'. Viewability was an idea for sports enthusiasts to watch TV coverage of matches in their gardens on sunny days, feet up, and simultaneously building up a tan.

I was a Test cricket fanatic and, one year, England looked like winning the series against Australia. Fine weather was in short supply and, one hot week-end, I decided to take our portable TV, a mains extension lead and my deckchair to the top of the garden to watch Botham at his best. To shade the picture and make it viewable, I cut a slot for the aerial in the roof of a cardboard supermarket box, inserted the TV set and pulled the flaps of the box to 90 degrees around the TV screen. It worked. I got nicely toasted and never missed a ball.

At that time, there was concern about office staff straining their eyes to view computer screens in shafts of sunlight, with no curtains or blinds to draw to produce shade. So I spent the rest of the weekend designing a simple cardboard kit, which could be adjusted to fit around different sizes of screen and held in place by an elastic strap.

On the Monday morning I asked my son Simon, who was in the business of registering companies, to register a £100 company called Viewability, with me as Managing Director and he and his brothers as Directors. We planned to advertise it in *TV Times* – possibly get it shown on TV – and visualised fortunes rolling in.

Not surprisingly, they didn't. For two good reasons. One was that, within a week, a manufacturer had announced a new kind of computer screen which could be viewed in bright light. The other was cost. We learned that professionally cut card, with hinged flaps, an elastic strap and a buckle, marketed in an attractive box, would cost, even if mass-produced, more than £6. And as my wife pointed out scathingly, 'If you're mad enough to want to watch cricket or Wimbledon in the garden, you can always get a cardboard box from the supermarket free.'

It was my first business venture and I lost £100.

The hunt for Nessie

The only time when the *TV Times* job and the ITN job did not meld together perfectly was when ITN sent Richard Lindley to report on an international Loch Ness monster hunt and *TV Times* sent me to cover it.

Don Horobin, Assistant Editor at ITN, had a son who was a sub-aqua diver and I believe it was he who convinced Don that Nessie existed and that the international team – who were equipped with sonar and a small, yellow research submarine – would prove it. Don would get the credit as the Man who Found the Monster and pulled off a great coup for ITN.

Some time previously, in Don's presence, I had scoffed at the idea of a monster in the Loch. I had spent a week for the *Evening Standard* and another with my family, roaming the Loch and talking to locals, police baillies and others who claimed either to have seen it or had theories about it. We even had our own 'picture of Nessie' – a 10 × 8 inch black-and-white print showing a line of four humps sticking out of the dark water, with no explanation in sight.

What the photograph did not show was the paddle-steamer which had passed by some five minutes previously, leaving a strong wake which bounced off the sides of the Loch and then disappeared before suddenly reappearing, without warning, as two criss-crossing currents several hundred yards behind the vessel. The criss-crossing had produced the four humps, which were mineral (water) not animal.

It was this photograph, together with several nods and winks from locals over some wee drams, that had convinced me that Nessie was, at best, a legend, not a modern fact.

Don had heard my explanation and probably made a mental note not to let me loose on the story. Instead, he brainwashed Richard, who arrived in the Drumnadrochit Hotel, near the entrance to Glen Urquhart, convinced that it was only a matter of time before the scientists, who were also staying there, announced that they had proof and enable him to break the news to the world.

ITN reporters are supposed to remain neutral and Richard was – and still is a fine reporter, but I listened aghast at some of his news reports from the Loch, which almost gave the impression that he had taken tea with Nessie that very afternoon.

The scientists were a fun bunch, especially in the evenings after they had made adjustments and taken test dives to 'prove out' their submarine, which was moored at the hotel's landing stage. After three days, they drew up an elaborate plan to reveal the presence of the monster – or monsters – if they were there.

Loch Ness converges slightly and reaches its narrowest point by Drumnadrochit Castle and the plan was to lay a sonar 'screen' across the deep water from the castle to the other bank, into which the creature 'S' would be driven, either by two boats carrying noise-generating machines or by the submarine. Synchronised timings were essential.

Richard decided to place himself aboard a steamer about the size of a tugboat and ride south with the noise-making equipment, from Inverness to Drumnadrochit. He suggested that I might like to travel north aboard another boat, towing a noise-making machine, from Fort Augustus to Drumnadrochit. Thus our pincer-movement should drive anything living into the sonar beams and the shape 'S' would show up on monitor screens, which could be televised, at 10 a.m precisely.

Synchronised timings were essential if an escape hole was not to be left around the sonar 'screen' and so it was arranged that 'my' boat would leave Fort Augustus at 7 a.m. sharp, while Richard's would leave Inverness at the much more comfortable time of 8.30. En route, we each had to stop and haul to the surface a bag of 'monster bait' – a mixture of bull's blood, flour and oats – to check for teeth marks through the protective muslin. We would locate the bags by the colourful marker buoys from which they were dangling.

I was introduced to Geoffrey, the scientist in charge of the Fort Augustus boat and to Duncan, the fisherman-owner, but we separated from the bar early because, in order to leave the southern end at 7 a.m., we would have to set out from Drumnadrochit at 4 a.m., which meant rising at 3.30.

When I reached the hotel jetty it was still dark but a temporary electric lamp revealed that Duncan's boat was about the size of a Thames police launch, smaller than the little yellow submarine – and, worse, that it was open to the elements save for half a cabin-top where the helm was located. But there was no time to get an extra sweater.

We set off at a steady chug-chug and soon any excitement about the adventure waned. The air was chilly and we took it in turns to hug the small diesel engine. Loch Ness is an enormous expanse of water – almost as far as London to Woking and nearly a mile wide in places – and it quickly becomes apparent to anyone out in a boat that the chances of finding a monster are considerably less than finding a mermaid in the North Sea, or winning the National Lottery. But because they are so slim, you develop a kind of conviction that you will do it.

We kept our hopes alive on cold sandwiches, as dawn broke to reveal misty hills, but there was just time to nip into the small general store at Fort Augustus and purchase a bottle of Glenfiddich before casting off and chug-chugging northwards.

I don't normally drink before 11 a.m. at the earliest, but that morning I was soon wishing I had bought two bottles of the malt, especially as I could not ignore the mournful, hang-dog expressions of my shipmates when I opened the first.

The sun came up and so did the bag of 'monster bait', still attached by cord to the marker buoy and still completely intact – not so much as a nibble from a fish, much less a monster, could be seen on the squelchy muslin. The sun dried it out and it began to stink.

We had been issued with 'walkie-talkie' radios and we tried to get permission to dump the bag overboard . But small radios were far from efficient in those days and we could raise nothing but hiss and crackle.

The 'noise-maker' was a joke. It comprised a cable with a tin can on the end, inside which three iron weights, tied to strands of the cable, revolved when the boat moved through the water. It was anything but scientific and, in my opinion, wouldn't have disturbed a baby much less Nessie.

The three hour journey up the Loch was spent scanning the water with binoculars and listening to the rattle coming from the can. Every so often, I would switch on the radio and call, 'Hello Richard, come in Richard, are you there Richard?' But it wasn't until we were almost at Drumnadrochit and could see Richard standing on the steamer's bow that the 'Hello Richard' drew a faint answer.

We allowed ourselves a moment of fantasy, visualising a shoal of monsters threshing around in the sonar beams, terrified by the noise-makers, not knowing which way to turn.

Then, six hours after our boat journey began, I cupped my hands and yelled at the sonar post on the bank by the castle. 'Hello

Peter and Vivienne (his first wife) with their children (left to right) Alastair, Simon, Duncan and Josephine, in 1969.

Peter autographing his book The ABC of Space.

Peter by Alan Shepard rocket at US Air Force Museum, Florida.

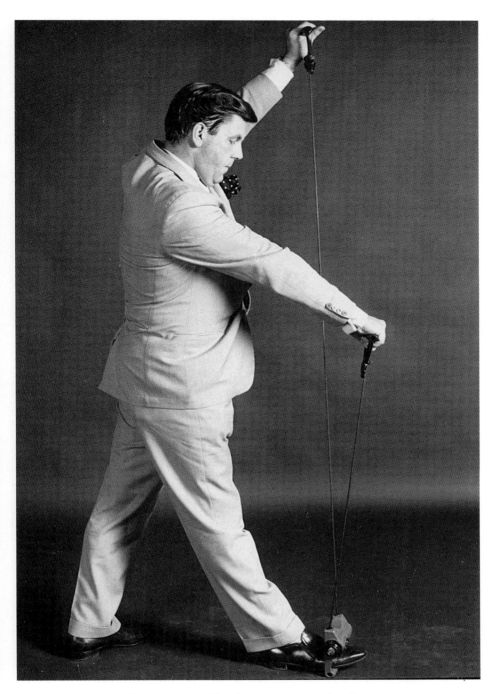

What is Peter doing? An exercise machine for astronauts, perhaps?

Peter being presented with one of several leaving gifts by Sir David Nicholas, CBE, the then editor of ITN.

Peter and three colleagues – MCC exhibition stand.

Peter with film crew from his own company, MCC.

Peter's houseboat, 'Moby Dick'.

Peter at his gate.

Helen and Peter, the day before their marriage.

Peter, photographed by Helen, in 1997.

Sonar. Any luck?' There was a long silence and our hearts began to beat faster. Perhaps Don and Richard were right after all. Then came a word which echoed mournfully down the Loch.

It was the word 'No'.

The pen is mightier than the purse

TV Times believed that the more I appeared on TV, the more the magazine would benefit, especially if I was introduced as Science editor of *TV Times* as well as of ITN. So, providing I completed the written work they needed, I had no problem in getting time away from 247 Tottenham Court Road to take part in programmes. Apart from regular trips to Anglia, Thames TV committed themselves (and their 'friend') to a long series of items in *Magpie* called *The ABC of Space*. At first once a week, then once a fortnight, Pete Brady would introduce a 'live' item, lasting anything from five to 12 minutes, under the heading of a different letter of the alphabet – 'A is for Astronaut', 'B is for Backpack, Beta Cloth and Back-up' and so on.

I was able to wheedle a lot of free film from NASA at Houston, who were delighted that British youngsters were showing keen interest in space. When the letter 'S' was reached, Thames TV had a model-maker build a 12 ft tall scale model of the Saturn V rocket for use in the studio and, for 'Spacesuit' I borrowed the realistic Apollo moon suit from ITN, complete with clumsy boots and goldfish-bowl helmet. *Magpie* dressed my sons in smaller versions of the suit and we all posed for a publicity photograph.

To go with the series, Thames decided to produce a book also called *The ABC of Space* with an introduction by Pete Brady and text by me. It was the first book to be published by Independent Television Publications, the publishing house owned by all the ITV companies and publisher of the weekly *TV Times*.

It was priced at 10s 6d and I was asked by the management to take a low royalty up to break-even point on costs and an 8 per cent royalty thereafter. To everybody's amazement, the book sold 50,000 copies in the first week and I ended up earning about £2,000, which was not part of their plan.

Unfortunately, far from being credited with helping their publishing enterprise off the ground, *The ABC of Space* only served to convince certain members of the Board of IT Publications that

I wasn't doing a full-time job as Science Editor of *TV Times* and that I was an expensive luxury which they could well do without.

A friendly director tipped me off that a motion was on the agenda for the next Board meeting 'to dispense with the services of Peter Fairley'.

Although the switch of career from Fleet Street had not turned out to be all that it was cracked up to be, I still drew satisfaction from being able to combine the visual with the verbal and I still very much enjoyed working with the rest of the staff at *TV Times*. I did not want to be sacked.

At the time, a TV series about Boardroom politics called *The Power Game*, starring Patrick Wymark, was running on ITV and I was hooked on it. So when the tip-off came, the immediate re-action was to think – 'What would Patrick Wymark do to thwart them?'

I decided to make a case for the defence and circulate it to the homes of all the Board members who were likely to be on my side, including Sir Geoffrey Cox, who was about to stand down as Chairman.

The three-page document included 18 detailed facts – including that I had written more words in the pages of *TV Times* since it started, than anyone else on the staff and never once been late with my 'copy'. It also listed a number of specific ways in which my appearance on ITN and other ITV programmes had brought in revenue for the programme journal and the actual sums involved.

There were two paragraphs of 'Opinion' and a 'Conclusion', the last words of which were, 'I do not see why, as I enter my '40s, I should apologise for doing well. I put my trust in *TV Times* – I think the management should now put its trust in me.'

It worked. I escaped redundancy. But sanctions were imposed.

When ITP decided to publish a whole batch of books for children, I found myself writing for no royalty at all – and no fee either. First came *Peter Fairley's Space Annual*, then a book about North Sea Oil called *North Sea Bonanza*, and finally, an illustrated book of gee-whiz information called *The World of Wonders*.

The last was designed to make youngsters stop and look more closely at the wonderful world around them – at man's ingenuity, at animal behaviour, life under the sea, life in outer space, sources of power, at challenges and conquests and at lessons from nature.

Three artists were commissioned to draw more than 300 illustrations and we were allocated a researcher, Andrew Thomas, who had previously worked for *The Guinness Book of Records*. Andrew, who was meticulous about accuracy and detail, started out as a mine of information and ended up a walking encyclopaedia. I shall never forget him poking his head around the door with an, 'I say, did you know. . . .?' or an 'I say I've just found out. . . .' It must have happened a hundred times or more and in the Foreword I wrote: 'In planning this book, we ourselves became excited and amazed at the ingenuity of some of the creatures and machines we were describing, compelled to probe deeper and learn more.'

But one wonder was never mentioned — the fact that we had only four months to research, write, design and get the lay-out off to the printer We made with one day to spare and I still had my job.

'Is there life in outer space?'

TV Times had its junior counterpart called *Look-in*, which also appeared on the bookstalls weekly. With interest in space high among youngsters, its Editor, Alan Fennell, was often needing background material and pictures of the various Apollo missions and, in the late '60s, we were constantly in and out of each others' offices — a relationship which paid off handsomely later.

Look-in also produced special supplements and books.

After *The ABC of Space*, IT Publications decided to publish six *Look-in* books for young people simultaneously. Always in search of ways to cut costs and increase profits, the management decided to do it as a joint venture with Severn House, another book publisher.

The others in the series were titled *Ponies and You, Have Fun with Origami, SOS Wildlife, Exploring Woods, Football, The Wild West* and *Have Fun with Sewing*. Mine was to be called — and I didn't choose the title — *Is There Life in Outer Space?* I was asked to get on with it as soon as possible.

It so happened that I had a 'holiday' booked for the following week, in order to go on location and film a documentary for the Dept of National Savings about the work carried out in its headquarters in Cowglen, a suburb of Glasgow. I had researched and written the script: the remaining task was to introduce a number of 'pieces to camera' and be seen walking through different departments.

The HQ at Cowglen seemed almost as large as Buckingham Palace and most of the top was given over to penthouse flats for visiting VIPs. As presenter of the film, I apparently had VIP status and was allotted a penthouse flat, with its own kitchen and bar.

The possibility of some form of life existing outside Earth had always fascinated me, especially since a team of American astronomers had published a research paper in which they calculated that there were ten thousand trillion other planets at just the right distance from their suns, with just the right temperature, for life to have evolved. Even the Cambridge radio-astronomy team, who had discovered the first pulsar (pulsating star) and later declared that the Universe began with one big bang, had nicknamed their first mysterious 'find' LGM-1 – LGM standing for Little Green Men – and a NASA group had just started to listen out with a computer-controlled radio telescope for patterns of signals from the sky which might indicate an extra-terrestrial intelligence.

I took a thick file of reference material with me to Cowglen and arranged with the film's director, Richard Collin, that whenever I was not wanted 'on set', I could take the lift to my flat and work on the book. He would call up whenever he needed me.

The book was 25,000 words long and I finished it within the week, although only by burning a lot of midnight oil. At the end, with a feeling of smug satisfaction, I decided to look up *The Guinness Book of Records*. But I quickly put it back on the shelf.

It recorded that Earl Stanley Gardner, creator of Perry Mason and the detective Chief Ironside, wrote an average of 10,000 words a day and worked on 17 novels simultaneously, while Frank Richards – creator of Billy Bunter contributed up to 80,000 words a week to the schoolboy publications *Gem*, *Magnet* and *Boy's Friend*.

My only consolation was that they hadn't also made a film.

Fired and hired

More substantial books were then asked for, including one explaining how TV works and the way of life for those on 'the

Box', called *Television Behind the Screen*. This time a royalty was offered, but again a low one.

Soon afterwards, there were further cut-backs at *TV Times* and I was asked by the management to accept six months' notice. By then, I was heartily sick of being made to feel an out-of-place prima donna so that when Peter Jackson described the fight he had put up to get me at least the option of taking salary in lieu of notice, I decided to quit and take all my trappings to ITN House.

Peter had also spoken to Nigel Ryan, then Editor, about my predicament and received an assurance that a shortfall of £5,000 a year would be at least made up by ITN, with plenty of opportunity to earn more under a new contract.

It was all rather sad but I had a joker card up my sleeve.

Shortly before Neil Armstrong and Buzz Aldrin walked on the Moon, *Look-in* was approached by a company called Space Spin-off Ltd to run a special offer in the junior *TV Times* of a replica of the Apollo 11 mission badge. Each Apollo crew designed its own mission badge, which the astronauts wore on the chests of their spacesuits and coveralls. The Apollo 11 badge was predominantly gold and blue and depicted an eagle landing on the Moon, with a small blue-and-white Earth in the distance. The replicas which Space Spin-off Ltd were offering were beautifully embroidered in up to nine different colours, with some 11,000 stitches in each badge. They had cost 50p each to manufacture; the company was offering them at 60p. Alan Fennell snapped up the idea, an article accompanied the badge offer and some 50,000 were sold.

I know these facts for a very good reason – I was 'Space Spin-off Ltd'!

On my visit to America to cover the launch of Apollo 9, I had asked NASA's public relations department for permission to reproduce the astronauts' mission badges.

'Providing it's for news, information or educational purposes,' was the answer. 'Strictly no advertising.'

I am an unashamed, addicted souvenir collector and no trip to the States to report Mercury, Gemini or Apollo flights was without its legacy of space souvenirs badges, crests on items of desk equipment, paper knives, ashtrays, little bronze plaques, first-day covers, postcards, 35 mm slide sets, models of rockets and so forth – and I had begun to think about extending the range and having them made and sold in Britain. The Apollo mission badges were the top attraction.

With the help of a friend in marketing and £100 of my own money, I set up 'Space Spin-off Ltd.' with the aim of promoting public interest in space in general and in 'space souvenirs' and 'space art' in particular.

Our first venture was the Apollo 11 badge.

We designed a visiting card and some note-paper and my marketing colleague went to see Alan Fennell at *Look-in*. He showed him the Apollo 11 souvenir badge as an example of what we would reproduce. Alan liked the idea and asked for a quotation for 12,000, 20,000 and 50,000.

The world of souvenirs was completely foreign to me but enquiries soon pointed to a Birmingham company, Thomas Fattorini, as perhaps the leaders in quality badge manufacturing. I was determined about two things – that the price should be within reach of children's pockets and that the quality would be first-class: those who bought a badge should feel that they were buying a souvenir of lasting value. I believed that we owed that, at least, to the Apollo astronauts who were risking their lives.

Fattorini's managing director gave me three prices over the telephone but added that he would need a guarantee, since we were an unknown company and we were talking about between £6,000 and £25,000 worth of merchandise.

Where was I to get that kind of guarantee?

One of my closest contacts at the National Research Development Corporation had been the general manager, John Duckworth, had moved to become a financial consultant to Rothschilds, the bankers. All we needed was about £13,000 so I went to see John in his luxurious new office in the City.

He heard me out, smiled and said, 'You wouldn't care to put another '0' on your figure would you, Peter?'

He explained that Rothschilds put a monitor on any sum loaned and the cost of monitoring a project had become so expensive that the minimum loan the bank would contemplate was £130,000.

I thanked him for his lesson in High Finance and left, slightly dejected. Next day, we had a bright idea. 'Would you like to come and have lunch at my club,' I asked Fattorini's MD, 'after seeing the lunchtime news go out from ITN?'

He took the bait. The following Wednesday, he arrived at ITN and, from the back of the Control Room, we watched Di Edwards-Jones direct (with unusual restraint) *News at One*. I could see he was fascinated. Then we walked 400 yards to my 'club' and I saw the surprise on his face as I signed him in to The Sportsman Club – a gambling club.

'Don't worry,' I told him, 'they do an excellent lunch here.'

I selected a Chateau Talbot '64 and fed him every 'inside' anecdote about ITN that I could think of. I steered him through the roulette tables after settling the bill and pressed a £5 note into his hand. 'Go on – try for both of us' I said.

An hour later – and more than £200 up – he looked at his watch in horror, We grabbed a taxi and I virtually poured him into the train back to Birmingham. He leaned out of the window and, to my delight, shouted, 'By the way, don't worry about the guarantee. . . .'

We added 10p per badge to Fattorini's price and Alan added a further 5p, and the Apollo 11 badge clearly caught the young readers' imagination because every mission badge that followed – 12, 13, 14, 15, 16, and 17 – was the subject of an agreement between *Look-in* and Space Spin-off Ltd but not before I had confessed my role in the company to Alan, who agreed to keep it quiet from the *TV Times* Board.

My colleague and I started to develop ideas and designs for other space souvenirs. We were fortunate in being able to draw on the talents of Malcolm Beatson, the very gifted Head of Graphics at ITN, during his spare time and within a year, we were not only marketing embroidered Apollo mission badges but mission ties, brooches, pendants, key rings and stickers.

Having become, like it or not, a familiar face on TV with an in-depth knowledge of the Moon programme, I was able to get at least a hearing in some unexpected places.

One was the Boardroom of Marks & Spencer in Baker Street, where I had lunch with several of the M&S directors and senior executives including those responsible for woollens and dressing gowns. I tried to persuade them to market sweaters with the Apollo mission emblems woven into them and dressing gowns bearing the embroidered badges on the pockets. They turned us down on grounds that the badges were too ephemeral – they liked long 'runs' of garments and they believed interest in Apollo would have waned while the 'runs' continued.

Another was Woolworth's, where I wangled an appointment

with the Toy Buyer. I was told that this was exceptional – some salesmen waited six months to see him.

When I checked in at the front desk of Woolworth's head office in Marylebone, it was like a scene from *Citizen Kane*. The waiting area had a ceiling as high as the nave of a cathedral with a desk like a Wurlitzer organ in the centre. A pimply youth sat at the 'organ', playing not keyboards but banks of switches linked to red and green lights. Around the walls sat 50 or 60 hopeful salesmen, many from Hong Kong or Taiwan, some of whom had clearly been waiting a long time.

Each time a red light went to green, the pimply youth would put down his *Daily Mirror*, look down a list and call out – 'Mr Chang – Mr Isaacs will see you now. Come this way please' – or something similar. He would then disappear to the lift for a few seconds before resuming his studies.

I only had to wait 10 minutes before my call came. One floor up, I knocked on the Toy Buyer's door, a Cockney voice shouted, 'Come in,' and I was in the presence of the Great One. He reminded me a bit of the actor George Cole. 'You've got 10 minutes,' he said.

I had sent him a set of embroidered mission badges in advance, but all he was interested in was seeing the emblems on metal button badges. He wanted them in groups of three, blister-packed onto coloured cards, with a short text about them printed on each card. There were only 11 emblems but by adding the generic badge of the whole Apollo programme – a graphic '17' – we made up four cards.

'Give me a quote for 20,000 cards,' he said. 'Anything else you got, connected with TV, that'll sell?'

I didn't mention the idea of packs of farm animals and characters from *Emmerdale Farm* that we had been toying with (by then we reckoned we might make our fortunes from such merchandise) but escaped to find a drink and think. Twenty thousand? That meant 60,000 button badges. But in metal? And in blister-packs? Where were we to find manufacturers who could handle the combination of materials?

I knew it was the wrong way to market the badges. Embroidered, they were works of art with an intrinsic value: in metal, they were throwaways. But you don't argue with Woolworths – a test marketing exercise in a few stores could lead to mass-production worth thousands.

He beat us down twice on our quotation but in the end we found a manufacturer, who also delivered the cards. But we never heard from the Toy Buyer again and knew it had been a flop, with virtually no profit at all.

Not much more came from an order from W. H. Smith for 10,000 plastic sheets of mission badge stickers. These looked 'interesting' and colourful but W. H. Smith wanted the sheets in clear, cellophane envelopes, centre-punched with a hole so that they would hang from a metal rod on a pegboard backing.

It was finicky, frustrating work trying to slide 10,000 floppy plastic sheets into 10,000 floppy covers. We had constant 'static' problems and the operation was not helped by hot, sticky weather. We were trying to miss out the 'middle-man' to increase profit margins but, by the end, I would gladly have given the money saved away to another pair of hands.

By the time the last men walked on the Moon, we had 21 different items in our mail-order catalogue, including Moon-car ties and cuff-links and a black, leather belt with a chrome-plated clasp which we called the 'Rendezvous belt'. One half of the clasp was in the shape of the CSM (Apollo Command and Service Module) the other half in the shape of the LM (Lunar Module). When the wearer clicked the two together, he or she was ' rendezvous-ing' like the real spaceships above the Moon.

I still have 200 of the damned belts in my garage, for we shut the company (with a sigh of relief) before they could all be sold. One day they may be valuable as antiques, but we could only see them at the time as a millstone.

Another business failure – ideas, yes, but too few resources to carry them through and not enough 'savvy' to get the margins right. But there were some laughs, not least when we took a stand for a week at the International Gifts Fair at Blackpool.

For this, we designed a completely black background with silver stars twinkling and the colourful mission badges along the front. I borrowed ITN's full-size replica of an Apollo astronaut, complete with helmet and backpack and positioned it by the entrance to the stand with a tape-recorder and closed loop of tape repeating non-stop. 'Hello, I'm Fred the spaceman. Welcome to Space Spin-off. Please come inside.'

On the third morning, two men in dirty mackintoshes paused to listen. By then I had got over my embarrassment at trying to sell our wares and stepped forward, rubbing my hands with a, 'Well, gentlemen, how may we help you?'

'I don't think you can,' one answered. 'We're HM Customs and Excise.'

'Ah, just the chaps.' I said 'I've got a query which I'm sure you can answer. Come in.'

One of our new 'lines' was an orange-and-black, stick-on sign reading 'SHORT VEHICLE'. It was a spoof on the sign 'LONG VEHICLE' carried by all lorries over a certain length. We were about to market it for Mini or small Renault drivers but we were not sure if it was liable for VAT.

As I led the two Customs men around some side tables, there was a clatter from the stand next door, where they were marketing imitation weapons and suits of armour. The black wallcloth between our two stands lifted a fraction. A voice hissed, 'Pssst, keep them occupied.'

The Customs men chatted about our range of space souvenirs and eventually decided that the 'SHORT VEHICLE' sign was non-VAT liable. They shook hands and moved on. After a couple of minutes, I dashed next door to ask what the fuss was about. I noticed that a fine display of dirks, claymores and lances had gone from the walls.

'We were marketing those as letter-openers,' they explained. 'Letter openers are not liable for VAT – swords and daggers are!'

Project X

The book which prompted the Anglia film about inventors was called *Project X* in paperback and *British Inventions of the 20th Century* in hardback. There were good reasons for using both titles.

When Frank O'Shanohun, who was handling the NIRDC's public relations, first came to discuss the book, he said that NRDC wanted to buy 3,000 copies to give away to captains of industry and opinion formers to celebrate the Corporation's 21st 'birthday'. But they could not afford 3,000 hardbacks at £1.75 a copy.

So it would have to be published as a paperback first and, under the terms of NIRDC's charter, it would have to try to recoup some of the money invested from sales to the public from station bookstalls, newspaper shops, bookshops like W. H. Smith etc. 'Ah,' I said, 'if it's got to compete with other paperbacks on bookstalls then we've got to have a picture of a nude on the front and a snappy title like . . . *Project X*.'

It so happened that one of the inventions which the NIRDC had backed was the 'hoverbed' – a machine for helping to relieve pain and speed the healing of severely burned patients by supporting them on a cushion of air coming through the mattress. The publicity picture taken, illustrating the bed in action, had shown a blonde in a bathing suit, lying face upwards with her legs apart.

'All you need do,' I suggested to Frank, 'is dress the woman in a bikini and re-shoot the scene in colour.'

That proved a bit more daring than the NRDC could stomach but they were happy with a montage of nine small photographs of inventions in circles of colour and they liked the title. My only problem was how on earth to justify calling the book *Project X*.

The top brass at NFIDC persuaded Harold Wilson (not because he is Prime Minister but because he was President of the Board of Trade in 1948 when we were set up) to write a Foreword. I soon found a justification for the title – the top-secret Enigma project (to invent a computer to help crack the German codes, carried out at Bletchley during the last war) was apparently carried out in a room simply marked 'Project X'.

Mayflower Books, who had previously published the paperback version of *Man on the Moon*, handled *Project X*. I was paid a flat fee of £2,000. The NRDC duly bought 3,000 copies and it was delivered to wholesalers on schedule. To my amusement, W. H. Smith placed it not under 'General non-fiction' but in a prominent position in their 'Spying and Espionage' section, (where it probably sold a lot more copies than it would have in the other!).

Harry Secombe also spoke

Writing a book, I suspect, must be rather like a woman having a baby. There is a short conception – the synopsis – involving two people (author and publisher a long period of gestation, during which not much appears to be happening ; increasing pain as the publisher's deadline approaches; acute pain when the manuscript is overdue and the author realises it is too late to opt out because he has spent the advance on royalties; moments of agony when the book is finally published and reviews are awaited, during which he vows never to write another and then – suddenly – it is all over and he is looking around for the next book baby to start.)

You soon forget the pain. Appearance on the bookshelves is a great analgesic and unlike radio and TV appearances, which are ephemeral, the printed word has a permanence which tempts the author to feel he has made a tiny contribution to history.

I was never able to write on the premises of ITN or *TV Times* or Capital Radio because they were news environments, full of ringing telephones and clattering typewriters. All my writing was done either at home, any time between 4 a.m. and 9 a.m. on weekdays, or at week-ends, or on trains or planes – a fact which, like the fact that I earned nothing from three of the eight books I had written, counted for nothing when the TV Times Board wielded their axe.

But *Man on the Moon* at least must have aroused interest at *The Yorkshire Post* because, out of the blue, came an invitation to speak at one of their Literary Dinners. I asked the lady organiser whether there were to be other speakers.

'Yes, two,' she answered. 'Harry Secombe (who had recently published his memoirs) and Leslie Thomas (author of several bestsellers, including *The Virgin Soldiers*).' I reckoned my contribution to the evening would go down like a lead balloon if I followed two of the funniest after-dinner speakers around at that time, so I asked if I might speak first. 'Sure,' she said. 'no problem.'

The *Post* booked us into the Merrion Hotel in Leeds and we changed into dinner jackets before taking seats in the Ballroom, where some 150 paying guests were already seated in groups of eight around circular dinner tables. I tried to enjoy the food and wine but all I could think about were the one-word reminders written on cards in my pocket.

Butterflies came and went as the chairman introduced me first as author of *Man on the Moon* and then, almost as an afterthought as ITN's Science Editor. I had plumped for serious fact rather than any attempt at humour. So I described how most of the book had been pre-written and then finished soon after ITN's coverage of the Apollo 11 splashdown and rushed to the printers. I told a few inside stories about the astronauts and ended by explaining the significance of Neil Armstrong's fluffed line 'One small step for man, one giant leap for mankind'.

'If the human race is to survive,' I went on, 'then, at some point in the future, we've got to find a way to get off this planet and onto some other – because our Sun is losing a million tons of matter every second in flares and explosions and one day it will no longer be able to support life on Earth. It will literally go out. That's why going to the Moon is so important – it's a stepping-stone to much longer journeys which men and women will need to make to ensure a future for mankind.'

There was some polite applause and then, as expected, Leslie and Harry made hilarious speeches which sent the audience into convulsions. I thanked God for having made me elect to speak first.

It is the custom at the Merrion Hotel to distribute a compli-mentary copy of the *Yorkshire Post* to each guest and, sure enough, a copy slid under my door soon after 7 a.m. I read the front page news in full and then turned to Page 2. To my amazement, it was dominated by the headline 'SUN GOING OUT SAYS SCIENCE MAN'. Below was an in-depth report of my speech.

I had not been aware of any Press being present at the dinner and obviously the reporter must have slipped away early to file copy because, at the very bottom of the story, there was a line printed in italics.

It read, 'Harry Secombe and Leslie Thomas also spoke.'

CHAPTER FIFTEEN

Daddy, you're not BBC

'Here, wait a minute – don't I know you?' the taxi driver said. 'I don't know whether you do or not,' I replied, ' but I'd like to go to the British Museum.'

He paused. 'Yeah, hop in – I've just placed you,' I climbed in. 'You used to play for Arsenal,' he said as I settled back.

It was wonderful. Only three months after the last men had returned from the Moon and here we were, back to near-anonymity – so essential to the personal privacy which most ITN reporters craved. Even Reggie Bosanquet, whom most regarded as a celebrity, was actually a shy man. That was certainly made plain when I asked him, as presenter of the Apollo 17 'special', to say a few words at the informal dinner-dance to celebrate the end of our Moon coverage. He rounded on me furiously. 'Don't you ever spring that kind of thing on me again without warning,' he hissed. And he meant it.

Andrew Gardner, Leonard Parkin, Sandy Gall, Ivor Mills, Trevor McDonald, Martyn Lewis, Julian Haviland – I don't be-lieve that any one of them welcomed celebrity status. We were news journalists, not movie stars.

What is a 'celebrity' you may ask? According to the dictionary, it is 'a person who is famous or notorious'. I like to think that none of us was notorious. Certainly, in my case, any fame was short-lived, but it still brought problems.

Immediately after the Neil Armstrong landing, I went on holi-day with the family. We decided to tow a caravan, partly to es-cape the public eye, partly because we couldn't afford much else. For most of the time, it worked – viewers do not expect to see TV 'personalities' in shorts and gumboots, which was my usual attire during that wet fortnight.

But there was one morning at Llanrwst in North Wales when I heard noises and opened the caravan door to find a cluster of giggling children holding out autograph books or scraps of paper with pencils. Some parent had spotted me, although my children were totally loyal – indeed they never let on until years later that two of them were being taunted and bullied at school because of my antics on screen. And I shall never walk along Eastbourne front again for fear of people secretly nudging each other and whispering, 'Isn't that the Moon man?' or 'Hey, that's Peter Fairley' – which is what hundreds did as we went for a late-afternoon stroll on the prom during that holiday in 1969.

I swear I caught more 'nudge-nudge–wink-winks' than the others because they were all over 6ft. tall and people tend to look down rather than up, when walking in the street.

Requests to appear at public functions began to come in. One, which eventually eased relations with my bank manager, was from Barbara Kelly, Bernard Braden's wife, who was not only a radio star but a much-admired panellist on the TV quiz show *What's My Line?*. Barbara had set up a business called 'Prime Performers', which guaranteed to find the right speaker, for the right occasion, at the right price.

She asked if I would like to go on her books to be available to speak after lunch or dinner – or open conferences or exhibitions – when her client was a science, medical or technology-based company. Would I? Her fees were heart-warming.

As a believer in the use of visual aids, I put a lot of energy and effort – and a few hundred pounds – into developing an illustrated lecture called 'AD 2000', which surveyed what the future held in store for Britain as a nation and the individual British family. It lasted an hour and was accompanied by 160 colour slides – two Kodak carousels full. It began with an audience grabber – a look at the wristwatch and a shock reminder – that, since the presentation started, X number of babies had been born while only Y number of people had died.

After showing the shape of the population explosion and trends toward a geriatric society, it looked closely at future sources of energy including nuclear energy, pollution and global warming, weather forecasting, new foods, fish farming, the future of the car, the ship, the aeroplane, the hovercraft and space exploration, before turning to more down-to-earth topics such as the future of the home itself, clothing, gardening, leisure and shopping.

All the information went on to cards (one card per slide) which could be held discreetly in the hand. It took weeks of work, re-searching the facts and then writing the cards in black felt-pen and some of the futuristic artist's impressions cost me £75 each but, at the end, I had a 'package' which could be taken down off the shelf, used at short notice and easily up-dated.

In fact, it was used 14 times, taking me to Miami, Paris, Ant-werp and most of the conference resorts around the coast of Brit-ain and brought in something over £10,000, which was a good motivation for overcoming shyness and standing on your own two feet. It is interesting, as the millennium draws near, to match the forecasts against reality. Some have materialised sooner than predicted, others are taking their time and a few have dropped out of sight.

Other Barbara Kelly commissions included launching two new motor oils for BP in a spectacular roadshow, put on in 12 differ-ent hotel ballrooms, where I and a giant can of oil appeared out of a cloud of steam and a succession of after-lunch and after-dinner 'entertainments'.

I am no comedian and starting a talk with jokes is an art. But shyness brought an unexpected benefit. On the first occasion where I was being paid a fee, I stood up and 'died' – no words came for several embarrassing seconds. While the brain strug-gled to remember the planned opening, I leaned forward and said quietly into the microphone 'He is shorter, fatter but perhaps slightly younger than you had expected.'

It brought laughter and broke the ice. From then on I never worried about speaking in public because that was exactly what every audience thought when I stood up; so I had a ready-made cover for the nerves

Even so, there was one after-dinner engagement which par-ticularly worried me, not least because it was at the North British Hotel in Edinburgh. The North British was known as the 'speak-er's graveyard' because the dining room stretched about a hun-dred yards to the left of the top table, a hundred yards to the right and only about 10 yards in front. So, if you were to be heard clearly, you had to keep speaking straight ahead into a micro-phone, which meant that you could only 'eyeball' a tiny fraction of the audience – the part directly in front of you.

The invitation was to speak at a dinner to open the 'First In-ternational Symposium on Charge-Coupled Devices'. On what? I had no idea what a Charge-Couple was except that the people at the symposium – and therefore my audience would be electronics engineers from all over the world. This meant that the 'He is shorter, fatter but slightly younger' opening would be useless because none of the many foreigners present would understand it.

A *Dictionary of Electronics* explained that a Charge-Coupled Device, or CCD, was 'a charge storage device based on a set of MOS capacitors formed in sequence on a chip, with a common earth plate' (ugh) or, alternatively, 'a form of semi-conductor TV camera device'. I preferred the alternative.

But what can you say to an audience of boffins whose whole world revolved around tiny 'chips' with a name which only they knew how to pronounce properly? Most of us would have put the 'd' in 'coupled' after the 'e' in 'charge'. Suddenly, after a good lunch on *The Scotsman* express to Edinburgh, I had an idea.

The organisers had sent me a massive wad of 'draft' conference papers as a briefing aid and, instead of dropping them smartly in the waste bin, I started to read.

They were better than I dared hope. If you put the 'd' in the wrong place and read them in the spirit of 'Charged Couples' and the context of a honeymoon, they were full of double-meanings – one long string of risqué jokes. I wrote my cards accordingly.

But would engineers – and particularly foreign engineers – appreciate risqué jokes based on their special jargon? Smutty humour is not for all men.

By the time the cognacs were served and sipped, I had decided to 'put a toe' into the humour pool and, if there wasn't so much as a ripple of laughter, switch immediately to the importance of CCDs to the future of television. But there was a ripple – and much more besides – and, fee apart, my final reward was when a Dutchman came up afterwards and said, 'Do you know, Mr Fairley, I shall never be able to take myself or my subject seriously again.'

James Bond and the Bonds

There was no National Lottery in those days. The only competition to football pools, tombola and raffles for the public's 'spare' cash took the form of bonds – Premium Bonds – selected by a machine called ERNIE.

ERNIE is an acronym for Electronic Random Number Indicator Equipment and it does indeed select winning numbers at random. But in 1975, few members of the public believed that and even fewer knew how ERNIE worked.

The man in charge of Public Relations and Publicity for the Department of National Savings at that time was a former stalwart of the BBC's News Information Service, Patrick Robertson, and I was delighted, as an ITN man, to be invited to research, script and appear in a film explaining ERNIE to the public. Apart from going onto the Central Office of Information's film lending library list, it was designed for showing to visitors who were about to see ERNIE in operation at Lytham St Annes in Lancashire.

Richard Collin was appointed the film's Director which meant that, when the camera was not actually turning over, filming would be fun.

Although the subject matter was factual, I was keen to make it a light-hearted film showing popular misconceptions as well as the truth.

On Her Majesty's Secret Service had just been released onto the cinema circuit and, as a James Bond enthusiast, it gave me an idea for how to open our ERNIE film. Why not start with a spoof – have Bond raid the Premium Bond headquarters and attempt to 'nobble' ERNIE and steal tickets with winning numbers?

We chose a location just outside Lytham, where there were some fine sand dunes. We hired a rubber dinghy, frogman's gear, a Mercedes car and the services of a beautiful chauffeuse. Richard said, 'I know just the girl – she's a Chinese model and she is stunning.' She was indeed.

The opening shot was to be sunset on the beach, waves gently lapping as the rubber dinghy crunched ashore – 'cut' . . . then a close-up of the frogman's flippers and 'wet-suit' dropping onto the sand – 'cut': then a distance shot of the chauffeuse looking out to sea – 'cut', then a ground shot of the Mercedes' door opening and closing and the limousine heading for Lytham, where the iron gates were to open in response to two flashes of the headlights – 'cut'.

The next sequence was to take place inside – black socks walking down a corridor, a silver key opening the door to the ERNIE room, a black gloved hand reaching for switches on a console and

– bingo – alarms would ring, lights come on full strength and I would appear saying, 'Some people will go to extraordinary lengths to win on ERNIE . . .'

That is what should have happened.

All went well until the Mercedes tried to get out of the sand dunes. Then, each time the engine whirred, the wheels bit deeper, scattering sand everywhere (including over the camera lens) but the limo stayed put. It took half an hour to smooth out the sand again and make it look virgin and we reshot seven times before it finally accelerated free.

Next, Lee Sum Sun, the chauffeuse, revealed that she couldn't drive. 'Don't worry, darling,' Richard said, putting a comforting but hairy arm around her wasp-like waist. 'When the time comes, we can fudge it. There's something I want to do first.'

He sat her in the back of the crew car, asked her to unbutton her high necked silk jacket and remove her bra, put the jacket loosely back around her shoulders and sit on the tailboard of the estate car. He clearly knew her well.

'When you see us flash our headlights, pull your jacket down,' he told her. To me he murmured 'I'll give that lazy sod, Sid, (the film editor back in Wardour Street) something to keep him awake – he's always complaining that film editing can be very boring.'

We set off in convoy – the assistant cameraman driving the estate, the Merc's owner driving the limo and Richard in my car, with the cameraman – camera at the ready – on the luggage rack. 'Turn over.' Richard shouted to the cameraman after we had gone about half a mile. 'Flash, Peter, flash.'

I flashed the headlights twice and watched pure silk slide down over the slender breasts of the Chinese girl as she smiled coyly at the camera. 'Keep it running.' Richard told the cameraman – and he did, for five minutes. Then he held his thumb up and silk travelled upwards again.

'Well done, Lee,' said Richard as the convoy halted outside the Premium Bond HQ's gates and we all got out. 'Now I know you can't drive but I want you to do something very simple. I want you to get in the limo and drive just 25 yards, straight towards the gates – then stop and flash your lights. The camera will be resting on the tarmac inside the gates. It's a private road, not the public highway. Do you think you can manage that?'

Lee Sum nodded. She climbed behind the wheel of the Merc,

the cameraman lay on the ground facing her and Richard shouted 'Action'.

Instead of moving slowly, the big car shot forward and crashed full tilt into the gates, which burst open – making the cameraman hurl himself sideways. He only just managed to hang onto his £20,000 camera. By a miracle, the Merc suffered only a bent bumper.

'Christ,' swore Richard. 'Women drivers.' But it wasn't long before we were all in the pub and he was cheering her up with a drink, or two.

Next day, there was a call for Richard on the car phone. 'Oh my God', he said to the cameraman, as he clicked off. 'Get onto Sid and tell him on no account to show those 'rushes' to anyone until he's found the striptease sequence – and binned it. I'm going to find Patrick Robertson and explain.'

The call was to say that the Director of National Savings was interested to see how the James Bond idea had worked. Richard had visualised him sitting in the viewing theatre, watching, when suddenly Lee Sum Sun would appear and strip off. Fortunately, Sid located the sequence in time and we all repaired to the pub to cheer Richard up with a drink, or two.

A tug on the sleeve

Different people have different attitudes to people in the limelight. Some studiously ignore them. Others pester them. But most of the strangers who recognised me during the years when I was on the Box frequently, were friendly, courteous and seemed genuinely pleased to have had the encounter.

Two questions came up, time and time again: 'How does an astronaut go to the 'loo?' and 'What do Reginald Bosanquet and Andrew Gardner say to each other at the end of the news?'

I soon became a world expert on faecal bags and Urine Collection Devices -indeed I used to carry a picture of them in my briefcase, to help the explanation but the other question was less easy. It varied so much.

Many people believed it was 'Rhubarb . . . Rhubarb . . . Rhubarb' – and indeed it was, but only once and then it was Gordon Honeycombe who said it, not Reggie (it made Andrew's jaw drop with surprise, in vision, so he was asked not to say it again).

Reggie told me that they either discussed an item which had just been in the bulletin, or how their performances had been that night or, occasionally, said something humorous. Andrew told me that they were careful with the humour after a deaf viewer wrote in and said she could lip-read.

Exposure on TV brought many invitations to speak at clubs, societies, school prize-givings and conferences. Fees from the conferences and Prime Performers' other engagements enabled me to buy the house of my dreams – a detached house with a wooden aeroplane propeller over the garage doors, named 'Pacific' after the owner, who had been one of the first aviators to fly solo across that ocean. But I made it a principle never to accept a fee for a charity engagement or for any request from part of our local community.

This brought an invitation from the local primary school, where my sons were taught, to speak at the opening of a new extension to the school buildings.

There was the inevitable platform party and the inevitable collection of floral hats and the Lady Mayor was to speak first.

Her Worship was well past her youth but she spoke to the point, if at length. Then she turned to me and said, 'We are fortunate indeed to have Mr Peter Fairley of the BBC with us today. I am told he is a scientist and no doubt will be telling us something fascinating about science.'

I stood up and spent a few seconds reassuring the audience that I would not be saying anything about science – not least because I had a degree in English but would like to say a few words about television.

As I spoke, I could see son Alastair – who was seven – starting to mouth something silently at me from the front row of the audience. I took no notice. I went into a little hobbyhorse of mine – the power of television for good or evil. Alastair kept on mouthing, I kept on speaking. To my horror, he raised his hand. 'Oh God,' I thought, 'he wants to go to the "loo!"' I grimaced at him but carried on with the homily.

Suddenly, ignoring the rows of parents, he mounted the steps and stood beside me. When I still took no notice, he pulled my sleeve.

'Yes, Alastair, what is it?'

'Daddy,' he said firmly, 'you're not BBC.'

There, he'd said it. The Lady Mayor's gaffe was out in the

open. I had deliberately not corrected her introduction at the time for fear of embarrassing her in front of parents and governors. Now there was no escaping it.

It's a common mistake,' I said, ' and it's true – I used to do work for the BBC, but not lately. Anyway, it really doesn't matter.' I turned to give her a reassuring smile. But her seat, which was near a side door, was empty. . . .

Change to news from Jupiter

Commissions to write and present films continued to come in during the mid 70s. One, to script and present a film for the Dept of the Environment about a new method for turning waste liquids from the home into what they called 'potable' (i.e. drinkable) water for the consumer, caused a stir for the wrong reasons.

I reckoned there was only one way to demonstrate confidence in the effectiveness of the new 'Waste Water Treatment' system – one stage of which involved passing the waste through columns of charcoal to filter out any organisms and that was to drink a glass of the water straight from a tap at the end of the process.

Next day I was violently sick. Near panic set in among the D.O.E. officials and engineers who were hoping to market the system not only to British water companies but overseas as well. Then I confessed to having had a 'dubious' shellfish meal in a local restaurant the night before and sympathy ceased.

Another film offer followed, this one from Mitchell, Monkhouse Associates the 'Monkhouse' being Bob, the associates including Denis Norden – to write and front a 15-minute movie which was to be used to open an IBM staff conference in Hamburg. 'What is it about?' I asked. 'Change,' was the reply. 'Yes, but what sort of change?' I queried. 'Just change,' was the answer. 'Can't tell you any more.'

So I sat down and tried to think of every imaginable form of change, starting with easily recognisable changes – like in the weather, or a new model of car – to invisible changes, such as the teaspoonful of skin which each of us sheds in bed each night and the loss of an average of 100 hairs off our heads every 24 hours.

We shot the film in front of that unchanging institution – Parliament. MMA promised to let me know the audience's reaction.

'How did it go?' I asked when they returned to London. 'And what was it for? Why the secrecy?'

'Well, IBM management, who were our clients, were very pleased with it,' they said. 'But we can't really speak for the audience. You see, it was being used to soften up the employees – make them see that change can be good – before the management announced the biggest reorganisation of jobs at IBM this decade.'

A film offer from the Army was vetoed by Nigel Ryan, then ITN's Editor, on grounds that 'it would tend to link ITN, through you, to support of an establishment body which could itself become a matter of public controversy'. I wasn't sure if he meant rivalry with the Navy or RAF or possible objections from CND and the anti-nuclear lobby, but it was the first time he had said 'No'. He explained: 'It is in part through ITN that people like yourself have become in demand by outside organisations and ITN does, therefore have a certain argument that you carry its reputation with you.' Goodbye £500 fee.

Then, because it was advertising, I had to turn down the offer to make a commercial for Mercedes cars. Goodbye £750 fee.

Since ITN was only guaranteeing me an income of £6,500, I could ill afford to turn down such offers but the benefits and pleasure from working there, with colleagues who, almost without exception, had a great sense of humour and who managed to make work fun, far outweighed the money.

One unexpected benefit, which was not of my choosing, was to pick up the *Daily Express* one morning and find that I was pictured (or rather sketched) reading the news from the surface of Jupiter!

Jeff Hawke – the creation of Sidney Jordan – had always been my favourite strip cartoon (if that is the word) and Sidney had decided to create a fictional mission to the planet Jupiter and one of its moons, which he called 'Europa'. Jeff took the risks: I reported his exploits. In one strip, a very good likeness of ITN's Science Editor was seen in a studio, with a starlit sky outside, reading notes to a microphone with the caption. 'Good evening – and welcome to the Jupiter News Desk.' A second view showed an audience watching him on a cinema screen as he said, 'Tonight, we hope to bring you live pictures from the surface of Europa, one of the 12 Jovian moons.'

There was one crisis scene where a pretty p.a. was shown in

the Control Room of the 'London TV Monitoring Station', anxiously reporting by telephone.

'The signals from Jupiter are faltering. Fortunately, they recovered.'

The drama lasted only a week before Jeff moved on to some other exploit, But I still have the seven strip cartoons, framed and hanging in my study, and of all the so-called 'trappings of glory' which I collected, they mean more to me than any other. I have always wanted to meet Sidney in person, if only to ask him. 'How did I get back from Jupiter? You never said. For all you care, I could still be out there.'

The Conquest of Pain

Despite the temporary return of Project Apollo to the news in July 1975, when a three-man U.S. spaceship physically 'docked' with a Soviet Soy spaceship high above Bognor Regis, it became increasingly hard, once more, to get science or medical news onto the main ITN bulletin – *News At Ten.*

Although ITN has an Editor, who chairs a morning meeting to plan the broad coverage of news each day, it is left to the Output Editors to decide what actually goes into each bulletin. Each programme – *News at One, The Five-Forty-Five Bulletin* and *News at Ten* – has two Output Editors, to allow for shift changes. I found, over the years, that while the early bulletin editors welcomed virtually all real news, each *News At Ten* editor had preferences – for example, David Phillips was keen on science and technology stories whereas Derek Murray (nicknamed 'Jokes') favoured political and trade union news and always seemed to want to limit my subject areas to one minute, or 1.5 minutes, in the bulletin.

I tried to get round the problem by studying the duty rota and delaying any stories which would 'hold' until a 'pro-science' editor was on. But after all the enthusiasm generated by the Moon missions, it was disheartening.

It did, however, leave time to get on with another book – *The Conquest of Pain.*

I had long been interested in the subject of pain, ever since my regiment the 8th Royal Tank Regiment – had received warning that it was to be posted from Catterick, Yorkshire to Korea, where the war was not going particularly well for it – 'our' side. I had spent the months, while the Regiment finished equipping itself with Centurion tanks and preparing to sail, training my mind and body to resist torture.

There had been reports of prisoners being captured and tortured by the Chinese and North Koreans and, out of a ridiculous sense of bravado, I wanted to feel able to 'tough' it out if I was captured. I gleaned whatever facts I could about the mechanism of pain from the few books available and tortured myself in my quarters at Catterick until I could 'stand' the pain from three types of torture needles under the fingernails, a cigarette lighter burning under the armpits and a cold bath with cold water from the shower dripping onto my forehead.

So when Reckitt and Colman, the British makers of aspirin, asked if I would write a book about aspirin, which they could distribute to doctors, I agreed providing it could be broadened into a book about pain in general, with the longest chapter being about aspirin. They agreed.

Despite the previous research and several existing files of cuttings on the subject, it still took nearly four years to research afresh and write and, by the end, I was vowing never to write another book again. But it brought me into contact with some remarkably courageous people, including a consultant orthopaedic surgeon, Ralph Denham, who drove four stainless steel screws through his own shin-bones in order to understand why a certain percentage of patients who underwent hip replacement operations felt pain afterwards from the 'spike' inserted into the centre of their femurs.

Until then, it was believed that there were no pain receptors in bone. Certainly none had been demonstrated. So was the patients' pain imaginary? Ralph Denham devised an ingenious experiment to find out.

When a small cyst developed on the palm of his right hand and he was forced to take time off, he persuaded his fellow orthopaedic surgeons at the Royal Portsmouth Hospital to give him a general anaesthetic and cut open both his legs to expose six inches of shin-bone.

Bones are sheathed, rather like cricket bat handles, in a flexible membrane called the periosteum. It is packed with nerves (it is these, not the bones themselves, which cause fractures to be so painful). Mr Denham asked his team to strip back the periosteum from one shin but not the other.

They then had to drill four holes in the bones – one completely through each shin, the other half-way through – and drive in four screws These were covered with dressings so that only the heads were visible.

When he became conscious again, the consultant could not tell which screw was which, nor from which leg the periosteum and its supply of nerves had been stripped. He slept satisfied. Next morning, one of his colleagues appeared with a screwdriver and tightened each screw.

'The result of the experiment,' Ralph Denham told me, 'was identical on both sides. The pain I felt had nothing to do with whether the periosteum was in place or not, it came from the bone. When my colleague applied a quarter-turn at a time, I could identify positively which screws had gone right through and which had only gone half-way. It was when the tips of the screws which had only been driven halfway touched the bone on the far side that it was agony – the ones which had gone all the way through, when turned, were only slightly uncomfortable.'

He added: 'Another interesting thing – the pain would die away after each quarter-turn, within a minute or so, but come back with each fresh turn. It was like a thumbscrew in a torture chamber.'

What a way to prove a point!

Some years later, I made a film based on *The Conquest of Pain* for Boots Pharmaceuticals and met Ralph Denham again. He said that, as a result of his experience. he had modified his hip replacement operation and now filled the cavity in the patient's femur with a special glue, before inserting the 'spike' of the prosthesis. Several thousand such operations have since been performed with no complaints of pain.

After signing the contract to write the book, I realised that it posed a particular challenge. It was due to be given away by Reckitt to doctors, as well as sold to the general public. How could the language and vocabulary possibly suit both readerships? The terminology had to be easy to understand, yet not 'talk down' to the medically qualified. The book had to have 'popular' appeal, yet act in the absence of anything similar – as a kind of reference book, quoting extracts from medical journals intact to back up statements?

The solution came, curiously enough, during an annual meeting of the Medical Journalists Association, when I saw that parts of the agenda were printed in italics. Why not print the extracts from medical journals – and technical discussions of interest to doctors – in italics also, so that the layman could by-pass those and 'move more rapidly through the book on stepping stones of simplicity'?

The Conquest of Pain received 21 favourable reviews and three of them mentioned this device, one saying that it was a 'first'. Whether it was or not, the publishers, Michael Joseph, had done a deal with Reckitt and Colman that the drug company would 'guarantee' a percentage of sales. I received a letter from the Dean of St Thomas' Hospital Medical School, saying: 'I am writing to tell you how much I enjoyed the book. I will make sure that it is made available in the Medical School Library and I very much hope that it will be read with interest by many undergraduates as well as post-graduates.'

Two years later, I updated it at the request of Charles Scribner's of New York, who then published it in America. Although, as in Britain, it eventually sold out, neither publisher risked going to a reprint because it was not a 'best-seller'.

It remains the only book covering the whole of man's attempts to conquer pain and could easily be updated again. Furthermore, I still get queries from medical schools about its availability. But the whole world of publishing has changed in recent years, especially with continuing rises in the cost of paper, and I have not so far been able to find a fresh publisher with the necessary courage.

A book well worth writing would be a *Writers' Guide to Publishers*, although *The Writer's Handbook* went some way towards that, in its 1996 edition, by introducing brief comments from authors at the end of its section on publishers.

Theft of a briefcase – birth of a game

Capital Radio continued to provide Londoners with what they wanted – tuneful music, consistent professionalism from its DJs and interesting current affairs programmes. The Board, chaired by Dickie (later Sir Richard) Attenborough with John Whitney as Managing Director, was always accessible to staff and gave sensible praise where praise was due. Advertising revenue poured in.

The place was full of characters with contrasting personalities and styles – urbane presenters like Michael Aspel and Gerald Harper, voluble talkers with encyclopaedic memories such as Tommy Vance and Roger Moffat and irrepressible geniuses like Kenny Everett, who tragically died some years later from AIDS.

One had a dual identity. Listeners (and later viewers) knew him as Michael Barry, the Crafty Cook. Staff and 'insiders' knew him as Michael Bukht, the station's first Programme Controller and a devout Moslem.

I first became aware of Michael Bukht's religious beliefs at 11 a.m. one morning when I arrived at Euston Tower and saw a man kneeling on the windswept pavement, praying to the East – the direction of Mecca. As I walked to the revolving entrance door, the man stood up and I saw his face. It was Michael.

We both said 'Hello' without turning a hair. He might just as easily have been buying a newspaper. Michael will always hold my respect as a man who was deeply sincere about his religion but never foisted it on others: he just wanted a few moments in the morning for prayer.

I became so fascinated by the hurly-burly of Capital Radio and the enthusiasm of its (mainly) young staff that I asked John Whitney if I might write a book about the station's first decade. 'I'm sure we'd all love it,' was the reply. ' If you need any information, just ask.'

I explained that it might take a year or so – it would have to be worked on when other work allowed – and borrowed an armful of documents. I decided to write as I researched and started next morning.

After I had written about 20,000 words of the manuscript, I took it to London to show 'the story so far' to Bryan Wolfe at Capital and ask for his comments. But I had to meet an ITN crew in Southampton first, to shoot a news story and so left the manuscript in a briefcase on the back seat of my car at Waterloo Station. The car was properly parked in a 'P' space on the ramp.

To my horror, when I went to collect the car, I found the rear offside window broken and the briefcase gone. Horror is an understatement. Every word in the manuscript – like all those in my previous books – was penned in long-hand and I had no carbon copy.

The only other item in the briefcase was a Philips Pocket Memo tape-recorder but I would have gladly have given the thief a dozen tape-recorders if only he had returned the manuscript.

After reporting the theft to an unsympathetic desk sergeant at Southwark police station, I searched the area for hours. Next day, I visited hostels and schools, offering a £50 reward for the return of the manuscript. But it never turned up.

I have to admit to not having the strength or imagination to start all over again. I told John Whitney what had happened and asked to be allowed to withdraw the offer. 'Of course,' he said sympathetically, 'I would do the same.'

The incident reminded me of Professor Denis Melrose of Hammersmith Hospital, who had written a thesis on animal kidney transplants while researching at the Keston laboratories of the Royal College of Surgeons. He left it in a briefcase on a London bus.

That, too, never turned up. Denis was so shocked that he could not face writing it all over again, either. So he changed direction in his research – and invented the world's first heart–lung machine, which helped to save thousands of lives.

I wish I could have done something equally useful. Instead I invented a game.

It was called 'Target – Moon!'. It was another attempt to keep the achievements of the Apollo astronauts alive in the public mind, especially children's minds. It was a board game with dice, a little like Monopoly, except that players scored points for making 'discoveries' or lost points for mishaps described on 'Space Mystery' cards. They ended up transferring into a tiny Lunar Roving Vehicle for a drive around a large graphic of the Moon in the centre of the board, where they would collect more points for 'discoveries' before finally 'blasting-off' back to Earth.

I turned for help to my old friends at *TV Times*. Eric Carter, the Assistant Editor, helped draw up the Rules of Play and provided half the money to patent the game. Gordon Moore and Eddie Pedder, Art Director and Picture Editor respectively, produced a blown-up graphic of the Moon for the centre of the board and Leo Armati, *TV Times'* New York correspondent obtained all the NASA photos we needed to illustrate the squares around the perimeter. Half the editorial floor seemed to get involved in playing the game, over and over again, in spare moments to test not only the rules but the popular appeal of the game.

We found a marketing firm in the East End of London, Mayplay Creations, who were enthusiastic to the point of manufacturing six trial games in illustrated boxes and taking a stand at the International Toy Fair in the Grand Hotel at Brighton to test it out.

We grew excited as the Fair opened, especially at the prospect of a premium offer to the millions of readers of *TV Times*, at a special price of 37 shillings and sixpence per game, which was under discussion at that very moment (Eric and I were due to receive an 8 per cent royalty).

I took a train to Brighton, then a taxi and finally a lift. I'm not sure which journey took longest but it was certainly no easy matter finding Mayplay Creations' stand, much less our game 'Target – Moon!'. It was tucked away on the top floor of the hotel, half-hidden by pillars and only accessible through phalanxes of mechanical monsters, cuddly dolls, farmyard animals, paint-boxes and other, attractively-presented board games. My heart sank.

It was no surprise when the letter came from Mr P. Solomons of Mayplay Creations, informing us that, 'with regret', his company had decided not to go into further production of the game 'due to lack of public interest'.

We should have had the guts to try again. But, as so often happens with journalists, our attention quickly refocused onto some major item of news and sidelines were abandoned and left to gather dust.

I still have one copy of 'Target – Moon!'. We still, occasionally, play it. But it remains a reminder of days when I was willing to dabble in almost anything in an effort to acquire money to pay not only the taxman but school fees.

Arithmetic and Miss *TV Times*

The wisdom of being selective about work – especially work under the spotlight of television – was borne out soon afterwards when I accepted fees to appear on Tyne Tees's, *The Kreskin Show*, and Granada's, *Wheeltappers and Shunter's Club*.

Kreskin was a Canadian stage clairvoyant, who used every technical device and piece of spoofery to convince audiences that he could read people's minds. Because of my association with the British Premonitions Bureau, he asked if I was willing to be interviewed on his show.

Kreskin had a patter and a highly-persuasive manner and the invitation came from him personally over the phone. I was flattered. Then, when Tyne Tees phoned to discuss the fee, I was hooked.

It was probably a mistake to have agreed because I was trying hard to be taken seriously as a Science Editor dealing in facts and, whatever talents Kreskin may have had, he was a showman and his show was full of what I call 'mumbo-jumbo'.

A surprising number of people remember the programme (for the wrong reasons). Although I remember little of what was said because the studio humidity matched that in the Malayan jungle, I spent the whole programme trying, while answering his questions, not to be noticed flicking huge drops of sweat off the end of my nose.

It was the TV equivalent of the radio broadcaster's nightmare – a 'frog' in the throat. Broadcasters usually have a 'cough key' to press, to cut out programme sound while they cough or get rid of a 'frog'. Or else they are trained to stop, apologise and clear the 'frog' unashamedly with their head turned sideways. I suppose I should have got out a handkerchief and unashamedly wiped the whole of my face. But nobody had trained me. So I was left to squirm.

Kreskin kept on sending me Christmas cards which read, 'Hope you feel cooler now – Kreskin.'

Another mistake was to be tempted by the fee to appear on *Wheeltappers' and Shunter's Club*, although I was also under a certain amount of pressure from *TV Times* to agree.

The Club was named after a genuine railwaymen's trade union club from the old London Midland and Scottish Railway days and was presented by a Master of Ceremonies, who called up stars and acts in the manner of *Old Time Music Hall*. The 'act' in which I was involved was the selection of the new 'Miss *TV Times*'.

Most of the programme had been given over to this beauty contest, which involved four contestants parading in bathing costumes, then smart evening dresses and finally being interviewed in 'comfortable' clothing of their choice. The judges included Pat Phoenix (of *Coronation Street* fame), George Best, the soccer star, and Larry Grayson, the comedian. I was the 'adjudicator', armed with a stop-watch, clipboard and pen, whose duty was to call 'time up' after each interview and to total up the judges' points in the commercial break and hand the MC a slip of paper indicating the names of 3rd, 2nd and 1st.

That was the big mistake – mine and Granada's. Granada had fallen into the trap of thinking that 'Science' automatically meant

'good at maths' and I had fallen into the trap of not finding out
enough about the role of 'adjudicator' before accepting it. Had I
known, I would have 'copped out', since maths was my worst
subject.

Commercial breaks usually last 2 to 2½ minutes. By the time 2
minutes of the 'Wheeltappers' break had elapsed, the sweat was
again running off the end of my nose and I had only totalled up
the figures on two of the judges' cards (nobody had thought to
supply a pocket calculator). I cannot remember who the MC was,
although I can still hear his gravelly voice and strong Northern
accent, but he saved my bacon that night by cracking a few im-
promptu jokes with Club 'members' and holding the camera on
himself until I had obviously finished.

Miss *TV Times* was duly elected. Flashlights duly popped
afterwards and we all went off to George Best's night club.

'Nice to meet someone good at sums,' said George as he bought
the first round of drinks. 'Good job we had you there, Peter.'

I have never let on until this day that, with sweat pouring and
pulse racing, I had had a total 'white-out'. I simply couldn't see
the figures much less add them together. I just guessed at the
winner. However, I kept the cards and, in the privacy of George's
downstairs 'loo', I added up the figures again.

The right beauty queen had won. But only by the margin of a
single vote. Phew!

Goodbye and Hello

When an invitation came to join James Goldsmith's new magazine *Now*, in March 1979, as Assistant Editor in charge of the
Modern Life section, it was difficult to resist. Firstly, *Now* was to
be an international news-oriented weekly, a little similar to
Newsweek, and should have offered plenty of opportunity, therefore, not just to follow up 'whiffs' of news but to indulge in
futurology, which I enjoyed. Secondly, the terms offered were
£25,000 a year, a pension and a car.

David Nicholas, who had taken over as editor at ITN, called
me stupid when I told him that I had decided to stay at ITN,
especially since the only guarantee of income I had was £9,500 a
year. But the truth was that the Goldsmith offer even in the form
of an official letter from his company, Cavenham Communica-

tions seemed to be too good to be true and because I enjoyed being part of the happy family working in Wells Street.

Almost immediately, a major news story developed – an energy crisis – and I found myself working with a writer-producer called Mike Chamberlain on a series of 'specials', explaining the crisis and examining 'alternative' fuels. With up to 5 minutes on offer for each report, it felt like the good old Apollo days again.

One of the 'alternatives' we examined – for motor cars – was alcohol. A BP research scientist had once told me that cars could run off spirits, albeit expensively. So we devised a scenario where the camera showed my Fiat slowing to a halt, apparently out of petrol, and then me buying a bottle of Scotch from an off-licence and pouring it into the tank.

To shorten the time needed 'on camera', we had my local garage make a small modification to the fuel tank so that the whisky did not mix with the residue of the petrol but went straight to the carburettor. We picked a quiet suburban road for the video recording – it had to be a 'one-off, once only' piece of action and we did not want traffic noise to drown the explanation.

Fortunately, whisky is not my tipple, so it didn't hurt to pour the whole bottle in without stopping, climb into the driver's seat and switch on. There was a certain amount of spluttering and one backfire – but it worked. I drove away.

'Now all you have to do is claim on your expenses,' said Mike. I can just imagine the Chief Accountant's face – 'to one bottle of whisky for car – £5.' But that was not the only problem.

Both the *News at Ten* Output Editors used the first two reports on consecutive nights, but the whisky-driven car was No. 4 in our series and, because reports of 5 minutes in length tended to be looked on as 'soft', feature-type material, it did not get used for a month – and then only in shortened form.

It was all rather depressing. But the depression soon lifted when I had a tip that a new drug was about to be launched by Smith Kline and French Laboratories which was a real breakthrough in the treatment of ulcers. Frank Hodson, SKF's Public Relations Director, confirmed it 'off the record' – but then offered a deal. 'If you will come and train our research team in giving interviews about this, I'll help you with some visual material and let ITN run the story the evening before we hold a Press conference and release the news generally.'

The offer was irresistible. The drug was called Tagamet and its importance was not only in its ability to relieve symptoms but to cure the duodenal or gastric ulcer or ulcers altogether. Medical research had been searching for such a drug for decades.

A week before the launch I travelled to Welwyn Garden City and put all six doctors and scientists involved through radio and TV interviews, as well as simulating a quick-fire Press conference. It was no easy task because the story was complex, especially explaining how the drug acted in the body. We had to turn, 'Tagamet is a histamine H–3 receptor antagonist which rapidly inhibits both basal and stimulated gastric secretion of acid and reduces pepsin output' into something understandable to the layman. In the end, we admitted defeat and decided that the best way would be to say it was 'extremely complicated' and switch quickly to some other aspect of the story.

It was an occasion when words needed a picture and I was lucky enough to be given a short sequence of animated film, explaining H-3 receptors and the way the drug acted on them, to use in my ITN report. Such film animation had cost more than £1,000 to create. Frank gave it to me free. Its value was underlined when, after *News at Ten* had broken the story, I had a phone call from David Rose, one of ITN's political correspondents. 'Peter, I've just watched your report about that new ulcer drug – is it any good?' he asked. I told him that I thought it was very good – a genuine breakthrough and asked why he wanted to know.

'Because I'm due to go into hospital tomorrow to have surgery on my ulcer and I don't think I will now,' he answered. David cancelled his hospital appointment went to see his GP who, after checking with SKF, prescribed Tagamet. The symptoms disappeared within a few days and have not returned. 'I regard myself as cured,' he told me, nearly 20 years later. Jim Burnham, who was in charge of the film editors at ITN at that time, tells a similar story. He, too, watched the report, persuaded his GP to prescribe Tagamet and has been ulcer-free ever since. Although Tagamet has been superseded, to some extent, by Glaxo's Zantac, it has given me real satisfaction to have helped save two colleagues from a great deal of discomfort and played a part in their full recovery. It was a 'whiff of news' of real value.

A big decision

David Nicholas decided to set up a proper Science Unit at ITN under Frank Miles, who had made an outstanding, behind-the-scenes contribution to our coverage of the Moon missions.

Many colleagues expected my nose to go 'out of joint', but which of us was chief and which Indian mattered not a jot to me – I was glad to have somebody else to fight for 'air-time' for science and medical stories.

However, two months later, an offer came out of the blue which I could not resist. It called for a big decision.

Socialism was still the nation's choice and James Callaghan had not long been in office as Prime Minister, when I was invited out to lunch by an old Fleet Street colleague, T. F. 'Tommy' Thompson. Tommy had abandoned aviation and then political reporting on the *Daily Mail* to found Opinion Research Centre.

ORC, as it was known for short, was then the most widely-quoted public opinion pollster on issues of the day and well respected by newspapers and politicians alike. What was less well known was the work it did for leaders of industry who wanted to find out what their workers felt on a variety of important matters, such as wages, holidays, rights and working conditions.

Tommy said he had 'a proposition'.

'There's a new mood in British industry,' Tommy explained, 'a will on the part of management to communicate more to their employees. Mind you, they're under threat from Jim Callaghan that, if they don't do something about it themselves, he'll bring in legislation to make them. We believe that we, at ORC, know the management's – you know the communications techniques.'

Tommy's proposition was that he and I – and his partner at ORC, a quiet, diminutive financial wizard called Hamish Nealon – should form a company to help British industry to communicate more effectively with its workforce. I said I would think about it.

Having not long previously rejected the offer to join *Now* and stay under contract to ITN, it seemed a bit shallow to change heart and leave for a totally unknown way of life, even if £20,000 a year was promised. But I have never shied away from challenges and, in any case, my total lack of financial acumen should be more than compensated for by Hamish's expertise as a

Financial Controller and his in-depth knowledge of the business world (it was rumoured that he and Tommy were already worth a million). Besides which, there was the whiff of an ITV technicians' strike in the air.

So, after only four nights of tossing and turning, I handed in my notice at ITN.

A lot then happened in a hurry. We managed to find ideal premises in Mortimer Street – just a block away from ITN House, which meant that it would be simple to walk to the studio for any appearances over the following three months, until my notice expired. We located Amanda Jacquet, who had been the most efficient Specialist Correspondents' 'temp' at ITN the year before, and asked her to work for us. We registered the company name – Management Communications Centre (MCC for short). And I starred in a film about pigs..

There is a saying in the film industry, 'Never work with children or animals'. I never found children a problem – they were a laugh a minute, especially those who appeared on *Magpie* – but I never wish to work again with a pig.

The booking came from Silkstream Film Productions of Pinner, who had been commissioned by the agricultural giant BOCM Silcock to make a movie about a new genus of pig called *The Masterbreeder*.

The creature looked like a black-and-white Wessex Saddleback with an unusually long, straight spine, firm flesh and a craving for sows. Its genetic history and cross-breeding had been so carefully arranged that, to maintain maximum value to any purchaser, it had to be reared like an aristocrat on an exceptionally clean pig farm.

We found one of these near Tring, in Hertfordshire, and I remember writing opening words to camera which went: 'They call this the Colditz Castle of the pig world. But the barbed wire on the top of the high, surrounding wall is not to keep the inmates in – it's to try to keep unwanted visitors out. The visitors they're worried about here are GERMS. Now let me introduce you to one of the inmates – he's known as "The Masterbreeder".'

We filmed me, in casual, country clothes, in front of the farm's front gate. It had vertical iron bars and looked very much like the entrance to a prison. We arranged for the pig's handler – a scientist – to remain out of sight in the doorway to a sty and only release the pig into the yard when he heard the words, 'Now let me introduce. . . .' The camera would then zoom in on the su-per-pig in the yard behind me.

'All ready? ACTION,' shouted Ted Hooker, the director.

I got my lines right but was amazed to see the whole crew be-hind the camera giggle and then guffaw. 'What was wrong with that?' I queried. 'Nothing wrong with you,' said Ted, who had the physique of Billy Bunter and looked as though he had just played one of his best japes. 'It was the pig.'

He finally stopped laughing and explained that the concrete base of the yard was made in two sections and one section had ended up about two inches higher than the other. The pig had come out of the sty, spotted the camera lights and apparently decided to see what was going on, walking towards them with two of its legs on one level of concrete and the other two on the other.

In other words, it had appeared, to the camera, to limp.

There was no alternative but to re-shoot. Even though a limp would be unlikely to impair sex drive or reduce fertility, we couldn't show an animal with a title like 'Masterbreeder' to have any kind of physical defect.

Porky (the pig, not Ted) was recaptured by the scientist and led back to the sty entrance for a second try.

Again, I got the lines right. But again, the crew burst out laugh-ing. 'What is it this time?' I said tetchily, because I had had my back to whatever had happened, as before.

This time, on the words, 'Now let me introduce you', the sci-entist had correctly released the pig but, instead of heading to-wards the lights, or snuffling at one or two slices of apple we had lain down on the concrete, it had shot out of one doorway – and scuttled at top speed into another.

It took us seven 'takes' before Ted was satisfied that he had the effect he was looking for 'in the can'. The rest of the 'shoot' was event-free.

He sent me a nice letter afterwards. It read: 'Very many thanks for all your splendid efforts. It is always a pleasure to work with real professionals.'

My dictionary gives, as one of its definitions of the word 'pro-fessional', 'an expert player of a game'. The pig was that all right.

CHAPTER SIXTEEN

Here We Go Again

A week after my notice to ITN expired, the phone rang in MCC's new penthouse offices above Universal Studios' London headquarters at 47, Mortimer Street. It was Pamela Juvenile, whom I knew socially and as the agent of both Gordon Honeycombe and Shaw Taylor.

'Are you going to be around for the next three weeks, Peter?' she started. I said I wasn't going anywhere.

'I've had an approach from a client who would like you to make a commercial for them,' Pamela went on. 'I can't tell you their name right now but they're quite respectable. They want you for a day.'

I was about to say the routine 'No' when I suddenly realised that I was no longer bound by the ethical rules of ITN. So I said 'Yes – providing I'm not going to be promoting baked beans or breakfast cereals or ketchup.'

'No,' she laughed, 'it's insurance. Anyway, if you're interested, how would it appeal if I asked for a fee of 15?'

'OK.' I said, thinking she meant £1,500 and adding sarcastically, 'I think I can just about manage a day for that.' My luck was definitely in.

She promised to 'get back within the hour' but was back in five minutes.

'OK,' she said, 'it's on. It's Pearl Assurance and they're delighted. But I could only get 12 not 15 – is that agreeable?'

I pretended to think it over for a second, then said 'Oh that'll be all right – after all, £1,200 for a day's work is not bad.'

'Twelve hundred,' she shrieked. 'Twelve thousand!'

I couldn't believe my ears. 'Gosh,' I said, 'I'd better go and buy myself a new suit.' Quick as a flash, she came back, 'Yes do. But they'll pay for that too.'

I tried to gulp 'Yes' but she rattled on – about date, time, location (Pearl's head office in High Holborn) and contact (a man from Pearl's advertising agency). 'Don't worry,' she ended, 'I'll confirm it all in writing. Thanks.'

So, in one day, I had found myself an agent and, in ITN terms, more than a year's extra salary. I took a taxi to Regent Street and bought a £250 suit, a cream shirt, burgundy tie and matching handkerchief from Aquascutum, before anyone could change their minds. I made sure I kept the receipt.

On recording day, I arrived early at Pearl Assurance to find a crew of 12 preparing the 'set' and fixing huge, silver reflecting boards along one edge of the architraved ceiling. The 'set' itself didn't take much setting – Pearl's head office was an ornate marble hall with columns, a long mahogany front counter and desks discreetly placed by the columns, where staff typed and prepared documents.

I was supposed to walk along the front of the counter, speaking to the camera and pointing to a sequence of cardboard notices on which words like 'Two years' and 'Five years' and figures like '5%', '7.5%' and '13%' were displayed .

I was given the Manager's office as a dressing and rest room, met the movie director and the man from the advertising agency and changed into 'The Suit'. My hands were trembling to the point that I had difficulty with 'The Tie' and then nearly spilled coffee down it. Finally, it was time to go under the strong lights and move to the first of the 'grouchos' (tape marks on the floor, indicating where an actor is supposed to stand and so called after Groucho Marx). I thought of a sunflower to calm the pulse, checked The Matching Pocket Handkerchief and faced the camera.

'When you're ready,' said the director. 'ACTION!'

I cannot remember the lines today but I had made sure that I knew them by heart that morning – after all, £12,000 was up for grabs. I pointed to the right notices on the right words, reached the end of the counter on time and, as far as I was concerned, had 'put a good 'un in the can'. 'Can I go home now?' I asked, tongue in cheek.

But this was not news, nor was it ITN – it was the world of advertising, where everybody has to justify the enormous budget extracted from the client and the size of the crew. Sure enough, someone found a reason to do another 'take' – and not just one, 46, in fact.

Each time, I retired to the manager's office, sat down and said quietly to myself, 'Mine not to reason why, mine just to take the money – and fly.'

Before lunch, virtually every 'retake' was due to some technical or lighting problem. The 'blondes' and 'red-heads' seemed to keep on producing shadows in the wrong places, or the Pearl Assurance staff working in the background, moved. But after lunch, I started to make mistakes, deserving the numerous 'that one down to you' from the director. There were two main reasons for this.

One was that there was no relaxing drink to go with the sandwiches and, when I asked if I might slip across the road to the pub for a 'quick one', the director (who was teetotal) said, 'I'd rather you didn't.' So, for £12,000, I didn't – but fell victim to tension instead.

The second reason was distractions behind the camera. To stop the public peering in at customers doing routine counter business or staff working at desks, Pearl had installed beautifully-etched, plate-glass windows, with the frosty effect extending to a height of about 6 ft. 3 inches – higher than the average passer-by. But whenever the lights went on for a 'take', the brilliance of the illumination made passers-by wonder what was going on inside, especially as dusk fell. So they kept jumping up to see over the etching.

If there is one thing that I have always had difficulty in coping with, it is someone moving directly behind the camera. That day, it was like addressing an audience of bouncing puppets and words kept failing me.

Supper-time came and we were still 'shooting' but, by now, only close-ups of the display signs on the counter. I took off the Suit and had a chat with the ad man. 'Why did you want me for this? I asked. 'Because you are a virgin,' was the answer.

A virgin? I did not know whether to take it as an insult or a compliment. But then he explained, 'You've never done a commercial before, so you're fresh. And because insurance is not what you're normally associated with, the impact on the viewer will be that much greater.'

'I see,' I said. 'When will the commercial go 'on air?'

'On Mondays, Wednesdays and Fridays for the next three weeks,' he replied. I asked at what time of day. I immediately wished I hadn't.

'We've booked slots before, during and after *News at Ten*,' was the answer.

I could see the look on the faces of the hierarchy at ITN. I tried to think of the sunflower but it wouldn't come. That night, I tried sheep, but they wouldn't come either. So I counted banknotes – twelve thousand of them.

It was worth a bit of insomnia . . .

Business under the belt

MCC flourished for 18 years, before the recession struck. Had I not bought out my partners after the first three years (they became more and more interested in making money while my priorities were to pay bills promptly and keep our suppliers and staff happy) the company might still be flourishing today. But 'cash flow' – their slogan – eventually became a trickle and then stopped.

In that timespan, we produced 217 films and videos, 28 management conferences – providing slides, written speeches and music – and ran more than 1000 Media Training Courses, including 30 for the Metropolitan Police. We also trained all London Underground's line announcers and every British Airways pilot, co-pilot and cabin crew instructor – between 1984 and 1990 – to improve their announcements to passengers over the p.a. system.

To help in the British Airways work, which was sworn to secrecy, we employed Bryan Wolfe (my old 'boss' at Capital Radio) and Bob Holness (of LBC radio, ITV quiz and BBC popular music fame) who has, in my opinion, the best modulated voice – and therefore the most interesting – in broadcasting.

Apart from classroom work, we carried out a lot of research among passengers and made a film, to introduce each course, called *Captain Who Speaking?* with me as presenter and narrator.

In it, one of the pieces of advice was to try to relate heights, speeds and distances to things which passengers can relate to – like '10 miles a minute' or 'roughly 300 yards a second' instead of '600 miles an hour' – and, instead of 40,000 feet, why not say 'Seven and a half miles above the ground' or 'That's roughly half as high again as Everest'.

A few years later, returning from shooting a recruiting video for British Airways called *Captains of the Future*, we were flying back to London from Glasgow, as ordinary passengers, when the Captain's voice came over the p.a. 'Good afternoon, ladies and gentlemen, my name is John Hastings and I'm your Captain. We'll shortly be flying over Blackpool – the visibility's good, so if you care to look out on the right-hand side, you may see the famous Tower.'

Well done, I thought. Nice, cheerful voice. Gave his name – not simply, 'This is your Captain speaking', and warned us what we might see in advance. Full marks. 'We're flying at a height of 32,000 feet.' Captain Hastings went on. Then he added .. 'That's roughly the equivalent of two thousand one hundred and thirty three double-decker buses, stacked one on top of the other.'

Evidently, I had been recognised coming aboard. Evidently, the Captain had taken our training to heart. Evidently, a reputation had not entirely vanished.

Francis Albert Bosanquet

Our decision to run Media Training Courses upset David Nicholas and Alastair (soon to be Sir Alastair) Burnet at ITN and I got a 'wigging', although there was nothing they could do about it (I no longer had a contract with ITN) and despite the fact that it was an early type of Media Training which had brought ITN the Tagamet exclusive before I left.

They did not go so far as to accuse us of 'helping the enemy'. But they believed that we were revealing tricks of the trade which would enable an interviewee to pull wool over the viewer's eyes.

I saw it differently – more as helping the interviewee cope with pressure and so give a more interesting interview. Fortunately, other ITN employees or ex-employees shared my point of view and we were never short of 'names' to do interviews or give advice on our Media Training Courses.

One such was Reggie Bosanquet who, even before he quit ITN, helped me to train the Board of Directors of Philips, the electronics group. Reggie's forté, in my view, was interviewing and, bless him, he agreed to do more to help MCC get better known.

Our next Media Training contract was to train all the European factory managers of Monsanto, the international chemical giant. The course had to be conducted at their Training Centre near Antwerp, using their own TV equipment

I arranged to hire a chauffeur-driven car to pick Reggie up at his flat in Chelsea and booked us onto a mid-afternoon flight to Belgium. It was a Sunday and Reggie had just spent Saturday night at a flamboyant country-house party given by Victor Lowndes, of *Playboy* magazine fame.

When we arrived at the flat, he appeared at the door, not with an overnight bag but with a large wooden rabbit hutch in his arms. A pretty, blonde girl aged about seven followed him. 'This is my daughter Delilah', he said, by way of introduction, 'and this is Hoppity'. A grey-brown rabbit put its face to the wire mesh, as if on cue. 'You don't mind if we take them first to Felicity's, do you?'

Felicity was Reggie's second wife, a tall, handsome blonde PR executive with a ready giggle, from whom Reggie had, sadly, separated prior to divorce. We loaded Delilah, bags, food for Hoppity and wooden hutch into the immaculate Mercedes, with the driver trying hard to give the impression that he did this kind of thing every day and that a bit of faeces-stained straw on his upholstery did not matter a damn. He knew his tip was coming.

As soon as we reached Felicity's house in Marloes Road, Kensington, Reggie leaped out and went to an entry-phone. Loud words were exchanged and I tried to cover the row by questioning Delilah about Hoppity. Eventually, he returned to the car looking flushed and disgruntled. 'C'mon Delilah – here, you help me with the rabbit, Peter.'

We drove off to London Airport with the little girl sitting forlornly on her pet's cage, outside her mother's flat. 'She'll be OK,' said her father. 'I think Felicity was having a snooze.'

We checked in, I tipped the driver £5 and Reggie went through to Duty Free. 'See you at the bar,' he muttered.

We drank two large cognacs and then it was time to board the Sabena plane. In flight, he ordered two quarter bottles of champagne and two cognacs to turn them into champagne cocktails.

Because of some by-law or other, in those days, Antwerp airport did not have its own taxi rank. You had to ring into the city to get a cab. 'OK,' said Reggie, 'while you're ordering the cab, I'll be in the bar.' He was in it for 20 minutes, while I watched for the taxi.

Monsanto had booked us both into the Intercontinental Hotel. At the Reception desk, we were asked to register. The registration card was one of those designed to be processed by a computer, where you are supposed to enter each letter of your name and address into a separate box and sign on a line at the bottom.

I did not know, although others at ITN did, that Reggie had a profound contempt for such forms. He showed it that evening. To my horror, I saw that he had filled in the little boxes to read F RA NC IS ALBERT SINATRA and scribbled Sinatra on the signature line at the bottom. Fortunately, they did not ask to see our passports – in fact the receptionist did not even look at the card. We arranged to meet in the bar at 7 p.m.

When I came down, Reggie was three-quarters of the way through a bottle of Chablis and was drinking a glass of Kir. He asked me to call the *Maître d'* and see if they had any oysters on the menu. We ordered oysters and a filleted Dover sole and I selected an expensive bottle of Mersault, I still felt in his debt, but only just.

We finished the Chablis and went to the table, where he ordered a Mirabelle, as an aperitif. I had never heard of a Mirabelle but the wine waiter explained that it was a white alcohol distilled from small golden plums.

Reggie's speech, by now, was becoming slurred. The Mirabelle seemed to improve things but, by the time he had downed six of the oysters, his pallor was a ghastly white. Suddenly, he got up, pointed to the remaining oysters and said, 'Give them to the barman,' and rushed out of the restaurant.

'*M'sieur* is very tired.' I said loyally to the *Maître d'*. 'He would like the barman to have the rest of his oysters. He won't be back.'

I spent an unhappy night, worrying about the Bosanquet hangover next day and what, for my company, was a VIP client. But to my amazement, he came out of the lift promptly at 7.30 a.m. as if nothing had happened. We were picked up by a Monsanto car as planned and I began to relax.

'A touch of rhinitis, Fairbags,' he explained on the six-mile drive to the Training Centre. 'I suffer from it from time to time.' But his complexion was turning greener and greener and, by the time we arrived, he looked a very sick man.

Monsanto had assembled a little reception party at the front door, to greet the 'TV star from England'. To my horror, instead of shaking hands, Reggie rushed past them, clutching his yellow bag of duty-free booze, and asked for the 'loo'.

He did not reappear for half an hour, by which time I had had to start the course because, with 12 managers to train, time was at a premium. I was just apologising for his absence due to 'an attack of hay fever', when in he walked, accompanied by a Belgian bearing a tray of glasses, some filled with Coke, the rest with orange juice.

During the opening lecture – advice on the Media and how they operate – I noticed Reggie downing glass after glass with his back to the class. When interviewing started, he was clearly feeling fine. He proceeded to conduct 12 first-rate TV interviews and showed no irritation when the Monsanto technician announced that he had failed to record any sound and so we would have to do them again.

He did not even grumble when lunch was 'dry' – orange juice or nothing.

The second batch of interviews were even better than the first. I then took the managers through radio theory and practice and we said goodbye. In the car on the way to the airport, I told Reggie: 'I have to be frank. There was a time last night – and again this morning – when I vowed never to use you as an instructor again. Then you did those brilliant interviews. How did you manage to pull yourself together?'

'Simple, Fairbags.' he answered, opening the top of his plastic duty-free bag. He pulled out a half bottle of brandy and a half bottle of vodka. They were empty. 'You can't see vodka in orange juice, nor cognac in Coke.'

Teetotal on the Tartan

Although I had been involved in reporting all the early oil and gas discoveries around Britain, I had never been on a North Sea oil production platform. About a year after MCC started up, the chance came to do so.

An old school friend, Clive Turner, had become Public Affairs manager for Texaco, the US oil giant and he needed a video in a hurry. The whole of his Main Board of Directors was flying over from America in two week's time, to inspect their £250 million investment in the North Sea known as 'The Tartan Platform'. The plan was to fly them out by helicopter from Aberdeen and let them spend half a day on the platform, watching a new test hole being drilled and oil being pumped ashore. The problem was that some of the directors were too old and infirm to cope with the helicopter flight and the metal stairways on the rig.

A video, shown in an Aberdeen hotel, would help to keep them occupied. Later, the 25-minute programme, called *The Tartan Report*, could be chopped into three and shown as part of a series of internal news magazine programmes which we created, called *Texaco Video News*. I hired a video crew and four of us and all the equipment were flown to the platform, which was about 117 miles off the Scottish coast.

Landing on an oil platform in the middle of nowhere is an unforgettable experience. At first, it is a tiny speck. Even from 700 feet up, it looks nothing. Then you close in and the scale is mind-boggling – to get a true idea of the size, the oil men put us in a skip out over the waves and winched us up 35 storeys, at top speed. It seemed never ending.

On arrival, we worked out a shooting sequence carefully – and compiled an inventory of all our equipment – and it was as well that we did. On the second day, we forgot a 'redhead' lamp, after completing a scene, and it took us nearly 20 minutes of walking to retrieve it, so large was the platform.

It was not only the three-decker platform which was large. I demonstrated to camera one of the nuts and bolts and one of the shackles used to secure equipment on deck. The stainless steel nut and bolt weighed 20 lbs. and was 18 inches long. I couldn't even lift the shackle.

We stayed aboard a week, during which the unpredictable North Sea stayed calm and the weather sunny. Texaco employed a former West End chef and the food was not only plentiful but of gourmet standard (it cost Texaco £10 per man per day). But no alcohol was permitted .

I worried a bit about that until it was pointed out that, with an investment of more than £250 million at stake, no risk of accident was acceptable. Then it made sense. Also, the rule applied to everybody and the penalty for breaking it, oilman or visitor alike, was to be held by the arms and ankles and tossed overboard into the sea – and they were deadly serious. I went teetotal for the week.

It was very satisfying being allowed enough time and a large enough budget to be able to tell, properly, a remarkable story of human achievement. It was the first time I felt glad to have left ITN.

We managed to get plenty of 'gee whiz' data into the report –

'taller than the Post Office tower, with 37,000 tons of steel and more than a quarter of a million nuts and bolts', 'an annual production of 33 million barrels of oil – enough to put 10 gallons of petrol into every car in Britain' – and so forth. And we included one statistic which seemed to put the value of North Sea oil to Britain into perspective once and for all.

Over a shot of the metering equipment installed by the Dept of Energy at the well-head in the control room, we showed figures to illustrate the words: 'By the time this Tartan field has been fully exploited, Texaco alone will have paid the Government £2 billion pounds (£2,000 million) in taxes – enough to build 4,393 primary schools or 588 miles of motorway.'

I often wonder how many of those schools or miles of motorway ever got built or, if they didn't, where the money went? It is a question which political journalists, for some reason, never seem to ask.

Operation 'Smash Hit'

Partly because my science reporting days had begun with the opening of the first nuclear power station and partly because I had changed roles and was now 'management', the Central Electricity Generating Board invited me to become a consultant to their Public Relations department in nuclear matters. I was asked to submit a list of ways in which MCC could assist the Board to improve its image.

Media training was one. Recording radio interviews and circulating tapes to local radio stations was another. Creating audio-visual, film and video productions was a third.

We made 23 different videos for the CEGB, several to be used for briefing local communities on the likely impact (and especially the benefits) of having a second (or even a third) nuclear power station built in their area. So we made *Sizewell 'B' – the Way Ahead, The Case for Sizewell 'C', The 'A', 'B' and 'C' of Hinkley Point, More Power for Wylfa, Search for a Site* and *Waste Without Worry*.

It was fun going on location with a three-man crew, picked not only for their skill but also for their sense of humour, with time to enjoy the countryside, find comfortable hotels off the beaten track and enjoy good food. I often used to say to the crew: 'You may not get paid well but you'll live well.' I was surprised to find that it was a rare attitude in the non-broadcast video industry, where crews often get booked into the worst 'digs' imaginable.

The power station productions were profitable, nonetheless. But there were other productions, not about power stations, which gave me more satisfaction.

The more I learned, from the inside, about nuclear engineering, the attitude to safety and the care taken over designing and building anything 'nuclear' including whole power stations, submarines and research reactors – the more convinced I became of the importance and value of the nuclear industry to Britain.

No longer a Media man, I was able to get access to the CEGB's Boardroom and the innermost thoughts of top scientists and engineers like Sir Walter Marshall, John Collier and John Baker – trustworthy men, whose No. 1 concern was public safety. As a layman, I needed convincing, but nothing was ever glossed over or falsified and we were never required to include anything in a video which was not fact or true.

Listening to Walter Marshall's analysis of what went wrong at Chernobyl and why, left me in no doubt that such a catastrophe could not happen in Britain and motivated all of us – me, camera crew, graphics artist, recording studio, video-editing suite and copying house, to pull out all stops and produce *Chernobyl Could It Happen Here?* within eight days of the event. It was only seen by CEGB nuclear workers (and later by MPs and opinion formers) but it served to allay the anxieties of a whole industry at a crucial time.

One safety aspect of the British nuclear industry which had always particularly impressed me was the strength and reliability of the ' flasks' used to transport 'spent' nuclear fuel rods from the power stations to the reprocessing plant at Sellafield. The ease with which Greenpeace and many media outlets were able to alarm the public about those flask movements by road and rail used to madden me (although, as part of the legacy left by a decade of CEGB policy to 'Tell the public only what it needs to know', it was understandable).

So I was pleased to be invited not only for MCC to make a video about them but to act as Master of Ceremonies, for four hours, at a public demonstration of their robustness The climax was to be the propulsion of a diesel locomotive, at 100 m.p.h., head on into a typical flask, which had been laid across the railway track at Old Dalby in Leicestershire.

The CEGB were inviting 1000 guests to witness the impact, but they all had to be in their seats in an adjacent field at least two hours before the event. This was for security reasons – Greenpeace and Friends of the Earth were known to be planning a demonstration and possibly some interference.

Our explanatory video was to be shown in marquees where guests would gather for coffee before finding their seats. It told the story of the fabrication of the fuel flasks, the materials used, the advanced welding technology involved and the previous strength-testing carried out – by dropping 100 ft from a rig onto concrete and then by intense heat from a fire. The whole transportation sequence was shown, including carriage of that day's flask by low-loader and the hoisting of it into position across the railway track.

Finally, the video showed the recently retired locomotive and the four coaches which were due to collide with it. We videoed a rehearsal of the 12-mile journey, as the train gathered maximum speed, to the point where the loco rounded a bend just before the straight piece of railway line where the flask would be waiting – the point where the spectators would first see it.

I made out the cards of commentary information for the Shannon file in good time and stayed at a hotel near Old Dalby overnight. The day was sunny and warm and there was an almost festive air about the site as CEGB staff prepared for their guests.

I was surprised to find that the commentary box was 30 feet in the air and reachable by ladder. It looked like a guard post in a PoW camp – indeed, someone told me it had once been just that, the PoWs having been German. The microphone worked. We started playing light classical music, dipping into it with facts and figures as more guests arrived and slowly building up the tension. I had worked out where the train should be passing – and at what speed – and so was able to give a running progress report for the final 15 minutes.

The box was such a good vantage point that, a few minutes before impact, I was joined by Walter Marshall and his wife Anne. None of us really knew what to expect and I had a hand ready to clamp my mouth shut if I felt in danger of bursting out with an expletive.

In reality, it was Anne Marshall who gave way to the tension.

The train and plum-red coaches looked so beautiful on that day, set against a tranquil background of woods and green meadows, that when it struck the flask and disappeared into a cloud of black smoke and a fireball, the sheer violence of it all caused her to burst into tears.

Fact or fake?

The PR men of the CEGB arranged a showing of our video of the crash in the lobby of the Commons. It contained clear pictures of the impact and the fireball from 10 different camera angles, in slow-motion as well as real-time, and ended with an 'I told you so' statement from Walter, standing by the intact flask.

As the demonstration had been a success, I was allowed to re-title the edited video *Operation Smash Hit.*

Unfortunately, MPs started to arrive at the video playback stand in the Lobby bearing a printed statement from Greenpeace. It alleged that the test had been rigged and cited four pieces of 'evidence'.

Firstly, it claimed, that bolts holding the diesel engine to the chassis of the locomotive had been deliberately left undone, so that it would fly through the air on impact and lessen the force of the blow to the flask (a large black object had been seen flying through the air after impact).

Secondly, that the locomotive was a Type 46 and not a Type 47 diesel and therefore not, as the CEGB claimed, the 'most aggressive' loco in Britain.

Thirdly, that the four carriages had been stripped of their fittings to minimise the train's impact.

Fourthly, that the flask had been carefully angled across the track, so as to protect its most vulnerable point – a pressure release valve.

Greenpeace accused the Board of 'blatantly lying'.

The CEGB men on duty at the House of Commons were thunderstruck. Their hopefully-convincing demonstration was ruined. Next day, the Press had a field day, with all the tabloids carrying banner headlines like 'Crash Test Rigged Says Greenpeace' and 'CEGB Told Blatant Lies'.

When a call came at 9 a.m. to go to Sudbury House and talk about ways of rebutting Greenpeace's allegations, I could well understand the anger of the engineers and PR men who had gone to such lengths (and spent over £1 million to reassure the public about the safety of those fuel flasks). Having spent a fortnight filming the behind-the-scenes story of the preparations, I knew the truth.

So we made a video, called *Fact or Fake?*, in a week. We interviewed the Head of Technical Support in British Rail's R & D Department, who pointed out:-

1) That security guards had protected the loco every minute for two weeks prior to the event and that he had inspected it carefully on the day: all bolts were in place and tightly fastened.

2) That concrete blocks were placed in the coaches to increase the force of impact – hundreds of witnesses who inspected the wreckage immediately after the crash had seen that for themselves.

3) The Type 46 diesel was heavier and sturdier than the Type 47 furthermore it was the only one which could be 'tuned up' to reach 100 m.p.h.

Next we interviewed John Hart, the engineer in charge of flask design, who explained that there were two vulnerable valves, not one, as Greenpeace had suggested. They were on opposite corners of the flask. So it was a physical impossibility to point both at the oncoming train simultaneously. The one which was, in fact, hit by the train had leaked less than one third of one pound per square inch of pressure. Had radioactive materials been inside the flask, that would have amounted to considerably less than the natural 'background radiation' from rocks in that area of Leicestershire.

Finally, Mike Shears of Ove Arup and Partners, the consultant engineers who had designed the test, pointed out that documents which Greenpeace had claimed indicated that the test was not 'the worst possible' scenario were three years old and had been based on computer studies and not even model tests. Model tests had 'flawed' their conclusions: the real-life impact at Old Dalby certainly was 'the worst possible scenario'.

Fact or Fake? and *Operation Smash Hit* were both shown in the Lobby of the House, 10 days after the first debacle, and seen by more than 300 MPs. Greenpeace, to their credit, called a Press conference to make a public apology (it was the first time they had ever done so). My company, MCC, were paid £12,000 for the video. And I received a tie from Ove Arup to add to my collection.

It is one of only 50 'struck' and shows, against a rich blue background, the front of a Type 46 diesel loco and a nuclear fuel flask
before they collided, woven in gold.

It reminds me not of the inexcusable failure of Greenpeace to
check their facts, but rather of the triumph of truth over scurril-
ous fiction. It also happens to go well with a blue suit.

Dinosaur on a golf course

After an invitation to speak to the Institute of Public Relations in
1980 about different communications techniques for telling company stories, I met a Norwich based PR man who needed urgent
help. One of his clients was a Swedish firm who were one of
the largest manufacturers of aluminium 'cladding' for modern
factories.

As a publicity stunt, the firm had decided to create a full-size
dinosaur in aluminium and present it to the Swedish town of
Norshopping to help celebrate the town's 600th birthday. A Czech
sculptor had been commissioned, who had drawn up scale plans
based on the bones of *Tyrannosaurus Rex,* the largest-known flesh-
eater, which he studied in the Natural History Museum in London. The work of welding aluminium spars and plates together
to form a replica of the beast had been carried out by the firm's
apprentices inside one of its large hangars.

The metal dinosaur, 40 feet long from fearsome teeth to ugly
tail, stood 25 ft high on two legs and weighed five tons. To give it
a useful function as well as making it an attraction, a ladder had
been fitted inside the hollow body, leading to a children's slide
down the tail. The hangar where it was built was 60 miles from
Norshopping : the problem was that there were four low bridges
on the road between the two.

The manufacturers had arranged for a helicopter of the Swedish Air Force to lift the dinosaur bodily, after a 'roll-out' cer-
emony at the hangar, and carry it to its final destination – a concrete
pad in a woodland amusement park.

Scenes of apprentices putting the final pieces of aluminium in
place, an interview with the sculptor, the 'roll-out', the lifting skywards by the helicopter and the journey across lakes and forests
to the amusement park were all to be recorded by TV cameras
and edited, as quickly as possible, into a video. The PR man

needed urgent help because the Swedish director he had hired had gone down with chickenpox. 'Is directing and editing within the scope of your company?' he asked. It certainly was.

On the day prior to 'roll-out', I flew to Stockholm and took a taxi for the 20-mile ride to the factory. I met the Swedish TV crew and we interviewed the sculptor and took shots of the apprentices before dusk fell.

Next day was sunny and the Air Force helicopter looked smart on the concrete apron outside the hangar. People were bustling about. The hangar doors had been partly opened to allow two huge rolls of paper to be hung across the gap. The idea was to set fire to these and, when well ablaze, push *Tyrannosaurus Rex* forward through the smoke and flames towards the camera.

The entire workforce and most of the local villagers turned out to witness the 'roll-out' It looked, indeed, like a fire-breathing monster as it came through the burning paper and we got some good pictures before boarding a second helicopter which was to act as a 'chase plane' for the journey to Norshopping.

All went well for about 20 miles. Then our pilot called up the Air Force pilot to warn him that one of the chains had slipped a little and the dinosaur was beginning to swing like a pendulum. Both helicopters immediately set down in a field of corn.

Adjustments were still being made to the chain when the farmer arrived in a mud-stained Volvo (what else?) and unleashed a torrent of abuse at the two pilots for the damage done to his ripening corn. He ignored the dinosaur – it was as though they were as commonplace as cattle on his farm – all he was interested in, apparently, was compensation. Names and addresses were exchanged and we all climbed aboard again.

After a further 20 miles, the radio crackled again and the Air Force pilot said he would have to deposit the dinosaur once more and return to his base (only a few miles away) to get more fuel.

This time he chose a golf course.

We had been lazing on the grass for about 10 minutes when, over the brow of a hill, came two golf balls, followed by four golfers – two in plus-fours. I shall never forget the looks on their faces as they saw *Tyrannosaurus Rex* glaring at them from the long grass beside the fairway, with an empty helicopter close by. Shock is too mild a word. One actually turned to run.

When they had composed themselves, they came forward again and spotted us crouched down behind the tail. I am not sure

whether Swedes guffaw, but those seemed to. After a few minutes, in which they put aside their clubs, climbed the internal
ladder and slid, one by one, down the tail, the Air Force helicopter returned and landed. More guffaws – then we hooked up,
took the strain on the chains and flew off again, one behind the
other.

I have it all on tape, including the lowering of the dinosaur
through fir trees onto a pad in the amusement park and the first
children to go down the slide. What I do not have is a record of
the tale which the golfers undoubtedly told when they reached
the '19th hole'.

Here we go again

The dinosaur airlift was the exception that proves the rule that
there is little humour in business and, in any case, this book is not
really about business – it is about news.

We were privy to quite a lot of newsworthy material but bound
by our own code of ethics not to communicate it until our clients were ready to release it. I took my satisfaction from being in
a position to decide how best – and at what length to tell stories,
from meeting employees who really appreciated being told what
was going on. From being able to hire former colleagues and
pay them swiftly (as opposed to the usual 'the cheque's in the
post' or 'the cheque's awaiting a second signature' or 'have you
sent an invoice?') and finally from working with talented artists
and video editors who would not look at a clock until the job
was done.

But I missed the world of journalism and, as company business
began to decline, so I started to dabble in travel-writing.

Everyone, it seems, wants to be a travel-writer and envies those
who fly, drive, sail or take the train or coach to interesting or
exotic places. But it is hard work, by any standards. However,
thanks to the *Evening Standard* policy of requiring reporters on
foreign trips to write features quickly about the countries they
were visiting (which is basically what most travel-writers do), I
had had some professional experience.

After Vivienne died of cancer, fate brought me into contact
again with Helen Gane, who had been Geoffrey Cox's secretary
at ITN when I first started to appear on TV. Helen is an excellent

photographer and shares my inability to lounge on a beach for long without getting itchy feet.

We married and had a hilarious honeymoon in China, which I wrote up as a humorous travel article for *Choice* magazine and Helen illustrated with colour pictures. We both got paid. We both became hooked, thereafter, on travel-writing.

It remained a holiday pursuit while I continued to run MCC. But by 1993, I was earning more from travel-writing than from business and was elected a member of the British Guild of Travel Writers.

The change of direction has so far led us into Siberia, Venezuela, the Caribbean, Costa Rica, Tanzania, Zanzibar, and several times to the USA as well as into six European countries. I had intended to retire – and, indeed, went so far as to start taking a pension.

Then I had a phone call from a friend in Cape Canaveral. 'Hey, Peter,' he said, 'a little birdie tells me that NASA has started serious studies into space tourism. Have you heard that?' I said I hadn't, but thanked him for the call.

The whiff of news was over powering. After I put the phone down, I said to Helen, 'If I were still at the *Standard* or at ITN, I would go to the Editor, tell him what I had heard and he would ask why wasn't I on a plane to Washington?'

'Why aren't you?' she asked.

I rang the Director of Public Affairs at NASA, who confirmed that the rumour was true. NASA and a conglomerate of 16 major aerospace companies, known as the Space Transportation Association (STA), were about to sign an agreement to carry out a year-long study 'with a view to establishing a US space tourism business'.

I booked a flight immediately to Washington, checked into a hotel in Arlington close to the STA's offices, and took the president, Tom Rogers, out to dinner that night. Next day, I had a long interview with Dr Jack Mansfield, the senior NASA administrator who would be signing the agreement and listened to some in-depth briefings, including one on the design of a 'space hotel'. Finally, I collected transparencies and 'stills' from the NASA picture library. It was just like old times.

Dr Mansfield even gave me a souvenir to take away – a paperweight made out of two pieces of special metal, welded together by a revolutionary technique. 'It is the development of these new materials and techniques which are the key to low-cost reusable spaceplanes,' he explained, 'and, therefore, to space tourism.'

Until then, tourism in space had been the stuff of science fiction or children's cartoons. Now, reputable engineers and scientists were discussing seriously the feasibility of sending ordinary people into space within five years – first in ones and twos, later in groups of 20. The first flights would be straight up-and-down 'hops' but, by 2010, they should be five- or six-day orbits of the world, with hours, rather than minutes, in which to take pictures and play weightless games, or splash about in a one-sixth gravity pool. And eight US states had started to put money into the design and development of 'spaceports' from which the holiday-makers would be launched and where they would land.

The adrenaline was really flowing on the flight home and I wrote a rough draft of my report instead of going to sleep. I felt the same excitement on the flight home as after the first briefings on Project Apollo. *The Sunday Telegraph* published the report as a full page feature on January 28, 1996, under the heading *Book a Day Trip to the Stars* and it broke the first news that a new era in travel had officially begun.

When I got home, Helen asked: 'Are you satisfied?'

'In a way, yes,' I answered. 'But I fear it might be a case of 'Here we go again . . .'

Index